"Uplifting . . . This positive volume should reassure parents and caregivers of kids with autism and any other disability that their kids are not broken, but, indeed, special."

—*Booklist*, starred review

"A long-awaited tour-de-force that parts the ever-expanding sea of books on the topic of autism. A must-read for anyone who lives with and loves a person with autism, this book should also be required for anyone who is striving to be a competent and humanistic professional."

—Pamela Wolfberg, PhD, Professor of Autism Spectrum Studies, San Francisco State University; Founding Director, Autism Institute on Peer Socialization and Play; and author of *Play and Imagination in Children with Autism*

"Prizant distils decades of working with autistic children and adults, and their teams, into practical advice for lowering stress, leveraging strengths and interests, building resilience, and importantly, embracing and celebrating difference. . . . Prizant's is a message of empathy, support and empowerment."

—*Nature*

"The reverence that Dr. Prizant brings to his work with individuals with autism and their families leaps out from every page of this remarkable book, enabling him to tell the story of autism in a deeply personal way that is at once inspirational and informative. The engaging, real-life examples interspersed throughout the book serve both to illuminate the experience of autism from the inside out and to expose the folly of viewing behavior separate and apart from the motivation that fuels it. That is epochal!"

—Diane Twachtman-Cullen, PhD, CCC-SLP, former Editor in Chief, *Autism Spectrum Quarterly*

"Prizant is a respected voice in the autism community, and the methods demonstrated here are backed by case study and experience. Parents, especially parents of the newly diagnosed, may find a ray of hope in the often bleak landscape of early diagnosis and the endless search for answers and information that inevitably results."

—*Library Journal*

"Elegant in its simplicity, *Uniquely Human* tackles extremely complex topics and how they impact school, home, and community. Compassion, learning, and supportive strategies—the three essentials for working with folks with ASD—are an integral part of this must-read book."

—Michelle Garcia Winner, speech-language pathologist and founder of Social Thinking®

"*Uniquely Human* . . . details stories that will resonate with parents or loved ones when a child is first diagnosed with autism. Families may find Prizant's approach . . . positive and uplifting."

—*Providence Journal*

"*Uniquely Human* is not just the perfect title for Barry Prizant's book, it's also an appropriate summation of Dr. Prizant's career. Though a clinical scholar, he is a humanist first, and always has been—a professional who is fascinated by unexamined lives that could be lived happily, yet aren't. With every brilliant, illuminating example in his book, he steers us away from the traditional fix-it mentality and toward the beatific, personally rewarding detective work that the entire spectrum world would be well served to adopt."

—Michael John Carley, parent-professional with ASD; founder of GRASP; and author of *Asperger's from the Inside-Out*

"A masterful treatise advocating for necessary changes in the way we see, understand, and provide services to persons with autism. This is a book for all parents and persons providing professional services to individuals with significant disabilities, not just those with autism. My hope is that this exceptional book will bring about the change in thinking and practice it is intended to do."

—David E. Yoder, PhD, Chair and Professor Emeritus, Department of Allied Health Sciences, University of North Carolina School of Medicine, Chapel Hill

"An excellent book that conveys what autism is like and how individuals with autism may be helped to build on their strengths and gain a greater social understanding. The approach involves much practical guidance for families and teachers, but it is refreshingly flexible and nondogmatic."

—Professor Sir Michael Rutter, child psychiatrist, FRCP FRCPsych FMedSci, Institute of Psychiatry, Psychology, and Neuroscience, King's College, London

"From the master clinician and scholar who taught us how to channel different learning styles into successful lives of learning and adaptation, *Uniquely Human* shines a light onto the vast possibilities of people with autism, showing that their lives represent opportunities, not disabilities; promise, not doom. Heed his detailed guidance because therein lies not only the secret for the fulfillment of every child's promise, but also the fulfillment of the promise of our entire society."

—Ami Klin, PhD, Director, Marcus Autism Center, Professor and Chief, Division of Autism and Related Disorders, Department of Pediatrics, Emory University School of Medicine

UNIQUELY
HUMAN

UPDATED AND
EXPANDED

A DIFFERENT WAY

OF SEEING AUTISM

BARRY M. PRIZANT, PhD

WITH TOM FIELDS-MEYER

SIMON & SCHUSTER PAPERBACKS

New York London Toronto Sydney New Delhi

Simon & Schuster Paperbacks
An Imprint of Simon & Schuster, Inc.
1230 Avenue of the Americas
New York, NY 10020

First Simon & Schuster trade paperback edition April 2022

SIMON & SCHUSTER PAPERBACKS and colophon are
registered trademarks of Simon & Schuster, Inc.

For information about special discounts for bulk purchases,
please contact Simon & Schuster Special Sales at
1-866-506-1949 or business@simonandschuster.com.

The Simon & Schuster Speakers Bureau can bring authors
to your live event. For more information or to book an event,
contact the Simon & Schuster Speakers Bureau at 1-866-248-3049
or visit our website at www.simonspeakers.com.

Interior design by Ellen R. Sasahara

Manufactured in the United States of America

7 9 10 8 6

The Library of Congress has cataloged
the hardcover edition as follows:
Prizant, Barry M. Uniquely human : a different way of seeing
autism / Barry Prizant, Ph.D.; with Tom Fields-Meyer.
pages cm
"Simon & Schuster nonfiction original hardcover."
1. Autism.   2. Autism in children   I. Fields-Meyer,
Thomas.   II. Title.
RJ506.A9P77 2015
618.92'85882—dc23 2014035241

ISBN 978-1-4767-7623-1
ISBN 978-1-4767-7624-8 (pbk)
ISBN 978-1-4767-7625-5 (ebook)
ISBN 978-1-9821-9389-8 (pbk updated edition)

To all autistic and neurodivergent individuals, diagnosed and not yet diagnosed, and their families, in the hope that this book will help them gain what they so deserve: understanding, respect, and a self-determined life.

And to all those who are devoting their lives to improving quality of life for autistic and neurodivergent people and their families, I respectfully urge you to *"look close enough / you'll finally see / that we're all uniquely human."**

---

* From the song "Uniquely Human," lyrics by Justin Anthony Long, from *Journey to Namuh*, The Miracle Project (2021).

CONTENTS

PART THREE: The Future of Autism

AUTHOR'S NOTE

THE underlying philosophy, values, and practices I share in this book are consistent with and in some cases derived from the SCERTS®Model (2006), an educational and treatment framework developed with my colleagues. The SCERTS Model prioritizes social communication, emotional regulation, and transactional support as the most important domains to focus on with autistic individuals. School districts, clinics, and agencies across the United States and in more than a dozen countries have implemented SCERTS. A more detailed description of the SCERTS Model appears at the end of this book.

PREFACE

WHEN *Uniquely Human* was published in 2015, I had no idea what kind of reception it would receive. I simply wished to share what I had learned from autistic people and their families over four decades, and to do so in a manner that was engaging and accessible. I was humbled and delighted that, practically from the beginning, the book was embraced by parents, teachers, professionals, and—most importantly—by autistic people themselves. In a few short years, it has become the bestselling book on the topic, translated into twenty-two language versions and earning the Autism Society of America's Temple Grandin Award for Outstanding Literary Work in Autism, among other recognition. Of the resources the Autistic Self-Advocacy Network (ASAN) recommends for parents, it's the only one written by a non-autistic author.

I have been gratified by the many parents who told me that *Uniquely Human* has changed their lives by giving them a new way to understand their children and renewed hope for the future, and by the many autistic people who have expressed gratitude for how accurately and respectfully the book reflects their life experience. One of my favorite responses was from Chloe Rothschild, an autistic young woman who first contacted me to tell me that my book was the hundredth autism book she had added to her library. (See Chapter 12.) Chloe, who has become a friend, told me that she carries a copy of the book in her purse or backpack, telling anyone who will listen that the best way to understand her is to "just read this book."

In *Uniquely Human*, I made the case that autism is not an illness, but a different way of being human. I have always believed that the best way to provide support is for non-autistics, and society in general, to collaborate with autistic people, to listen and better understand each person's experience, and change what we do in providing appropriate support if and when it's needed.

This message is also at the center of the burgeoning neurodiversity movement, which acknowledges and celebrates the wide range of human minds and lived experience. Since the book's publication, that perspective has moved from the fringes to the mainstream, with television shows, movies, and novels prominently featuring autistic and neurodivergent individuals. A wide range of celebrities—from the climate activist Greta Thunberg, to the actor Anthony Hopkins, to Tesla CEO Elon Musk—have not only acknowledged that they are on the autism spectrum but attribute their success to their unique minds. Millions of people have become familiar with such minds on TV shows such as "Love on the Spectrum," and "Atypical." Even "Sesame Street" has added to its cast an autistic Muppet, the delightful Julia.

What's most significant is that it's autistic people who are spearheading many of these developments—organizing events, speaking out, sharing their stories and perspectives, and setting the cultural and research agendas.

For this edition, I have updated and expanded *Uniquely Human* largely in response to what autistic individuals are telling us and the experiences they are sharing. While in the past such voices were heard mostly at conferences and smaller gatherings, technology has made it far easier to amplify autistic voices more broadly. In 2020, I launched "Uniquely Human: The Podcast," cohosted and co-produced with my friend Dave Finch, a bestselling author and audio engineer who is on the spectrum. The podcast has given us a forum to hear and share the stories of dozens of people on the spectrum, from Morénike

Giwa-Onaiwu, a Black professor, author, and social justice-activist; to Ron Sandison, an evangelical minister; to Danny Whitty, a non-speaking self-advocate with expertise in the culinary arts. From Carly Ott, an autistic bank vice president; to Scott Steindorff, an executive producer of feature films and TV shows; to Domonique Brown, an autistic TV actor; to autistic children and adults sharing their "enthusiasms."

Those conversations, my continuing consultation work with agencies serving autistic people of all ages and abilities and their families, our weekend parent retreats, my involvement with the Miracle Project programs in Los Angeles and New England, as well as the Spectrum Theater Ensemble in Providence, R.I., all have helped inform many of the changes in this new edition, which are reflected in these areas:

Language. The way we speak about and describe autistic and neurodivergent people is constantly evolving. The first edition of *Uniquely Human* used what's known as person-first language, typically mentioning a "person with autism," or "person who has autism." The majority of autistic people now express a preference for "identity first" language, which refers to people as "autistic" or "on the autism spectrum." We have shifted our language accordingly.

The terms *neurodiverse* and *neurodivergent* have also come into common use, though their meanings vary. In some cases, they're used to acknowledge that every mind is unique, and there is no "normal" mind. We use these terms to refer to those who are autistic or have other differences, which may include conditions such as ADHD, learning disabilities, and mental health conditions as well as autism. In most cases, when the term "autistic child" or "autistic person" is used, the comment is relevant for those other neurodivergent individuals who do not have a specific autism spectrum diagnosis. We use the term "neurotypical" for those who are not autistic, neurodiverse, or neurodivergent.

I occasionally make reference to Asperger's syndrome, which for many years was a diagnostic subcategory of Autism Spectrum Disorders in the Diagnostic and Statistical Manual of Mental Disorders (DSM) of the American Psychiatric Association. Although in 2013 the term Asperger's syndrome was dropped as a separate sub-category of autism in its most recent edition (known as the DSM-5), it continues to be used commonly to describe people with average or higher cognitive and language ability paired with challenges in the social realm as well as sensory and other challenges common in autism.

In referring to individuals who do not (or do not yet) communicate by speaking, I use the term "nonspeaking" and similar language. Others may commonly refer to such people as "nonverbal," but many such people truly are "verbal" as they use words and other symbolic means to communicate through sign language, iPads, and other alternative means, even though they do not use speech as their primary mode of communication.

Many people use the term "self-advocate" to refer to autistic or neurodivergent teens and adults who play an active role in steering their own lives, express their opinions and preferences, and exert control over decisions about their accommodations, schools, employment, and living arrangements. Some prefer the more general term "advocate," as many self-advocates have gone on to support and mentor others on the spectrum and educate the neurotypical public and especially those serving neurodivergent people. I have chosen to use the more common term "self-advocate" when referring to autistic or neurodivergent individuals who play an active role in advocating for themselves or others.

Age and Diversity. Autistic self-advocates have highlighted that autism research and discussions are often overly focused on children and teens and neglect to consider the significant issues and experiences of adults on the spectrum. I have made an effort to speak more broadly about people on the spectrum, not just children, and to address many of the issues facing adults. This edition also includes updates about some children and teens who have become adults since *Uniquely Human* was first published.

Events far beyond the world of autism have highlighted the importance of acknowledging and addressing the diversity of humankind in order to be as inclusive and respectful as possible. I have made an increased effort to represent a diversity of life experiences, perspectives, and voices throughout the book.

Emerging issues. Autistic people have brought new attention and urgency to a number of significant issues, including how and when to disclose an autism diagnosis; embracing autism as an identity; and the overlap of autism with race, gender, sexual orientation, and other aspects of one's identity. Chapter 11 delves into those matters, as well as highlighting some of the exciting approaches that are enabling nonspeaking autistic people to give voice to their experience and share their stories.

Many autistic self-advocates and organizations, most notably the Autistic Self-Advocacy Network (ASAN), have adopted a slogan made popular by disability-rights activists: "Nothing about us without us." These words resonate with my values and have guided the approach I have taken for four decades by collaborating with and inviting autistic self-advocates to speak to my classes, at our live conference events, and on our podcast. In this new edition, I expand upon these efforts to elevate and amplify the voices and perspectives of people on the spectrum, so many of whom are now dear friends and colleagues.

To be clear, I do not claim to fully understand the lived experience of autistic and neurodivergent people, and certainly am not putting forth indisputable truths. I am sharing what I have learned in my lived experience of a half century of sharing time and collaborating with autistic and neurodivergent people and those closest to them, with a focus on what is most helpful in supporting these individuals and their families.

Not long ago, I marked fifty years of working with and learning from autistic and neurodivergent children, adults, and their families. When friends ask when I plan to retire, I always reply that I am among the fortunate people whose personal and professional lives are intertwined—each informs and inspires the other and is the fuel that energizes my own personal growth and quality of life. With boundless gratitude, I look forward to continuing to learn and grow along with the many people who have given my life such meaning and purpose.

A Different Way of Seeing Autism

N OT long ago I was meeting with a group of educators at an elementary school when things suddenly got personal. I was there in my role as a school district consultant for programs serving children with special needs, and as the meeting was breaking up, the principal asked to see me privately. I figured that he wanted to discuss a staff issue, but the principal—an intense, serious man—closed the door, pulled his chair close to mine, looked me in the eye, and began telling me about his nine-year-old son.

He described a shy, quirky, and solitary youngster who had grown increasingly remote and isolated, spending much of his time playing video games by himself and rarely mingling with other children his age. Then he got to the point: a psychologist had recently diagnosed the boy with Autism Spectrum Disorder. The principal leaned forward, putting his face within inches of mine.

"Barry," he asked, "should I be scared to death?"

It is the sort of question that has become all too familiar to me. Almost every week I speak with parents who are intelligent, capable individuals, often confident and accomplished in other realms. But when these mothers and fathers encounter autism, they become disoriented. They lose faith in their own instincts. Facing this unexpected and unfamiliar territory, they feel bewildered, frightened, and lost.

A few years earlier, the person asking was a world-renowned musician. He and his wife had invited me to observe their four-year-old daughter. The girl had not been responding well to intensive autism therapy that required sitting for long periods and responding to directions and commands. Her parents wanted a second opinion about the best approach to helping and supporting her. On my first visit to the family's sprawling home, the father gestured for me to follow him into another room.

"Can I show you something?" he asked. He reached behind an upholstered chair and grabbed a paper shopping bag, then stuck his hand inside and pulled out a toy. It was a Bumble Ball, a battery-powered, textured rubber toy with a motor inside to make it vibrate when it was switched on. I could see that it had never been removed from its original packaging.

"I bought this for my daughter last Christmas," he said apprehensively. "Was that a bad thing? I thought she would like it."

I shrugged. "I can't see how it could be bad," I replied.

"Well," he said, "her therapist told me it would make her more autistic."

It made no sense: a brilliantly talented celebrity known for his forthright, confident stature was so paralyzed by the words of a relatively inexperienced therapist that he was scared to give his own daughter a toy.

For more than four decades it has been my job to help parents like these, people from all walks of life who are struggling with the realization and reality that their children are on the autism spectrum—and to support the educators and various professionals who work with these children. More and more often I meet parents who have been thrown off balance—who suddenly feel perplexed, sad, and anxious about their children, not knowing what an autism diagnosis means for the future of their child and their family. Then, as they begin to seek clarity and direction from online resources and social media, they become immersed in the wilderness of autism controversies and often find themselves overwhelmed.

Their distress and confusion stem partly from information overload. Autism Spectrum Disorder is now among the most commonly diagnosed developmental disabilities; the U.S. Centers for Disease Control estimates that as many as one in forty-four, or 2.3 percent of school-age children, are on the autism spectrum, and fifteen to twenty percent of the general population have neurodivergent conditions. A flood of professionals and programs has emerged to serve these children: physicians, therapists, schools, afterschool programs. There are karate classes and theater programs for autistic children, sports camps and religious schools and yoga classes. At the same time, charlatans and opportunists with minimal or no experience—and even some with professional credentials—advertise their approaches as "breakthroughs" or as the only way to "recover" a child from autism. Unfortunately autism treatment is a largely unregulated enterprise.

All of this has made life even more challenging for parents. Which professional to trust? Who can explain your child? Which treatment will succeed? Which diet? Which therapy? Which medication? Which school? Which tutor? Years down the line, autistic adults and their parents continue to struggle with choices about health care and living arrangements.

Like any parents, these mothers and fathers want what's best for their children. But, struggling with a neurodevelopmental condition they don't understand, they don't know where to turn. Even those families who have been on the autism journey for years find themselves perplexed by new stages and challenges along the way. What will my son do after his school years? Who will care for my daughter after we're gone?

My job for five decades has been to help them transform their desperation into hope, to replace anxiety with knowledge, to turn self-doubt into confidence and comfort, and to help them see as possible what they thought was impossible. I have worked with thousands of families touched by autism and neurodivergent conditions, helping them to reframe their experience, trust their own instincts, and in turn build healthier, fuller lives. That's what I hope this book will help you to do, whether you are a parent, a relative, a friend, or a professional working to support these individuals and their families, or whether you are autistic or neurodivergent yourself.

It starts with shifting the way we understand autism. Again and again I have witnessed the same phenomenon: parents come to perceive their child as so radically different from others that the child's behavior seems beyond comprehension. They have come to believe that the tools and instincts they would bring to raising any other child just won't work with a child who has an autism diagnosis. Influenced by some professionals, they see certain behaviors as "autistic" and undesirable and perceive their goal as eliminating these behaviors and somehow fixing the child and "defeating" autism.

I have come to believe that this is a flawed understanding—and the wrong approach. Here is my central message: The behavior of autistic children and adults isn't random, deviant, or bizarre, as many professionals have called it for decades. These people don't come from Mars. The things they say aren't—as many professionals still maintain—meaningless or "nonfunctional."

Autism isn't an illness. It's a different way of being human. Autistic children and adults aren't sick; they are progressing through developmental stages as we all do. To help them, we don't need to change them or fix them. To be sure, we should address co-occurring biomedical or mental health issues to reduce suffering and improve quality of life.* But what's most vital—for parents, professionals, and society as a whole—is to work to understand them, and then change what *we* do.

In other words, the best way to help a person on the autism spec-

---

*While many autistic individuals experience co-occurring medical issues—including gastrointestinal and sleep disorders, allergies, migraines, and ear infections—that can result in severe health challenges, many are free of these conditions, which are not definitive of autism.

trum change for the better is to change ourselves—our attitudes, our behavior, and the types of support we provide.

How to do that? First, by listening. I have worked at the highest levels of academia and served on the faculty of an Ivy League medical school. I have published my work in dozens of scholarly journals and books. I have addressed conferences and presented workshops in every state and across the globe, from China to Israel, from New Zealand to Spain. Yet my most valuable lessons about autism have come not from lectures or journals. They have come from children, their parents, and a number of extremely articulate adults—both speaking and nonspeaking—with the ability to explain their own experience of being autistic or neurodivergent.

One of those is Ros Blackburn, a British woman who speaks more insightfully than practically anyone I know about what it feels like to go through life autistic. Ros often repeats this mantra: "If I do something you don't understand, you've got to keep asking, 'Why, why, *why?*'"

This book is about what I have learned over half a century of asking why—what I have come to understand by learning what it feels like to live on the autism spectrum, constantly coping with a world that can be endlessly challenging because of differences in your neurological wiring.

Concerned parents and caregivers share the same kinds of questions: Why does he recoil from my hugs? Why does she rock her body? Why can't he stay seated at the dinner table? Why does she repeat lines from movies over and over? Why does he hit his temples with his fists? Why is he terrified of butterflies? Why is she mesmerized by ceiling fans? Why does this person find certain sounds and smells so overwhelming?

Some professionals simply categorize these as "autistic behaviors." Too often the ultimate goal of professionals and parents is to reduce or eliminate these behaviors—to stop the spinning, stop the arm flapping, stop the repeating. Or to get the individual to comply with demands, accept hugs, sit still, stop rocking, stay at the dinner table with "quiet hands, quiet mouth, quiet body." All of this without asking, the simple question: "Why?"

Here is what I have learned from my years of experience and from Ros Blackburn and other autistic people: There is no such thing as autistic behavior. These are all *human* behaviors and *human* reactions based on a person's experience.

When I present workshops and seminars about autism, I often tell the audience that I have never seen an autistic person do something that I haven't seen a so-called neurotypical person do. Of course, many people find this difficult to believe. So I make it a challenge. I ask the listeners—usually parents, teachers, and professionals—to name a behavior that they consider definitive of autism, and I predict that I have witnessed it in a neurotypical person. Immediately people in the audience raise their hands.

"How about repeating the same phrase over and over one thousand times?"

Plenty of kids do that when they're asking for an ice cream cone or how much longer the drive will be.

"Talking to yourself when nobody's around?"

I do that in my car every day.

"Banging her head on the ground when she's frustrated?"

My neighbor's "typical" son did that when he was a toddler.

"Habitually biting your fingers?"

Lots of people bite their fingernails when they're nervous.

Rocking, talking to yourself, pacing, jumping up and down, flapping your arms, zoning out? We all do these things. The difference, of course, is that you might not have seen it as persistently or as intensely (or at an older age) in a typical person. And if we do engage in such behavior, we generally make sure we're not doing so in public.

Ros Blackburn says people stare when she jumps up and down and flaps her arms. They're simply not accustomed to seeing an adult act with such abandon. She points out that it's common to see people on TV doing just what she does, after they've won the lottery or a game show. "The difference," she says, "is that I get excited more easily than you do."

We're all human, and these are human behaviors.

That's the paradigm shift this book will bring: instead of classifying legitimate, functional behavior as a sign of pathology, we'll examine it as part of a range of strategies to cope, to adapt, to communicate and deal with events in our world that feels overwhelming, frightening, or just too exciting. Some of the most popular autism therapies make it their sole aim to reduce or *eliminate* behaviors, or to train an individual to passively comply with directions. I'll show how it's better to enhance communication abilities, teach life skills, build coping strategies, and offer supports that will help to prevent behavioral patterns of concern. This approach provides the foundation that naturally leads to more desirable behavior, builds self-confidence and self-determination, and improves quality of life for autistic people and those who support and love them.

It's not helpful to dismiss and pathologize what these individuals do as "autistic behavior" or "aberrant behavior" or "noncompliant behavior" (a phrase used by many therapists). Instead of dismissing it, it's better to ask: What is motivating it? What purpose does it serve? What is this person feeling? Does it actually help the person, even though it looks different?

Autistic people are complex human beings and I don't have simple answers, but I can offer ways that will lead to a better understanding of children, teens, and adults on the autism spectrum, and the family experience. The stories in *Uniquely Human* span my career across many different settings and roles: my early work in summer camp programs, positions in university departments and hospital clinics, and twenty-five years in private practice. They also describe my experiences consulting for more than one hundred public school districts, for hospitals, private agencies, and families, and from many years of traveling the world leading training workshops and consulting. The weekend parent retreat I have facilitated for twenty-five years has given me the opportunity to learn from parents and develop many deep and enduring friendships, witnessing the journeys of families and autistic individuals from the early intervention years to the midlife years. Finally, through many conferences and workshops, I have met and presented with international leaders of the autism self-advocacy movement, as well as courageous autistic "unsung heroes," many of whom have become valued friends and collaborators.

This book offers a comprehensive approach and value-based mindset that underlies my research and work with colleagues, my experience with families and professionals, and especially the insights shared by people on the spectrum from whom I have learned so much.

It's the book I wish I had been able to read more than five decades ago, when I first lived with and cared for autistic children and adults. Many professionals enter the autism field because of a personal connection—a child or a relative on the spectrum. I happened into it almost by accident. After my first year of college, I landed an un-fulfilling summer job in a New York City print shop. My girlfriend was teaching music at a sleep-away camp for children and adults with disabilities. A couple of weeks into the summer, she phoned to tell me there was an opening for a counselor. I applied, got the job, and literally overnight found myself, at just eighteen, responsible for a cabin full of boys with a variety of neurodevelopmental conditions.

For a boy from Brooklyn, the isolated rural setting in upstate New York felt like a primitive wilderness. But I was even more unprepared for the people I met. One eight-year-old boy in my cabin seemed remote and disconnected, but he had a knack for repeating phrases or whole sentences he heard. Another camper, a young adult known affectionately as Uncle Eddie, lumbered and spoke as if in slow motion because of his seizure medication. He had the endearing habit of offering compliments without inhibition. "Hi Barry," he'd say. "You look *sooo* handsome todaaay."

I felt like I was entering a different culture with different rules of relating and being, full of people who acted very differently from anyone I had met. Yet I soon became so comfortable and so thoroughly enjoyed my campers that I wanted to understand more. In particular, why did these people struggle so much with communicating their thoughts and feelings, and how could we help them? Why were they so easily upset about seemingly minor issues such as changes in routine or loud noises? That initial experience inspired me to study child development and developmental psycholinguistics, and then speech and language pathology, and eventually to go on to earn a doctorate in communication disorders and sciences.

This book might have also helped me understand one of my closest friends from my childhood in Brooklyn in the 1960s. Lenny was a brilliant student—skipping two grades before high school—and a talented self-taught guitarist. He was a musical genius, stealing guitar licks from Eric Clapton and Jimi Hendrix before the rest of us had even heard of them.

He was one of the most interesting people I knew, and also one of the most anxious, unfiltered, direct, and abrasive. Peers were put off by his frequent comments about his own superior intelligence. When Lenny lived in his own apartment as an adult, his shelves were lined with his extensive collection of records and first-edition comic books, all in plastic sleeves, impeccably organized and catalogued. But his kitchen sink was routinely overflowing with dirty dishes, his clothes strewn everywhere. Lenny had perfect SAT scores, eventually earned two master's degrees and a law degree, but had a difficult time keeping a job because he had trouble getting along with people.

Still, if Lenny knew you well and trusted you, and if you had common interests, he was as loyal and caring a friend as I have known. Though I frequently found myself in the position of explaining Lenny's eccentric and off-putting ways to acquaintances—most people thought him rude and arrogant—it took decades before it dawned on me, long after we had lost touch, that he probably had Asperger's syndrome. (Asperger's wasn't a formal diagnosis in the United States until 1994.) When Lenny died in his sixties after years of chain smoking, it struck me that his life surely would have been easier if he had been aware of being on the spectrum and if those around him had better understood what was causing his unusual habits and often brusque manner.

Finally, this is the book I wish I had been able to share a few decades ago with the parents of Michael, one of the first little autistic boys whose family I came to know well. I was a newly minted PhD, teaching at a large university in the Midwest, and Michael was the nine-year-old son of an English professor. Like many autistic children, Michael had a habit of fluttering his fingers in front of his eyes and staring at them, apparently delighted and captivated. For long stretches he would sit, mesmerized by the movement of his own hands. His teachers and parents routinely badgered Michael to dissuade him: "Michael, put your hands down. . . . Michael, stop looking at your hands!" in their effort to "extinguish the stim." But he persisted, eventually learning to enjoy secretively peeking at his hands during routine activities such as playing piano.

Around that time Michael's grandfather died. Michael had developed a very close relationship to his grandfather, spending time with him every weekend, and the death was his first experience of loss. Of course he felt confused and anxious, repeatedly asking his parents when he would be able to see his grandfather again. They explained that Grandpa was in heaven and that someday, in the very distant future, Michael would surely join him there. Michael listened intently, then replied with a single question: "In heaven, are people allowed to look at their hands?"

When Michael considered the idea of eternal bliss, that was what came to mind: not angels and harps and eternal sunshine, but a world where he could watch his own fingers flutter when he wanted to and not be reprimanded for something that he so enjoyed and that gave him a sense of peace.

His simple question taught me much about Michael and about autism. I have seen hundreds of autistic children who visually fixate on something: their fingers, a toy they carry with them, a fan, garden sprinklers. You could call that "autistic" behavior, or you could watch, listen, pay attention, and ask why they do it. When I have done that I have learned what underlies a fixation like Michael's: he finds it calming and grounding; it provides a sense of predictability; it's within his control, it's "self-regulating." With that understanding and insight, behavior like Michael's isn't so strange—it's a unique way of being human.

This book's scope encompasses the full spectrum of autism, including the most extreme challenges facing individuals of all ages and their families. I am well aware of how debilitating and stressful some patterns of behavior can be. I have cared for individuals who are so overwhelmed by pain or confusion that their behavior becomes unpredictable, dangerous, destructive, and even harmful to themselves and others. In these extreme cases, most of these individuals have complex co-occurring medical or mental health issues such as allergies, gastrointestinal problems, bipolar disorder or severe motor-speech problems. I have directly experienced injuries (bites, bruises, scratches, broken fingers) while attempting to support people in extreme states of distress. I have lived with autistic people who also have sleep disorders, and I have experienced the frustration of trying to ensure proper nutrition for individuals with highly restricted food preferences. I have dealt with children and adults who have become lost, have fled, or have unintentionally put themselves and others in danger.

While I don't claim to have experienced the chronic level of stress and concern that a parent might, I know those concerns and fears intimately. From observing and supporting countless families, I have learned this important lesson: Even under extremely challenging circumstances, our attitudes about and perspective on autistic people and their behavior make a critical difference in their lives—and in ours.

That is the message I hope to share in this book—one that can eliminate the fear I sensed from the principal and the musician and replace it with awe and love. It's the heart of what I taught a few years ago at an autism workshop in Nanaimo, a small city in British Columbia. Throughout the two days there a young father in a baseball cap sat in the front row with his wife, taking it all in but not speaking. The moment the workshop ended, he rushed up to me, hugged me, and buried his head in my shoulder.

"You have opened my eyes," he said, "and I will always be grateful."

I hope this book will open your eyes—and your ears and your heart. I hope to capture and share the unique spirit of the many autistic and neurodivergent children, adolescents, and adults I have known—their enthusiasms, their sense of wonder, their honesty and sense of justice, their loyalty and innocence. I will also describe the many obstacles I have seen these individuals and their families overcome. I don't claim to know firsthand the lived experience of an autistic person, but I am hoping you learn from my half-century of sharing my personal and professional life with so many autistic children, adults, and their families. Despite the challenges you may experience as a parent, family member, educator, or one of the many people who share their lives and help individuals on the spectrum, my hope is that understanding what it means to be uniquely human will make your experience, and ultimately, your life's journey with these distinctive people deeper, more awe-inspiring, and more joyful.

PART ONE

———

Understanding Autism

CHAPTER 1

Ask "Why?"

THE first thing I noticed about Jesse was the fear and anxiety in his eyes.

I was visiting a small New England school district when I heard about an eight-year-old boy who had recently transferred from a nearby district. There he had earned a dubious distinction: administrators called Jesse the worst behavior problem they had ever encountered—stubborn, noncompliant, aggressive.

It wasn't difficult to understand why, given his challenges. Jesse, a sturdy boy with straight brown hair and wire-rimmed glasses, struggled with severe social anxiety, extreme sensitivity to touch, and difficulty processing language. He also had a seizure disorder that was detected when he was a toddler, about the time he lost the ability to speak. He communicated with little more than guttural sounds and grunts, pushing away people and objects or physically leading people to what he wanted.

Since it was so difficult for Jesse to make his needs known, he often seemed aggravated and miserable. He sometimes took out his frustration and anxiety on himself, pounding his fists against his thighs and his forehead, covering his body with bruises. When teachers tried to direct him from one activity to the next using a physical prompting, hands-on approach, he often reacted with flailing limbs or by pushing them away with his arms or legs. Reports from the previous school described kicking, scratching, and biting episodes escalating into fits so severe that almost daily, three or four adults had to pin the boy down to subdue him, then isolate him in a "time-out" room. The staff had interpreted all of this as willful, uncooperative behavior. But Jesse's mother knew better. She understood that his actions were his way of communicating—a direct reflection of his confusion, pain, agitation, and fear. When she explained to the administrators that her son struggled with sensory challenges that made him unusually sensitive to loud noises and being touched, they had been dismissive. Clearly, they insisted, the boy was displaying noncompliant behavior. In their eyes, Jesse was strong-willed, stubborn, and defiant, and their response was to try to break him—to treat him as a trainer would treat a horse.

What did these educators offer to help Jesse learn to communicate? Practically nothing. The district's policy was to focus first on training compliance, controlling a child's behavior, and, only after achieving success, to address the area of communication. The primary goal, as stated in his individualized education plan (IEP), wasn't helping him gain the power to express himself, but rather getting him to be compliant.

They had it all wrong.

I had heard so many awful things about Jesse that I was intrigued to come face-to-face with him. When I finally did, I didn't observe any of what I had heard described—not the defiance, not the aggression, not the willful disobedience. What I saw was a boy who was understandably frightened, anxious, and constantly on guard, often experiencing fight-or-flight reactions. And I saw something else: Jesse's extreme vigilance and anxiety were manifestations of the inevitable damage that occurs when people—however well meaning— completely misunderstand the behavior and experience of autistic individuals.

How does this happen? The short answer is that caregivers, and even professionals, neglect to ask "Why?" They don't listen carefully or observe closely. Instead of seeking to understand the person's perspective and experience, they simply try to manage the behavior.

Unfortunately this deficit-checklist approach—categorizing behaviors simply as deviant or typical—has become the standard way of determining whether a person is autistic. We say a person is autistic if he displays a combination of traits and behaviors that are deemed to be problematic: difficulty in communicating, trouble developing relationships, sensory sensitivities, and a restricted repertoire of interests and behaviors, including repetitive speech—known as echolalia—and actions, such as rocking, arm flapping, and spinning. Professionals observe these "autistic behaviors" and then assess the people who display them by using a sort of circular reasoning: Why does Rachel flap her hands? Because she's autistic. Why has she been diagnosed with autism? Because she flaps.

Following this approach means defining a child, or even an adult, as the sum of his deficits. How best to help such a person? By managing those behaviors or attempting to get rid of them: to halt the rocking, to squelch the echoing speech, to reduce the flapping. And what denotes success? The more we can make the person look and act "normal," and to comply with demands, the better. As a prominent behavioral therapist put it, the goal is to make an autistic person "indistinguishable" from a neurotypical one.

This way of understanding and supporting autistic people is sorely lacking. It treats the person as a problem to be solved and to be fixed rather than an individual to be understood. It fails to show respect for the individual and ignores that person's perspective and experience. It ignores the fact that their neurological differences mean autistic people learn, communicate, and experience everyday life differently.

It neglects the importance of listening, paying close attention to what the person is trying to tell us, whether through speech or patterns of behavior.

On top of that, in my experience it doesn't work—and often makes things worse. Many autistic adults who as children were subjected to "deficit-checklist" and compliance-training approaches have recounted how difficult and even traumatic those experiences were. And research has documented much higher rates of anxiety in those individuals. In the words of the autistic author Paul Collins, "Autists are the ultimate square pegs, and the problem with pounding a square peg into a round hole is not that the hammering is hard work. It's that you are destroying the peg."

What's more helpful is to dig deeper: to ask what is motivating these behaviors, what is underlying these patterns. It's more appropriate, and more effective, to ask "Why?" Why is she rocking? Why does he line up his toy cars that way, and why only when he arrives home from school? Why does he drop to the floor or flee when asked to enter a busy gym? Why does he stare at his hands fluttering in front of his eyes, and always during English class and recess? Why does she repeat certain phrases when she is upset? Although each person is an individual with her own reactions and experiences, in order to answer, "Why?" and learn how to be of assistance, it's helpful to listen to what autistic people say about similar behavioral patterns they experience and what's the most helpful response.

The Challenge of Dysregulation

Usually the answer is that the person is experiencing some degree of *emotional dysregulation*. When we are well regulated emotionally and physiologically, we are most available for learning and engaging with others. We all strive to be alert, focused, and prepared to participate in activities in our daily lives. Our neurological systems help by filtering out excessive stimulation, telling us when we're hungry or tired or when to protect ourselves from danger. People on the autism spectrum are unusually vulnerable to everyday emotional and physiological challenges, primarily due to underlying neurological differences in the way their brains' wiring works. So they experience more feelings of discomfort, anxiety, and confusion than others. They also have more difficulty learning how to cope with these feelings and challenges.

To be clear: Difficulty staying well-regulated emotionally and physiologically should be a core, defining feature of autism. Unfortunately professionals have long overlooked this, focusing on the resulting *behaviors* instead of the underlying *causes*.

If you know an autistic person, consider what makes this person *less* able to stay well regulated: problems in communicating, environments that are chaotic, people who are confusing because they talk or move too quickly, unpredictability and unexpected change, excessive worry about things that are uncertain. Then there are associated challenges, such as sensory sensitivities to touch and sound, motor and movement disturbances, sleep deprivation, allergies, and gastrointestinal issues. For some, a history of stressful and traumatic experiences—combined with strong memories of them—adds additional complications.

Of course autistic people aren't alone in experiencing these challenges. We *all* feel dysregulated from time to time. Speaking in front of a large audience, you might feel sweat collecting on your brow, your hands might quiver, your heart might race. Wearing a scratchy wool sweater might be so irritating that you can't focus. When your normal morning routine—coffee, newspaper, shower—is thrown off by an unexpected intrusion, you might feel out of sorts for the rest of the morning. When we associate people, places, or activities with difficult or stressful incidents, we try to avoid them. When these factors accumulate—you miss sleep, you're under a deadline, you get stuck in traffic, you skip lunch, and then your computer crashes—it's easy to become extremely agitated.

We all have these challenges, but people on the spectrum are unusually ill equipped to deal with them because of their neurology. That makes them far more vulnerable than others—that is, their threshold can be much lower—and they have fewer innate coping strategies. In many cases, sensory-processing differences can also contribute to dysregulation: autistic people may be either highly sensitive or undersensitive to sound, light, touch, and other sensations and therefore less able to manage. In addition many autistic people are innately unaware of how others might interpret their actions when they are dysregulated. Or the unhelpful reactions of others may add additional stress, further contributing to the dysregulation.

Feeling emotionally dysregulated affects different people in different ways. Often the reactions are immediate and impulsive. A person's behavior may shift suddenly and unpredictably, with no apparent cause. When a child is exposed to a loud noise, for instance, he might drop to the floor. I often see children refuse to enter a gym class or the school cafeteria. Their teachers might mistakenly believe that this is willful disobedience, a planned attempt to escape an activity the child doesn't enjoy. The reason is typically much deeper than that: the child can't bear the volume or quality of the noise or the chaos of the setting. Or an adult who becomes confused and agitated when she finds the sidewalk blocked by construction on her habitual walking route home from the library, and she returns home full of anxiety.

When I worked in a preschool autism program based in a hospital, the children ate lunch in the classroom on trays brought up from the hospital cafeteria. Once a teacher and I led the four- and five-year-olds to the cafeteria's kitchen so they could see how the trays were cleaned. At exactly the moment we arrived, the industrial-size dishwasher spewed forth steam and suddenly emitted a high-frequency *SSHHHH!* Instantly all the children dropped their trays, some covered their ears and screamed, and they ran for the exit. It was as if a monster had suddenly appeared, inches from their faces.

That's dysregulation, sudden and visible.

Sometimes the cause of dysregulation is less obvious. While visiting a preschool where I consulted, I was walking outdoors with Dylan, an autistic four-year-old, when suddenly and without warning, he dropped to the ground and refused to proceed. I gently picked him up and helped him along, but soon he dropped again. As I helped him again, we heard a dog barking. He immediately panicked and tried to run away from the sound. It dawned on me that Dylan, with his hypersensitive hearing, had heard the dog all along, but its bark had been so distant that it hadn't registered with me. What might have appeared as uncooperative, random, or defiant behavior was in fact a very understandable expression of fear.

That too is dysregulation.

Many autistic children (and some adults) flap their arms, either as an expression of their level of excitement or to calm themselves. When Conner felt joyful, and sometimes when he was anxious about a transition between activities, he did what his parents called his "happy dance." He stood on his toes and stepped forward, then back, while flicking his fingers in front of his eyes. A previous therapist had advised Conner's parents to respond with a firm "Hands down!" And if he didn't comply: "Sit down, sit on hands!" (To their credit, his parents ignored the suggestion, instead helping Conner to label his feelings or easing transitions by telling him what to expect.)

It's easy to dismiss flapping or rocking or dancing as "autistic behavior." But parents raising children on the spectrum, and the professionals who work with them, need to look through a different lens. Like detectives, we need to examine and consider all available clues and work to discern what is underlying or triggering a particular reaction. What is making the child dysregulated? Is it internal or external? Is it visible? Is it in the sensory realm? Is it pain, or physical discomfort, or a traumatic memory? In most cases the child can't explain the behavior in words, so it's up to those close to him to sort through the clues.

Coping Strategies and Regulating Behaviors

Here is the important irony: Most of the behaviors commonly labeled "autistic behaviors" aren't actually deficits at all. They're strategies the person uses to feel better regulated emotionally and physiologically.

In other words, when they're helpful, they're strengths.

When a child with extreme sensory sensitivities enters a noisy room and cups his hands over his ears and rocks his body, this pattern of behavior is simultaneously a sign of dysregulation and a coping strategy. You could call it "autistic behavior." Or you could ask "Why is he doing that? Does it appear to help?" The answer is twofold: the child is revealing that something is amiss and that he has developed a response to shut out or control what is causing him anxiety.

Consider Sam, the dancing teenage barista at a Toronto Starbucks who was captured on a video that attracted millions of online views and an invitation to Ellen DeGeneres's talk show. "I concentrate a lot better when I dance," he told Ellen. In other words, Sam's constant movement—which some might have viewed as stigmatizing and a deficit—actually helped Sam to stay focused and coordinated, enabling him to get a job and do it well.

Whether or not we realize it, all humans employ these rituals and habits to help us regulate ourselves—soothe ourselves, calm our minds and bodies, and help us cope. Perhaps, like many people, you find public speaking unnerving. To calm yourself, you might take a series of deep breaths or pace back and forth while you speak. That's not exactly the way humans typically breathe or behave in public, but an observer would not judge this as deviant behavior. The person would understand that it's your way to cope with the stress of the situation and to soothe your nerves so that you can do your best.

When I return home from a day of work, I immediately check the mailbox, then sort the mail, placing bills in one pile, magazines in another, and tossing what I don't need in the recycling bin. It would take a significant distraction for me to skip that small but important ritual; then I would feel out of sorts on some level until I took care of it. It's a calming routine; it's how I come home. When my wife has had a bad day or feels worried, she organizes and cleans. If I come home and find my personal items I left around the house in a pile, and our home is more immaculate than usual, I know that something is bothering her. Religious services include layers of comforting rituals—chanting and praying, symbolic gestures and body movements—to enable people to let go of the worries and trivialities of everyday life and enter a higher spiritual realm. And mindfulness practices, such as meditation, Tai Chi, and yoga, are defined by rituals that focus on achieving a state of emotional and physical well-being.

For autistic people, comforting rituals and coping mechanisms come in all varieties: moving in particular ways, speaking in various patterns, carrying familiar items, closing cabinet doors, lining up objects to create predictable and unchanging surroundings. Even proximity to certain people can serve as a regulating strategy.

After coming home from a busy school day, Aaron, who was eight, had a habit of placing both palms on a table in front of him and then rhythmically jumping in place. His parents noted that the intensity and duration of his jumping were a good barometer of how stressful his day had been. Just as infants are comforted and soothed by being rocked, and toddlers run in circles to stay awake, we all use movement to modulate our emotional and physiological arousal. If autistic people feel underaroused, they may increase their alertness by climbing, spinning, bouncing, or swinging. If they're overstimulated, they might calm themselves by pacing, squeezing their fingers, staring at a fan or repetitively chanting a phrase.

Many people call these simply "behaviors." Again and again I have heard parents or educators describe people on the spectrum as having "behaviors." Don't we all? It's only in the field of autism that the word *behavior*—without any modifier—has a negative connotation. "Our new student, Sally, has really got a lot of behaviors," a teacher will say. Or "We're working on getting rid of Scott's behaviors." Others use the term *stim* or *stimming* (for repetitive, self-stimulatory behavior), terms that once had, and in some approaches still have, negative connotations. In earlier decades many researchers aimed to rid children of stims, some employing punishment and even shock as a means to eliminate "autistic behaviors."

Thanks to the insights and advocacy of many autistic adults, we now understand that stims often serve a self-regulatory function, helping a person feel grounded when the sensory environment is overwhelming, or when they feel anxious, afraid, or even bored. Or one might stim because it is enjoyable, fun, and creative. Prue Stevenson, an Australian autistic artist, creates visual and performance art based on her stims. "We have reclaimed stims as our own," one autistic person told me.

So we should not view these merely as *behaviors*. They are most often *strategies* to cope with dysregulation or simply to engage in something fun and grounding.

When an American psychiatrist named Leo Kanner first introduced the autism diagnosis in 1943, he noticed a striking trait among the children he described. He called it "insistence on preservation of sameness" (a trait still considered definitive of autism). Indeed many autistic people regulate themselves by trying to control their surroundings or other people's behavior—by seeking sameness. That isn't a pathological symptom. It's a coping strategy.

Every time Clayton returned home, he would survey every window in the house, adjusting the blinds so they were all at exactly the same height. Why? He was trying to ground himself by taking control and making his environment predictable and visually symmetrical. Others habitually eat the same foods, close all the cabinet doors in the classroom, watch the same video over and over, or insist on sitting in the same chair every day. Peter, a young man I know, insists that we greet his classmates in a particular sequence at the start of the weekly expressive-arts class he attends on Zoom.

Are rituals like Clayton's and Peter's indications of Obsessive-Compulsive Disorder? Actually their impact is quite different. True OCD behavior is disruptive and rarely serves to make the person feel better. In other words, the need to repeatedly wash one's hands or to touch every chair before leaving a room can interfere with everyday activities. But when an autistic person seeks out the same clothing or music or creates visual order by organizing items or a sequence of events, it's because the child has learned that these things help him to emotionally regulate so he can be more available for learning and engaging.

A couple once brought their seven-year-old son, Anton, for an initial evaluation at the clinical practice I ran. After a colleague and I interacted with the boy and observed him for a while, it was time to chat with his parents, so we gave Anton some paper and colored markers to entertain himself.

As we conversed, Anton was intently drawing. He carefully took one marker at a time, removed the cap, wrote down a number, replaced the cap, and put the marker back in the can, then repeated the process with different markers dozens of times. When we took a break and looked at what he had drawn, I was amazed. Anton had created an elaborate grid of numbers from 1 to 180, arranged in order, by systematically alternating seven colors. The result was a tidy, precisely ordered sequence of rows of numbers with the diagonal columns creating a rainbow of color. This was a boy who could speak only a single word at a time and echo a few phrases, but he had kept himself calm and engaged for some thirty minutes by focusing his attention on creating this ingenious visual display.

"He's never done anything like this before," his mother told me.

The drawing revealed not only that Anton's mind was more nimble and complex than we could have imagined, but also that he had devised his own ways to keep himself regulated. In this new environment, with adults—some unfamiliar—conversing around him, he found a way to remain grounded. Another observer might have concluded that he was stimming. I call it *self-regulation* (and remarkably creative).

Sometimes what helps a child self-regulate is an object. One boy would keep a particular stone—small, black, and polished—with him at all times, the way babies hold security blankets or stuffed animals. It calmed him; it regulated him. When he lost it, his father was anguished. "We've tried all kinds of other black rocks," he told me, "but he knew they weren't *that* rock." Eventually the boy found a replacement, a ring of plastic keys. Ron Sandison (see Chapter 12), an autistic author, minister, and speaker, described with great affection his reliable childhood companion, a stuffed prairie dog named Prairie Pup, that for many years he would carry wherever he went.

Often autistic children mouth, chew, or lick things to regulate themselves, just as many people habitually chew gum or enjoy crunchy snacks. Glen would pick up twigs on his kindergarten playground, lick them, and often chew them. He constantly gnawed on pencils in the classroom, and his mother said that he chewed on his sleeves and collars so frequently that the family's clothing bills were rapidly mounting. When I observed Glen in class, it was clear that he would seek things to mouth or chew at the times he felt most dysregulated: during unstructured times (such as recess), transitions, or when noise increased. Working with his occupational therapist, I suggested better ways to provide the sensory input he craved: offering crunchy snacks (carrots, pretzel nuggets) and a rubber toy or tube to chew on. We also provided a variety of supports to decrease his level of anxiety and confusion.

People as Regulating Factors

One of the many harmful myths about autistic people is that they are isolated loners who neither need nor seek relationships. That's not true. In fact, for many the presence and proximity of another trusted human being is the key to emotional regulation. The McCanns had recently relocated to a new town, where their four-year-old autistic son, Jason, was enrolled in a public preschool program. His mother asked the school to give the boy scheduled movement breaks—chances to go outside or to the gym once or twice daily—and she requested that his eight-year-old brother join him. Since the boys were adjusting to the new environment, she felt it would be helpful to both, since they were so mutually attached. Not only did Jason regulate himself by getting the movement he needed, but he experienced the regulating presence of a familiar and trusted person, his brother.

Sometimes autistic people become dysregulated if a particular person is absent. Seven-year-old Jamal repeatedly asked his teacher, "Mommy at home?" One therapist suggested that the teacher answer affirmatively just once, but then ignore repeated questions. The ignoring only made Jamal more anxious, and his questioning became louder and more urgent. I suggested instead placing on his desk a photo of his mother at home and assuring him, "Mommy's at home. You will see Mommy after school." That reduced his need to question and helped him focus on schoolwork.

A third-grader named Caleb benefited from a different kind of companion: an imaginary friend he called Stephen. In class Caleb would sometimes insist on saving the seat next to him for Stephen. On the playground he would pretend to play with Stephen. His teacher said Caleb tended to invoke Stephen only in difficult moments: transitions between activities or settings or at particularly chaotic times. When I visited as a consultant, his young classmates told me Stephen was Caleb's make-believe friend who helped him because he was autistic. They understood! Clearly Caleb was using the imaginary friend as an emotional regulatory strategy, a way to soothe himself in difficult moments.

"Should we discourage this?" the teacher asked. As long as it wasn't making him less present or engaged, I assured her, it seemed a useful strategy. As Caleb made friends and became more comfortable, he mentioned Stephen far less frequently, and then not at all.

Some strategies are verbal. Many autistic people display echolalia, the repetition of spoken language, repeated either immediately or sometime later (see chapter 2). This too has often been dismissed as autistic behavior and irrelevant, nonsense talk. But echoing serves many functions for autistic people, including emotional regulation. A boy might ask over and over, "Going swimming this afternoon?" One could label the child an incessant questioner and aim to stop his echoing. Or we could ask "Why does he need to do that? What purpose does it serve?" Perhaps he has a need for things to be predictable. So the questioning is both a sign of feeling ill at ease and a coping strategy he employs to get information so he knows what to expect, reducing his uncertainty and anxiety.

Some autistic people not only repeat themselves but dominate conversations, sharing great amounts of information about a favorite topic (say, geography, Disney movies, dinosaurs, or train schedules) and may not consider the other person's thoughts, feelings, or interests. This too can be a sign of dysregulation, or an intense interest in sharing information. For a person who has difficulty grasping subtle social cues and who finds the unpredictability of typical conversation stressful, speaking incessantly on a familiar and beloved topic might provide a sense of control. As an autistic man once told me, "Entering into a free-flowing conversation is like stepping on to a mine-field. Something you say or do might blow up in your face." That may be why Paul, who is in his thirties, almost always greets me with "Hi Barry. You first visited me when I was four years old at the Stonehill preschool, right?" It's his ritualized way of initiating conversation, essentially his way of saying, "Hi Barry, how're you doing?"

I often see people go an extra step, trying to control *both* sides of the conversation. Some feed their parents lines to say: "Ask me, 'Do you want Cheerios or Frosted Flakes?' Ask me!" Many children repeatedly ask questions when they already know the answers: "What's your favorite baseball team?" "What color is your car?" "Where do you live?" If I intentionally and playfully give the wrong answer, they immediately correct me. So why did they ask? Doing so might be yet another effort to exert control, to increase predictability and sameness in the face of the anxiety triggered by social conversation. At the same time, it shows the child's desire to connect and stay engaged socially.

The Importance of Understanding "Behaviors"

Once you understand the role emotional regulation and dysregulation play in autism, it's easy to see why "deficit checklist" approaches to treating autism prove ineffective. They can actually cause *more* anxiety for the person involved, particularly when they aim to decrease strategies that help the person. These methods define certain traits and behaviors as autistic, viewing them only through the lens of pathology, and then focus on "extinguishing" them (a term many behavior therapists use). They fail to delve into the true motivations underlying the behaviors, and they often blame the person for being noncompliant or intentionally manipulative rather than recognizing that the individual is successfully using appropriate strategies—however unconventional in appearance. If they succeed at eliminating these behaviors, what they're really doing is stripping the person of coping strategies and communicating that what the person is doing is offensive or wrong, possibly leading to low self-esteem, depression, and a sense of oneself as flawed and incompetent. A better approach is to recognize the purpose and value of such behavior and, when necessary, to teach other strategies to stay well regulated.

Seeking to eliminate behavior without fully understanding its purpose is not only unhelpful; it also shows a lack of respect for the individual. Worse, when such efforts are common, it can make life more difficult for the autistic person and over time erode the individual's self-worth, making the person feel "I've screwed up" or "I'm being bad again."

That was the case for Lucy, an eleven-year-old. Her public school teachers had reported that Lucy, who did not yet have a reliable and effective communication system, was an unhappy and extremely aggressive child, prone to unpredictably lunging and clawing at the faces and necks of teachers and therapists. When I spent a morning observing her in my role advising the district, the problem became clear. Much of the work the educators and therapists were doing with

Lucy consisted of compliance training, such as exercises in which they repeatedly asked her to match pictures and images on cards or to point to pictures on command.

I quickly deduced why Lucy appeared to be lunging at her teachers. In the midst of the activity, the assistant abruptly changed course. She stopped showing pictures and instead wrote Lucy's name on a card, placed it in a row with other cards, and asked the girl to identify it. Almost immediately Lucy dove toward the young woman, trying to pull on her blouse in protest. Why? The therapist had shifted the pattern, changing the rules without warning. When a highly anxious child craves routine to understand the world, it's no wonder a sudden change throws her off and triggers an extreme reaction.

To test my theory, later that day I watched Lucy stroll with a teacher along a familiar school hallway. Then I suggested that the teacher alter the route from the usual routine. When she did, Lucy, suddenly upset, again lunged and grabbed at the teacher's neck and blouse just as she had before. I took no pleasure in instigating that reaction, but it drove home an important point to the teacher, who simply saw Lucy's behavior as an intentional effort to "escape" from activities.

It was clear that the grabbing wasn't *aggressive* behavior; it was both a protest and a plea for support at a moment of extreme confusion. Lucy didn't intend harm. She was confounded during a familiar activity; she had become more anxious and dysregulated, approaching a state of panic.

How Adults Can Cause Dysregulation

Lucy's experience shows how the various people in an autistic person's life can actually be the cause of dysregulation. When I lead autism workshops for parents and professionals, I often tell the audience, "Raise your hand if your behavior has ever been the primary reason your child, student, or adult client experienced a full-blown meltdown." After some nervous laughter, virtually every hand goes up. We're not bad people, I point out. We might be acting with the best of intentions—asking a child or older person to stay in a noisy and challenging social activity just five more minutes, for example, or complete two more math problems. But that's all it takes.

Of course we can also play a significant role in helping people cope. If a child is hypersensitive to sound, a parent can offer noise-dampening headphones. Often a child will repeatedly ask a question—"Going to the park this afternoon? Going to the park this afternoon?"—even after the parent has repeatedly answered. Instead of answering directly, a parent might say, "Let's write down the answer and put it on our daily calendar so we don't forget." That not only acknowledges the child's concern and helps calm and reassure her in the short term; it also provides her with a model, a strategy to keep herself regulated in the future. In the same way, we can encourage an autistic college student to advocate for himself by explaining to his professor that he may need to take a movement break during a long lecture to stay focused.

Often the most important things we can do to help are to acknowledge and validate a person's feelings of dysregulation, yet teachers and others frequently overlook this basic measure. I made a consultation visit for eight-year-old James, when he was having a particularly difficult day. James was a sweet, wiry, and active little boy with saucer-like eyes who sometimes had unpredictable and uncontrollable episodes of dysregulation. One of his favorite parts of the day was gym class, an opportunity to expend energy and relax his body. But on this particular day, the gymnasium was being used for class photos. Autistic children often find such changes in schedule challenging and confusing, so it wasn't surprising that James had reacted with dismay. The teachers offered to take him on an extended walk, but that didn't meet his need to regulate.

"But I *need* to go," he said, then screaming, "I need to *move in the gym.*"

By the time I was called from another part of the building, James's meltdown had become so severe that the teacher had taken him out of his classroom to a small conference room, where he was hiding under a table, growling and refusing to come out. Previously a therapist had suggested the staff ignore such behavior to avoid reinforcing it with attention. Instead I offered James a beanbag chair he liked and a weighted stuffed animal, a frog, that he liked to hold when he needed to calm himself. I slid them both under the table to where he was curled up in a fetal position.

"James," I said calmly, "I think you're upset because you couldn't go to gym today."

"Couldn't go to gym," he echoed. "I need to *move*."

Slowly I scrunched my body under the table and scooted toward the boy. Sitting beside him, I acknowledged his feelings of confusion and anger and offered some words of encouragement: "Everybody's feeling sad because they know you're upset."

Taking in my words, he slowly calmed down and turned in my direction. "No pictures tomorrow?" he finally said. "Go to gym tomorrow?"

"Yes," I said, "you will go to the gym tomorrow."

James emerged voluntarily, quietly walked out of the room, and asked to take a stroll in the hallway. His teachers said he recovered far more quickly than when they had ignored him.

What James needed wasn't to be ignored, and his reaction clearly told us that. The regulating routine he relied on had been interrupted. The rules had changed without warning. His expectations were not met. He needed someone to be present and to listen, acknowledge, and validate his feelings.

Near the end of the school day, a school aide flagged me down in the hallway and brought James over to me, holding his stuffed frog. "Dr. Barry, I just want to say goodbye," James said. "And my frog wants to say goodbye too." It was not the first time that a simple gesture from a sweet child brought a tear to my eye.

A parent or teacher can make a difference, positive or negative, merely with tone of voice or energy level or by being predictable—or surprising, accepting, or intrusive. If a stranger, or even a relative, tries without warning to offer a hug to an autistic child, the child might react defensively. But the same child might not mind a hug if she does the initiating. Once when my British friend Ros Black-burn visited the United States, I accompanied her to several speak-ing engagements where I introduced her to acquaintances. When people moved in close to her personal space with great excitement and energy—"Ros! It's *so* great to meet you!"—she would often step back, even recoil, stiffening her body and assuming a protective, guarded posture. But when people stood farther away, moved slowly, and spoke more slowly and calmly, Ros responded with much greater ease and confidence.

Sometimes offering the best support means suppressing your instinctive, emotional reaction. Barbara picked up her four-year-old son, Nick, at preschool every day at 3 p.m. One day, on her way there she got a flat tire and had to wait forty-five minutes for a tow truck. She alerted the school, but her son was so dependent on his fixed routine that she worried in the meantime how Nick would react. Would he panic? Would he have a meltdown?

When she finally arrived, Nick was sitting on a mat in the "quiet corner" of the classroom, frenetically rocking, looking disconnected, lost, and distraught. All of the other children had been picked up, and he was the last one waiting. The teacher told Barbara that Nick knew she would be coming, but feeling anxious herself, Barbara felt the urge to dash to reassure Nick. Instead she paused, took a few deep breaths, walked over slowly, and calmly and sat down next to him. "Nick, honey, Mommy's here," she said in a soft, measured tone. "Everything's okay." Gradually Nick looked up at her, stopped rock-ing, and echoed, "*Mommy's* here, Mommy's here, Mommy's here." He stood up, took her hand, and silently led her to the door. Barbara understood that to help Nick recover she herself needed to stay well regulated.

Her moment of restraint was emblematic of an important idea: Instead of trying to change how an autistic person reacts to us, we need to pay close attention to how *we* react to the person.

The Power of Listening and Building Trust

I learned that lesson in a larger way from my experience with Jesse, the eight-year-old whose difficult behavior had proven such a problem at his former school. At his new school, where I consulted, we clearly needed to work to build trust and help him see school in a positive light. My approach, whenever possible, is to work as a member of a team rather than presuming I have all the answers. In collaboration, parents, teachers, therapists, administrators, and others involved in a child's life can develop and execute the best possible plan. When his new school team first assembled shortly after Jesse arrived, nearly everyone agreed that Jesse wasn't aggressive but rather defensive, scared, and confused.

"We're going to have to build trust," I told the team. Jesse didn't speak, and since the previous school made compliance training— not social communication—its priority, he lacked an effective way of communicating. He didn't have control over how he spent his time, or even an understanding of what to expect, since his teachers didn't utilize visual schedules, which help prepare kids and make things more predictable. While his teachers and therapists had been focused on getting him to behave, he had been fighting to express himself and survive.

He was routinely dysregulated and had no way to share how he felt or what he needed—other than for people to back off.

His new school team immediately focused on giving him tools to communicate, using cards with picture symbols and photos, and always presenting him with choices to ensure that he felt some degree of autonomy and dignity. We gave him a schedule so he could know what to expect. We understood that he had severe sensory challenges, so an occupational therapist created a plan with various sensory strategies to help him regulate his body. As part of his morning routine, for instance, he would sit in a rocking chair in a quiet area in his classroom while an occupational therapist massaged his hands with lotion and then massaged his forehead; he found deep pressure calming. I once joked that they should have called the room Spa Jesse.

Within weeks the team had organized Jesse's photos and picture symbols into a communication book to help him express himself by pointing to what he wanted or wanted to do. (This was before iPads were available.) The book included activities he found regulating, such as running in the gym, head squeezes, massage, and listening to music. The therapist let him choose the hand or arm he wanted to have massaged and also taught him to massage himself. Now able to communicate, Jesse—previously so anxious and frightened that he swatted away anyone who came near—became comfortable interacting with classmates and teachers for extended periods. He spent part of his days in mainstream classrooms, supported by an aide, and only a few months after his arrival, his teacher reported good news: for the first time in his new school, Jesse had flashed a broad smile. For the first time in his life, Jesse was delighted to head off to school each day.

What was different? At the previous school, the staff had focused on getting Jesse to comply, to follow their plan—not on listening to him, not on communication. Now the focus was fostering social communication and finding ways to support a well-regulated emotional state. His new team gave him a sense of control over his life—not unlimited, open-ended control but choices within a predictable structure. They taught him things he could do independently to feel a sense of control and stay well regulated. They helped him understand that they were there to support him, not to control him.

To be sure, he still had his share of struggles and some challenging days. But over time they became less frequent and Jesse opened up, clearly feeling more comfortable in his classes, around people, in his own skin. In middle school Jesse continued to progress and took on two different jobs. Working with a neurotypical classmate, he collected paper from classrooms for recycling. He also delivered mail to classrooms. Though Jesse wasn't a fluent reader, the staff established a color-coded system to help him sort the mail. In the process he had opportunities to interact with adults and peers. With the help of a speech-generating device, Jesse carried on brief conversations with the teachers as he delivered the letters and packages each day.

No meltdowns, no hitting, no resistance, and lots of smiles based on lots of trust.

The boy who had appeared to be so frightened, bruised, and alone was now staffing the school store, selling snacks and drinks to class-mates and teachers, collecting money and making change. He cel-ebrated completing middle school by attending the end-of-the-year dance with a friend. Later, in high school, this teenager, who had once been so anxious and unpredictable that staff would steer clear of him in the hallways, worked as an assistant to the chemistry teacher. Jesse so excelled at keeping the beakers and test tubes in order on the shelves (with the help of a visual guide) that the teacher said the lab had never been so organized.

I clearly remember a moment at a team meeting when Jesse was ten. Two years earlier his mother had given up on the previous school district, frustrated and angry at the way Jesse was treated as a behav-ior problem. Now she looked around the table at the therapists, the teachers, and the staffers with tears in her eyes.

"You saved my son's life," she told the group.

If we had, it wasn't through heroic measures or brilliant insights. It was because instead of trying to change Jesse, we listened, we ob-served, we asked why, and we changed our approach based on what we saw and heard. We recognized what was making him feel dysregu-lated, and we helped give him the tools to cope and to exert some control over his own life. Most importantly we helped him under-stand that people cared about him and were worthy of being trusted.

If that approach can work for Jesse, it can help almost any child.

CHAPTER 2

Listen

D AVID taught me to listen.

David was an energetic and joyful little four-year-old who seemed to be in constant motion, bouncing like a pinball from place to place. Observing him in his preschool classroom when I was beginning my career, I came to understand that although David spoke a great deal, almost all of his speech came in the form of echoes. Instead of typical, creative speech and language, he had his own kind of communication: either he would mimic what he had just heard someone say, or he would produce a phrase or sentence that could seem completely out of context or even nonsensical. Sometimes he immediately echoed what he heard; sometimes it was hours, days, or months later.

David had a fascination with textures and tactile sensations, and he had a particular affinity for my sweaters. One day I was working to encourage him to take turns with me putting pieces in a puzzle, but I could tell he was distracted. In the unabashed manner young children have, he began picking tiny wool pills from an arm of my sweater and then the front, examining each ball up close, holding it to his eyes and rolling it between his thumb and index finger. Instead of protesting, I decided to follow his interest.

"See that, David?" I said. "That's a piece of fuzz."

"That's a piece of fuzz, fuzz, *fuzz*," he repeated, excited that I was interested in what so fascinated him.

I listened as he delighted in playing with the tiny ball of wool, and then in playing with the word itself, seeming to enjoy the sensation as it crossed his lips: "That's a piece of fuzz, fuzz, fuzz! That's a piece of *fuzz!*"

It was obvious to me how happy this combination of touch and sound made David, so I saw it as a way to connect with him and draw more of his attention. The next day I brought a bowl of cotton balls. That enchanted him. I placed the balls around the room and devised a game, asking David to follow my verbal cues and hunt down the cotton balls—on a chair, say, or under a stuffed animal. Clearly something about the textures excited him, making him more present and eager to connect with me. Imposing activities on him might have provoked resistance, but by following his interests and his energy I discovered that David would be motivated, even persistent in finding his own ways to communicate. His learning could be joyful rather than stressful.

One day we had the children create an art project with paints, but instead of paint brushes, we used pieces of sponge. Afterward David discovered bits of the cut-up sponge on the floor of the classroom. Just as he had with the fuzz balls, he began picking them up one at a time, closely examining each as he rubbed it between his fingers, savoring the texture.

"That's a piece of sponge," I said.

"That's a piece of sponge," he echoed, glancing at me. "That's a piece of sponge, sponge, *sponge!*"

Again I could see the joy he derived from the combination of the feeling of the material, the sound of the words coming out of his mouth, and sharing his discovery with me. As he clutched the bits of sponge in his cupped hands and looked at the others on the floor, he began to dance around the room on tiptoes, making brief, furtive glances in my direction. "That's a piece of sponge, sponge, *sponge!*" he kept saying. "That's a piece of *sponge!*"

The real revelation came the next day. By then the classroom had been cleaned. We had cleared away the art project and someone had straightened up and vacuumed away all the debris. When David arrived in the classroom, though, he returned to exactly the spot in the room where a day earlier he had come upon the sponge bits. I watched as he repeated his dance, shifting his gaze to me and saying, "David, that's a piece of sponge, sponge, sponge! That's a piece of sponge!"

Consider this: What if a visitor had happened into the classroom that day to observe the children? Imagine such a person watching this little boy coming into the room, full of energy, and then performing a little dance and babbling on about a sponge. The visitor might easily have dismissed the behavior as absurd. Or silly. Or random. Was he hallucinating? Had David lost his grip on reality? Or did he simply not understand the word *sponge*?

But if you had been in the room the previous day, if you had shared the conversation with David that I did, if you knew about his enthusiasm for new textures, then you would have understood exactly what was going on. This little boy was remembering and re-enacting his experience of the previous day—not only the facts of the experience (the materials used in the art project) but, more important, his own feelings of excitement about it and his connection with me.

He was telling a story.

Reframing Echolalia

Anyone who has spent time with an autistic person who speaks is familiar with this tendency to repeat words, phrases, or whole sentences or songs, often ad infinitum. Indeed echolalia is one of autism's defining characteristics. In children who can speak it is often among the first indications to parents that something is amiss in a child, when, instead of responding or initiating with the child's own language, the child echoes words or phrases borrowed from others.

> Mother: Honey, you want to go outside?
> Daughter: You want to go outside?

Those initial exchanges take many forms: the child repeats snippets from videos she's watched, announcements on the subway, greetings from teachers, animal noises, or even select phrases from an argument her parents had at home. Anything can become an echo. Utterances children hear at moments of great excitement, pain, anxiety, or joy seem to take on a life of their own, becoming the source of echoes, with the child seeming to relive the moment and the emotion that accompanied it.

A colleague once asked me to visit an elementary school to offer insight about an autistic fifth-grader named Eliza. When I arrived at the classroom to observe her, the teacher gestured for me to come in and take a seat. But when I approached Eliza, the girl suddenly had a worried look on her face, cautiously looked in my direction, and said three words: "Got a splinter!"

I wasn't sure I'd heard right. A splinter? But I proceeded with my friendliest and gentlest demeanor and sat nearby, only to hear Eliza repeat the same words, "Got a splinter! Got a splinter!," as she anxiously watched me out of the corner of her eye.

I looked at her hands to see if she might have hurt herself, but the teacher spoke up. "Don't worry," she told the girl. "Barry's a nice man. He's just visiting today."

Eliza repeated verbatim, "Barry's a nice man. He's just visiting today."

That seemed to calm her, but it only made me wonder what feelings Eliza was experiencing and what was going through her mind to make her say "Got a splinter!" What was she talking about? Did it have anything to do with me? Was it just random? And why had the teacher responded in that way?

When I asked the teacher later, she explained that Eliza had suffered a painful splinter on the playground two years earlier. Since then she had used the phrase "Got a splinter!" whenever she felt anxious or scared.

Just as Eliza's teacher knew what she meant, and just as I fully understood and delighted in David's celebration of the sponges, parents and others close to a child often comprehend exactly what the child is saying—and why. "Oh, that's a line from a *SpongeBob* episode he watched last year." Or "He heard his teacher say that when there was a fire drill at school last month." Or "I said that to him when I gave him a bath last month!" Or "That's what the announcer on *The Price Is Right* says."

Yet these same parents grow apprehensive when they hear some "experts" speak of echolalia through the lens of pathology—when they're told that echolalia is just another "autistic behavior" that interferes with learning, a problematic trait that's considered an obstacle to the child's ability to fit in and appear "normal."

That's a mistake and is wrong.

Certainly on the surface it looks that way, and based on the mistaken advice of some professionals many parents worry that this persistent echoing hinders the child's ability to connect with other children, to develop relationships, or to learn language and participate in school. They may be told that it isolates the child, marking him as quirky, different, or weird.

Some ill-informed professionals reinforce their beliefs by labeling this kind of communication "silly talk" or "video talk" (since so many of the phrases come from movies and TV shows). They convince parents that echolalia has no value and work to arm them with strategies to stop it. Early in my career it was common for educators and professionals to use harsh and negative techniques to get children to stop these speech patterns. Therapists would respond to a child's "silly talk" with loud, annoying (to the child) noises such as clapping their hands near the child's face, the way you might try to dissuade a dog from barking in the house. In one school I visited, teachers would squirt lemon juice in a child's mouth to punish "undesirable" behavior and remind her to speak in turn or get back on topic. More recently practices have become less harsh and aversive; some involve ignoring the child (known as "planned ignoring"). Some professionals instruct parents to hold up an index finger to the child and issue a firm command: "Be quiet!" or "No talking!" or "No silly talk!" All of these approaches share the same goal: stopping the talk. Many autistic adults exposed to these behavioral "contingencies" as children now indicate they were upsetting, frightening, and even traumatizing.

I have long believed that this is wrong, that these professionals were misunderstanding echolalia and that the responses they were prescribing were not only misguided but maybe even harmful. In their attempts to make children appear more "normal," these "experts" were plainly ignoring what were clearly legitimate attempts at communication, and—worse—they were disrupting the child's process of learning to communicate and connect with the world.

How I Came to Understand Echolalia

Shortly after I earned my master's degree in speech and language pathology, I landed what felt like a dream job. As part of my required clinical fellowship, I was offered a position at the Buffalo Children's Hospital Autism Program. (People are sometimes surprised to hear that such a program existed in 1975, but I can vouch for its existence and excellent quality.) That year I worked as a speech and language specialist in a classroom with five young boys, all of whom were on the spectrum. At the same time, I was conducting a pilot study, observing these boys to try to understand what specific role echolalia played in their communication and language development.

One reason I wanted to study echolalia was that many of the judgments about autistic children had been made by people who had no training or knowledge about children's language and communication development, or child development in general. They were behavior therapists, specialists in developing programs to reduce undesirable behavior and increase desirable behavior. Most shared the belief, and many still do, that echolalia was in the "undesirable" category of behavior without really understanding it. In Ros Blackburn's terms, they hadn't asked "Why?" They saw themselves as the experts and didn't demonstrate the respect to try to understand the child's or the parents' perspective.

I suspected that there was more to this kind of speech than just random or pathological behavior. My observations, and my training in psycholinguistics and speech-language pathology, had taught me that echolalia was far more complex than "meaningless parroting," that this kind of speech served a purpose, or possibly many different purposes. And I wanted to test this hypothesis.

Up until that time the limited research on echolalia had been conducted in the more artificial, contrived conditions of a laboratory. Mine was a social-pragmatic study; that is, I studied language as the children used it in the context of everyday activities and settings. I watched these little boys in the classroom. I observed them at home. I videotaped them as they interacted with peers and siblings. In short, I observed them and listened to them as they lived their lives.

It was the first time I had worked with so many children who displayed echolalia, and as I got to know them well, I could see that for none of them was this meaningless speech. These little boys were communicating, and using echolalia for other purposes as well. In talking with their mothers and fathers, I found that the parents had similar perceptions.

I first saw it in David, the same boy who had celebrated over the sponge pieces. Every time one of the teachers or aides would say "No!" to David in a way that indicated displeasure, he would react the same way. He would skip around the room, repeating in a voice with strong negative emotion, "We don't slam doors. We don't pee on the wall." Those ten words told an entire story. He wasn't saying them as an order to someone else; nor was it random or silly—though, admittedly, the adults in the room found it quite entertaining. David had been scolded before, and this was his way of acknowledging the social import of the moment: "We don't slam doors. We don't pee on the wall." It meant that he comprehended that the adults disapproved and he was being reprimanded. Whatever he had been doing fit into the same category as door slamming and urinating: things you're not supposed to do in the classroom. He was attuning to the emotion behind the message and indicating in his own way, "Understood."

I learned that the echoing could also communicate important information and feelings. One afternoon Jeff, another boy in the class, seemed less energetic than usual, but since he wasn't yet communicating directly, we didn't know why. Then he started approaching the various adults in the classroom, got close to their faces, and made a noise we hadn't heard before: "Doo-aaah! Doo-aaah!" As he said it, he opened his mouth wide and extending his jaw downward with the prolonged "aaah."

He continued that pattern through the entire afternoon, pacing around the classroom but then finding his way back, making eye contact, and repeating those two syllables: "Doo-aaah! Doo-aaah!" My first impression was that he was playing with sounds, seeing how it felt for various noises to emanate from his mouth. Hard as I tried, I could not discern what he was trying to say—though it was clear from his approach, his intent expression, and his persistence that he was trying to communicate something. He was seeking and expecting a response.

When Jeff repeated his "Doo-aaah!" again the following morning the teacher phoned his mother to investigate. She didn't even have to pause to figure it out. "Oh," she said, "we think he might be coming down with a cold."

We waited for more. "And?"

"Well, when I think he's getting sick, I tell him to open his mouth and do 'Aaah.' "

It made perfect sense. Jeff was trying to tell us that he didn't feel well. He had a cold, or maybe a sore throat. At his developmental stage, he was unable to explain that in his own words, so he was acting out a scene for us, reenacting what he had heard his mother say at home: "Do 'Ahh!' "

Out of context it meant nothing; it was a little boy making funny sounds. But we kept asking "Why?" With some careful listening and probing, I understood Jeff perfectly.

I did a lot of listening that year. With a federal grant from the Department of Education's Bureau of Education for the Handicapped, I recorded twenty-five videotapes of the boys in everyday activities: in school during playtime, at lunch, and during individual and group therapy sessions, and at home with their siblings and parents, over the period of a year. I spent months analyzing the children's speech, gestures, and actions, and in the process, I identified 1,009 distinct echoes and categorized them (as good academics do) into seven functional categories. I distinguished immediate echolalia (when a child repeats a word or phrase on the spot) from delayed echolalia or "scripting" (when the speech is repeated hours, days, or even months or years later).*

The bottom line was this: These little boys were communicating in all sorts of ways. Sometimes they were affirming what they understood. Sometimes they were taking turns, as one might in conversation. Sometimes they were repeating words as a way of rehearsing something they were going to say later. Sometimes they were repeating certain sounds because the sounds themselves were calming, as chanting a mantra might be. Sometimes they were talking themselves through the steps of a process or reasoning through the situation aloud to reassure themselves. Sometimes they were echoing to support emotional regulation, telling themselves not to be anxious or afraid.

In other words, they were using language for the same purposes we all do.

We just had to listen, observe, and pay attention.

---

* I focused on immediate echolalia for this study, but later studied delayed echolalia with Patrick Rydell, a student of mine, and we reached similar conclusions.

An Alternative Way of Communicating

The more I have listened over the years, the more I have developed my ability to recognize and make sense of the echoes I hear in autistic children and even adults who use echolalia. Does echolalia ever appear to have little apparent communicative value, in the sense that we cannot decipher the meaning or purpose? Of course. For example, when individuals who are otherwise nonspeaking blurt out words or phrases, it's now referred to as "unreliable speech." They are not intending to use the words or sounds to communicate. (See Chapter 11.) But most of the time, with careful listening and a bit of detective work, it becomes clear that the child (or adult) is communicating—in his own unique way. My research has proven that, and other researchers have found similar results.*

Aidan, for example, was an adorable three-year-old whose ability to speak wasn't developing as expected but who showed a knack for picking up whole chunks of language. Most typically developing children add a word at a time to their vocabulary (*mommy*, *daddy*, *baby*), combine the words flexibly, and then build short sentences ("Mommy hug." "Daddy eat cookie."). Instead Aidan would surprise his parents with whole phrases and sentences, sometimes quite sophisticated grammatically. At four he would greet people he met not by saying "Hi" or "Hello" but with a line from his favorite movie. He would cock his head to the side, squint his sparkly eyes, and ask, "Are you a good witch or a bad witch?"

Of course that is how Glinda, the Witch of the North, greets Dorothy in the famous scene from *The Wizard of Oz*. It's a dramatic moment. Dorothy has just landed in Oz when a tiny glowing bubble shows up, gradually growing in size as it nears, then suddenly bursts,

---

*Inspired by our research, Marge Blanc addresses this issue and the research in her book *Natural Language Acquisition on the Autism Spectrum: The Journey from Echolalia to Self-Generated Language* (Madison, WI: Communication Development Center, 2013).

and Glinda appears, looking like a fairy princess in a gown and holding a wand. She approaches Dorothy and says those immortal words: "Are you a good witch or a bad witch?"

What more powerful example could there be of one person greeting another? This boy wasn't speaking gibberish; he was capturing the essence of what it means for one human being to encounter another. (Later his teachers and therapist taught him to use the more conventional "Hi, my name is Aidan." As much as his mother appreciated that, she missed her son's more distinctive greeting.)

Sometimes children echo to narrate their way through an experience—even the most mundane experiences. That was true of Bernie. He was a high-arousal, high-energy youngster, and much of his communication consisted of enthusiastically repeating things he had obviously heard from other people, including his mother. He had an uncanny ability to re-create the speaker's accent. When I worked in his school decades ago, I would sometimes be in the men's room with him when suddenly I heard his voice emanating from a lavatory stall, sounding exactly like his mother: "You done now, boy! Now wipe yo' butt!" Being of African-American descent, and being raised in an urban area, his echoes reflected characteristics of what was then called Black English, and is now referred to as AAVE (African-American Vernacular English). When he echoed things I had said, his speech clearly reflected my Brooklyn accent as he knew I was from "New Yawk."

Often children use echoes to tell us what they're thinking, but rarely in ways that are immediately obvious. The father of Kyle, a young autistic boy, once invited me to join the two of them on a sailboat in Narragansett Bay, Rhode Island. In the middle of a lovely afternoon, we were anchoring in a little cove when the boy began running up and down the deck as he anxiously leaned over to peer into the water.

"No dogs! Dogs bite!" he kept saying with increasing urgency, looking back at his dad. "No dogs! Dogs bite!"

No dogs? We were out on the water, with no other boats nearby—

no people, no animals. Just waves and wind. What could he have been talking about? His father knew exactly what he meant. "He's asking if he can go swimming."

I asked the father to explain. He told me that Kyle had a fear of dogs. When he felt anxious about his safety, that was how he expressed it: "No dogs! Dogs bite!" Now he wanted to go swimming in the shallow cove, but he wasn't sure whether this was a safe place, so he was asking. With that phrase he accomplished three things: he expressed his fear, requested permission from his dad, and made sure it was safe. And when his father responded "It's okay, it's safe! No dogs!," Kyle jumped in with great glee.

Every Family Has a Language

As stories like these illustrate, echolalia offers lessons not just about language and communication development but about raising children. Many parents look to doctors or therapists to be the experts, appealing to them to explain their children. Over time I have come to realize that the best approaches to providing effective and meaningful support for autistic children and adults center on the family, and those close to the family. Parents almost always know their children better than anyone else does. Adult siblings and grandparents often have a great depth of understanding about the autistic person with whom they have shared so much of their life. And based on innumerable shared experiences over so many years, every family develops its own language: its own familiar phrases, its own terms, its own shorthand. In other words, every family develops its own culture that allows for mutual communication, understanding, and support.

Each family has its own native culture, and outsiders are most often alien to that culture. So rather than parents relying on outsiders, such as professionals, to make sense of things, the professionals need to rely more on the insiders: parents, their children, and other family members. When parents ask me to explain their child's habit of repeating phrases and words (or any perplexing pattern of behavior), my first response is always to turn the question around: "Well, what do you think?" Usually they can tell me—or at least make an educated guess. In either case they often provide important information about their child that I was not aware of, and in the process their expertise about their child is validated—they feel respected and valued as a member of a collaborative partnership with professionals.

For one study I sent parents questionnaires asking about their experiences of echolalia. Nearly all of their autistic children used echolalia, for which the parents had their own explanations: "Sometimes he does it to keep something in mind to help him understand it better." "Sometimes she uses it to request something." "That's how he takes his turn when he doesn't understand." "When he echoes he's saying 'Yes.'" Nearly all of them found meaning in their children's unconventional speech.

Echolalia as a Learning Strategy

In fact, I found that echolalia serves an even more vital purpose for many autistic children: it's a path to acquiring language. In the simplest terms, it works like this: Many autistic children struggle with communication, but they tend to have a very strong memory. So they learn language by hearing it and repeating it back, either immediately or with some delay. As the child continues to grow socially, cognitively, and linguistically, she begins to discern the rules of language, but she does so, in part, through a "gestalt" learning style, using echolalia to breaking down the memorized chunks of speech.

Of course that doesn't mean it's easy to live with. I always tell parents that just because it's functional, may provide the stepping stones to language development—and is vital to their child's developing communication—that doesn't mean it won't drive you crazy at times! The fiftieth time your daughter repeats the same line from *Frozen*, your head might be ready to burst. The hundredth time your son says, "We don't slam doors. We don't pee on the wall," you might feel like slamming the door yourself. But it's important to take heart in two things: first, the knowledge that this kind of communication serves a purpose for the child, and second, that it represents an ever-evolving developmental process. Over time the echoing will most likely lessen as a child's creative language system develops, though of course progress comes at different rates and at different times in every child.

Parents and others can help a child learn to use more creative language—instead of echoing—through various strategies, including simplifying the language they use with the child, breaking down echolalic chunks into words and smaller phrases, adding gestures, and introducing visual supports and written language. For example, a father might say to his daughter, "Please go over to the refrigerator and get some milk and cookies." The child might fill her "turn" in the conversation by merely echoing the sentence, or part of it, but not really respond. Then the father might simplify the complex sentence by dividing it into segments: "Go to the refrigerator (while pointing). Get milk. Open the cabinet. Get cookies."

Another strategy is to introduce photographs, pictures, or written words on visual displays or iPads instead of exclusively using spoken language. This can help a child understand more readily and rapidly, making it less necessary to use echolalia as a strategy to understand.

For some children it's helpful for the child to write or type what they want to say. This can improve the ability to formulate language rather than relying on retrieving memorized chunks. Most autistic people are stronger using visual ways to express and understand language than communicating purely by hearing and speaking. Some nonspeaking autistic individuals with more automatic and unreliable forms of echolalia are able to type or spell to communicate complex thoughts or feelings. While it's crucial to acknowledge and understand the intentions, functions, and different types of echolalia, it's equally important to help the child move to more creative, self-generated language and more conventional ways of communicating through speech or other augmentative or alternative means.

Many children who use echolalia persistently when they are young use it less and less as they mature, but when faced with challenging circumstances or difficult moments of dysregulation, these individuals may revert to echoing. Elijah, a middle school student, was a passionate fan of Broadway musicals, in particular *The Lion King*. Though Elijah had significant academic challenges, particularly in subjects requiring high-level comprehension of abstract language, he attended mainstream classes in his public middle school so he could benefit from sharing time and developing relationships with neurotypical peers. For the most part he thrived there, except when he felt overwhelmed and anxious about the more challenging academic work. As his anxiety increased, Elijah would stand up in the middle of his history class and start singing "Circle of Life" at the top of his lungs, first in English, then in German (which he'd learned from videos he'd found on the Internet).

The teachers at his school wanted to honor Elijah's creative spirit, but it can be disruptive to have a student break out in show tunes in history class. So I asked Elijah why he sang during this class. His explanation: The teacher was talking too quickly, and Elijah couldn't keep up. He had a difficult time paying attention, and this was Elijah's way of regulating himself emotionally to decrease his anxiety. The song was just another form of echoing, what some professionals have referred to as "scripting." He wasn't being bizarre or displaying random behavior; he was coping, the same way another person might play a favorite tune in his head when feeling bored or stressed (but without projecting it publicly).

Working with his teacher, parents, and others in the school, I sought a less disruptive way for him to calm himself. In addition to the songs, Elijah also liked drawing the *Lion King* characters. So we suggested that he bring a sketchpad to class, and later a small whiteboard and markers, so that when he felt anxious, he could quietly draw instead of interrupting the class. (Years later, Elijah became an artist, selling his work at craft fairs and creating greeting cards.)

Another teen who benefited from that kind of alternative outlet was Justin, a talented artist. When he was eleven, a small local café agreed to host a show of his artwork. His parents welcomed the opportunity to work on his social greetings, so he spent time rehearsing how he would greet the friends and strangers who might come to the show. The night of the opening he shook hands and welcomed the first few guests appropriately, but as more and more people arrived, Justin became increasingly anxious and overwhelmed. So in place of a standard greeting, he asked, "Who's your favorite cartoon character?" (Justin loved animation, and many of his pictures were cartoons.) Even when he knew the individuals well, he forgot the greetings he had prepared and instead blurted out his question, showing little interest in the answer. The anxiety in his voice seemed to increase with each repetition. Justin repeating his familiar question was like Elijah singing *Lion King* songs. In each case the echo provided a way to cope despite the feelings of anxiety.

To replace Justin's unusual greeting with a more conventional one, his parents prepared an index card with reminders of what to say in social situations. It wasn't a script, but it had some key words to remind him to stay engaged in conversation and to thank his friends for coming, rather than reverting to his familiar question. Knowing he had that visual and written reminder was enough to help Justin through social situations in which he felt overwhelmed and anxious.

Echolalia also serves a basic developmental purpose. A child cannot become a creative and fully functional user of language merely by repeating memorized words or phrases, but echolalia is a start. For many of these children, it's the first step in understanding the basic concept that they can use their body as an instrument to produce speech that expresses wants, needs, observations, and feelings. And in that way they can connect with other human beings.

Even some autistic adults who have progressed through stages of echolalia to more creative, conversational language say that much of what they say is based on "scripts." Julia Bascom, executive director of the Autism Self-Advocacy Network (ASAN) shared that she retrieves what she wants to say from her "store of utterances."

Listening Encourages Communication

All of that makes it important for parents to listen to their autistic children and family members and not be dismissive of this type of communication. One of my early mentors, the late Dr. Warren Fay, a speech and language specialist who worked at what is now Oregon Health & Science University, put it this way: If we don't yet fully understand what echolalia is all about, shouldn't we at least give the children the benefit of the doubt?

Consider the perspective of the individual, who is desperately trying to communicate, despite the neurological challenges that come with autism: social anxiety, sensory overload, often language-processing challenges. When that child's early attempts to communicate are met with harsh orders recommended by some professionals to "be quiet!" or "stop the silly talk!" it's not only unhelpful; it's actually discouraging efforts to communicate and work through the challenging process of figuring out what speech, language, and communication are all about. Besides, shutting down these attempts at communication may provoke even greater stress and confusion so that the person may react by avoiding certain people, shutting down, and giving up. As noted, in more extreme cases, autistic adults who experienced attempts to suppress or "extinguish" their echolalia recall these experiences as stressful or even traumatizing.

My simple advice: Listen, observe, and ask "Why?"

When parents, teachers, and caring professionals do that—when they pay close attention to words and gestures and context—they often understand intuitively that echolalia is part of the process of learning to communicate. I watched that happen in Namir, a little boy I first met when he was two and a half and captivated by Disney videos.

That's a common theme in the children with whom I have worked. Animated movies of all kinds hold a particular fascination for children on the autism spectrum, capturing their attention like almost nothing else. Why? Many children find the predictability and consistency of animated characters (as well as the music) comforting, a welcome contrast to the unpredictable nature of real people in everyday situations. In *Despicable Me* or *Madagascar*, the characters' vocal, facial, and body language is exaggerated, making emotions easier to decipher for such children, and even adults. Many autistic people also find the clear delineation of good and evil characters an appealing alternative to the more nuanced gray areas they encounter in real life. And repetitive viewings engender a reassuring sense of familiarity and mastery.

Many parents express concern that their children are spending too much time focusing on *The Lion King* or *Shrek*, worried that this is harmful to their development. Therapists or other professionals often compound their fears, cautioning that repeated viewing of these movies can serve to exacerbate the behaviors or somehow intensify their child's autism. Parents often ask me if these movies are only serving to provide more fodder for "silly talk," more useless phrases for children to echo.

I learned from Namir and his parents to take a longer perspective, a more nuanced view. As a three-year-old, Namir seemed lost in Disney films. Much of what came out of his mouth consisted of snippets from *Peter Pan*, his favorite. Instead of using language to interact with other people, he would repeat lines from the movie to himself, sometimes seeming oblivious to the real human beings surrounding him.

Others might have tried to dissuade him by reacting with demands to stop using such speech, convinced that this "meaningless parroting" was hindering his progress. Instead Namir's parents listened to him—and joined him. They bought *Peter Pan* action figures and interacted with him as he acted out imaginary scenes with the toys. They honored his interest and supported his engagement, so that Namir felt listened to and respected.

In time his play progressed. He showed increasing understanding of what he was saying. He was still using the phrases he had picked up from *Peter Pan*, but he found ways to use the Disney dialogues in their appropriate social context. Like Aidan, the boy who employed *The Wizard of Oz* line to greet people, Namir began integrating the snippets of speech spinning in his head as a way to connect with other people.

As he learned to use language more creatively, he used the "Disney talk" more selectively, when it was appropriate to the social context and his own intentions. When he wanted someone to leave, for example, he would say, "Tinker Bell, I hereby banish you forever!" By encouraging his unique efforts to communicate, Namir's parents dramatically aided his development. Between preschool and elementary school, he transformed from a boy who seemed lost in a world of random scripting and playing alone to an interactive and social little boy.

When his fourth-grade teacher assigned the children to do a research project on a famous American, Namir chose Walt Disney. And when he produced a lovely report, his parents took another opportunity to celebrate their son—and the value of having faith in one's own child.

CHAPTER 3

Enthusiasms

SOMETIMES a single word can change your perspective forever.

I once invited the late Clara Claiborne Park to speak at an annual autism fundraising conference I helped organize. Clara, who was an English professor at Williams College, was the mother of Jessy Park, a gifted autistic painter. Clara and her husband, David, were pioneers in the autism world. In the 1960s they were among the founders of the National Society for Autistic Children, the first advocacy organization of its type and the forerunner of the Autism Society of America. And in 1967 she published *The Siege*, the first widely read memoir written by a parent about raising an autistic child. I was privileged to get to know Clara and David early in my career and savored every opportunity to spend time with them.

Jessy displays many classic characteristics of autism. She struggles with social interactions, has difficulty expressing herself in speech, and recoils if someone touches her without warning. Over the years Jessy's parents appreciated and supported her deep interests, many of which became themes for her vivid, rainbow-colored paintings: architecture, prime numbers, clouds, odometers, quartz heaters, constellations, streetlamps, ATM machines, and many others.

After her speech at the conference, Clara, then in her late seventies, took questions from the audience. "I'm curious about your daughter's obsessions," someone said. "How have you dealt with them?"

"Obsessions," Clara repeated, contemplating the question for a moment. "Hmm. We've always thought of them as *enthusiasms*."

Clara and David had a particularly constructive attitude toward the many subjects that attracted their daughter's focus, no matter how unusual they were. Clara explained that if something truly gripped Jessy's attention, she and David would seek ways to steer Jessy's interest in a way that would help her.

That wasn't always easy, since her taste was so unpredictable. For a time Jessy focused on quartz space heaters. She admired the design; she categorized the styles and brands; she would carefully examine their parts. That enthusiasm gave way to another: the logos of rock bands. She would pore over album covers and photographs in magazines, closely scrutinizing the letters and graphics. She began integrating quartz heaters and rock band logos into her paintings, many of which have hung in museums and been featured in gallery shows. Rather than directing her daughter away from her interests, Clara treated Jessy with respect, assuming there were reasons for her fascinations—that to Jessy it all made sense.

Autistic children and adults develop all kinds of enthusiasms, talking nonstop about or focusing endlessly on subjects like skyscrapers, animal species, geography, particular kinds of music, sunrise and sunset times, or turnpike exits. Perhaps focusing on one topic gives the child a sense of control, of predictability and security in a world that can be unpredictable and feel scary.

Building on Enthusiasms

Still, some parents and professionals view these deep interests as yet another undesirable symptom of autism, one that makes it even more difficult for the child to fit in. Often their instinct is to discourage the child, to redirect his attention and suggest a wider range of interests that are more socially acceptable and conventional. But discouraging an enthusiasm can be just another way of dismantling a strategy that supports interest and engagement and that helps an autistic person feel better regulated. When we attempt to discourage or remove sources of interest and joy we miss out on opportunities for learning and building trusting relationships. A more helpful approach is to do as Jessy Park's parents did and use the enthusiasm as a way to expand the person's outlook and improve quality of life.

That was the case with Eddie, a fourth-grader who showed little interest in reading the stories his teacher assigned as part of the standard reading curriculum. He didn't seem to have difficulty reading and didn't typically avoid doing schoolwork. Rather he found the subject matter too abstract and the stories irrelevant to his life experience.

When I met with his talented special education teacher, Kate, in my role as consultant for the district, I suggested that we make an effort to find a hook that would draw him in to his academic work. Surely we could discover *something* that would motivate him to read and write. Was there anything that seemed to engage Eddie? Kate had noticed one thing: Eddie liked to spend time closely examining license plates on the cars in the school lot, then later enjoyed matching plate numbers and cars from memory.

A casual observer or a teacher who was less attuned might not have registered that a child's interest in something as mundane as license plates could actually become an opportunity. I suggested that Kate pay attention to that particular interest. Perhaps it might inspire an idea to engage Eddie.

When I returned a month later, she was excited to show me a project Eddie had recently completed. Working from a plan Kate had helped Eddie to create, he had spent time photographing each car and license plate in the school lot. With help from his teacher and the school office, he matched each car with the staffer who owned it. Then he met with each car owner, photographed the person, and conducted an interview to get to know the person: Do you have any hobbies? Are you married? How many children do you have?

Over time he assembled the photographs, documented the interviews, and developed a PowerPoint presentation for his class. Not only did the project serve its purpose, offering Eddie the chance to focus on reading, writing, research, and organizing material, but the experience had also proven transformative. The same child who had seemed disengaged and unmotivated to read went about his project eagerly, engaging with teachers, gathering information, and assembling it to share with his class. It also provided an opportunity to work on social and communication skills, as he proudly presented the finished project to his classmates, then fielded their questions.

His parents could not have been more surprised or delighted. At our next team meeting to review Eddie's progress, Kate explained the project and its goals, and Eddie's father's eyes were wide with amazement. "He did *what*? He interviewed *teachers*?" he said. "That's *incredible!*" When Kate showed him photographs of Eddie presenting his project to a roomful of classmates, his father was overwhelmed. Eddie was achieving things his parents couldn't have imagined. He was progressing academically and socially, and his self-esteem was soaring.

Other parents might have disapproved of a teacher who engaged their child in a subject as trivial as license plates. Another teacher might have insisted that Eddie read the same stories his classmates were reading, whether he liked it or not. Another school might not have been open to an alternative, individualized academic approach, instead letting the child struggle (and possibly fail) in the standard curriculum. But Eddie's success didn't require extra money or radical innovation, just a teacher who paid close attention and had the instinct to see an enthusiasm as a strength. Kate did this by focusing on what was most motivating for Eddie, and she used his interest as a powerful inspiration for learning. She saw enthusiasm as a source of potential rather than an impediment or a problem.

What Inspires Enthusiasms?

Why do people on the autism spectrum develop enthusiasms? To answer that, it's useful to consider how all kinds of people take comfort in hobbies, passions, and collections. If you were to visit my home, you might be surprised to see that I have a glass china cabinet holding more than a hundred pieces of walrus tusk in various shapes and sizes. Years ago, on a visit to Vancouver Island, I first came across Inuit ivory carvings, and something about them appealed to me. (The ivory walrus tusk used is acquired legally by native peoples who hunt walrus for food, clothes, tools, and materials for indigenous crafts.) Perhaps it was the shiny appearance of the ivory or the way its smooth texture felt in my hands. As I expanded my collection, part of the allure was certainly the detail and visual appeal of the carvings—the way the craftsmen carved the raw material into the shapes of walruses, bears, and whales. For whatever combination of reasons, I began collecting these pieces and found emotional satisfaction in the process.

I don't think of myself as obsessive, but, like a lot of people, I have gone through various phases of collecting. When I lived in the Midwest in my thirties, on weekends I drove to used-furniture stores and farm auctions in search of antique furniture. Later it was old quilts, then Navajo rugs; after that antique clocks and piano stools and antique slag glass lamps.

That I maintain these modest collections doesn't make me unusual. And that's the point. Nearly everyone has passions and interests. They fill a need; they give us pleasure; they make us feel good for reasons we may not always understand. They're part of being human.

Why, though, do so many autistic people display a far greater tendency than others to have these strong passions? Why do their enthusiasms often seem exponentially more powerful than other people's interests? As with any kind of hobby or pastime, it often begins with an emotional connection and response. An experience feeds a basic neurological need to be engaged, to appreciate beauty, and to experience positive emotion. When an autistic person develops an interest, we must assume that the particular subject of the interest is a good match for that person's neurophysiology and serves an important function. An adult with Asperger's syndrome explained to me that because connecting socially is challenging, many autistic people direct their energies into their areas of interest, leading, in some cases, to stronger and more focused passions.

Michael's focus was on music. When he was eight, long before he could engage in conversation comfortably, he demonstrated the gift of perfect pitch. He could hear the horn of a passing car and spontaneously identify its musical note. Suddenly distracted, he would look up and exclaim, "B flat!" Later he would hear a song on the radio, then sit at the piano and re-create it on the first attempt. He also could immediately transpose songs into other keys on request.

As many as 15 percent of autistic people demonstrate these high-level natural talents or gifts, known as savant skills, but most do not. Many others have "splinter skills"—strengths, such as rote memory or artistic and musical talent, that stand out relative to their overall profile. These unusual abilities are rooted in different learning styles, based on differences in how the brain processes and retains information. Some children feel drawn to information, activities, or tasks that jibe with their learning styles. Some like concrete and factual information that can be easily memorized; others enjoy activities that require good visual-spatial judgment, such as fitting things together. An older child might effortlessly memorize countless facts and details about dinosaurs or sports teams. A toddler might easily complete complex puzzles.

Some parents of younger children or those with greater developmental challenges confide that they show no such surprising skills, talents, or interests, at least not yet. Still, children might demonstrate clear preferences for particular kinds of sensory stimulation. Perhaps they seek visual, auditory, or tactile stimulation by flicking their fingers in front of their eyes, producing particular vocal patterns, or exploring specific textures through touch. Children are often drawn to certain toys because of the sensory input they provide. One toddler I worked with seemed magnetically drawn to electric fans of all kinds. If he knew there was a fan in a room, he would practically fight to get in to see and feel it, and when he encountered a fan, he would inspect it closely from all angles. Something about the sensation— feeling the breeze, seeing the spinning, feeling the vibrations, or the combination of them all—excited him, captured his attention, and heightened his alertness.

The King of Carwashes and Other Remarkable Tales of Passion

Once a child becomes aware of such a preference, what begins as a pleasurable sensory sensation often transforms into a focus of attention, interest, and preoccupation. The child seeks out what brought the positive feelings, and it can occupy his thoughts at all hours of the day.

Carwashes caught Alexander's attention. From an early age, when his father took the family car for its occasional cleaning, Alexander was simultaneously fascinated and frightened—by the sound, the splashing water, the brushes, the sight of the cars making their way through. Alexander couldn't explain why, but he begged his parents to take him back again and again so he could watch and listen. They visited so often that the owner of the local carwash befriended the family, welcoming Alexander to help out at the entrance by waving his arms to direct drivers into the wash.

His parents didn't understand what motivated Alexander's fascination, but they could sense how thrilled and happy it made him. Other children savored amusement parks or fast cars or ski slopes. Their son delighted in car washes. Whenever the family traveled, they sought out carwashes and mapped their journeys accordingly, visiting carwashes from Florida to Maine. At each stop on the tour, Alexander excitedly stood outside, surveying the grounds and taking in the operation the way another child might watch an NBA game or an action movie.

When he was ten, his parents contacted the International Carwash Association to request brochures they thought Alexander might enjoy. To their surprise, that led to a dream vacation for Alexander and his family—not a trip to Disneyworld or Hawaii but to Las Vegas, as an honored guest at the association's annual convention. He was so filled with excitement that for three nights he could barely sleep. His interest continued into adulthood. Alexander 's father calls him the King of Carwashes. Decades later, as an adult, he still loves going to car washes.

Then there was Chad. His passion was garden sprinklers. Everywhere he went as a child and teen, he would search the ground for pop-up sprinklers. At a park crowded for holiday fireworks, Chad would keep his eyes to the ground, searching out the sprinkler heads. When he found one, he would pull it up to identify the maker. At age eight he could tell a Toro from an Orbit from a Rain Bird. When he drew pictures in art class, along with the animals and trees he always included a sprinkler head popping up from the ground and shooting a spray of water into the air.

What inspired his fondness for garden sprinklers? Perhaps it started with a sensory experience: perhaps Chad was intrigued by the sight and sound of sprinklers popping out of the ground, then mysteriously disappearing, or the gentle sensations of water sprinkling the grass. Over time his interest morphed into a preoccupation. In unfamiliar surroundings he found it difficult to focus on anything else until he surveyed the area and found the sprinklers. And while it certainly wasn't what was occupying the attention of other children his age, his parents appreciated that their son had found something that brought him joy. Other dads took their kids to baseball games or fishing. Chad's dad surfed eBay to purchase secondhand sprinkler heads. Chad would give them names and toted them to school in his backpack. His dad drew smiley faces on the sprinkler heads. Sometimes Chad took them to bed with him at night like stuffed animals.

These deep interests can help children stay more engaged and attentive. They can be used to motivate learning and to enable participation in situations that might otherwise be difficult. That was true for Ken, an autistic teenager. From a young age Ken was fascinated with drawing—not so much artistically but simply focusing on drawing lines on paper. Over time he became interested in solving mazes, staring intently at a page while using a pen or pencil to make his way through the labyrinth. The appeal for Ken wasn't just drawing lines; it was solving problems. Each maze offered a sense of logic and order, a beginning and an end.

Wherever the family went, Ken would bring his maze books. Though he communicated very little through speech—he was learning to use a speech-generating device—his parents always brought him to meetings of his educational team, as they knew he could understand far more than he could say. Merely sitting and listening to a meeting would have proved challenging, but Ken's stack of maze books helped him to stay in the room. While he did his mazes, he was engaged in the meeting, looking on intently when he was interested in the conversation, turning his attention back to his maze when he wasn't. With this strategy Ken was able to stay focused and well regulated by shifting his attention away from the more demanding task of following the conversation to an activity with which he felt more competent.

Many autistic people find it helpful to bring a toy or other item or an activity related to an enthusiasm to settings that may pose difficulties, such as restaurants, family events, or larger group activities at school. Almost any enthusiasm can help in this manner. Five-year-old Vinny's interest was Oreck vacuum cleaners. When Vinny was feeling overwhelmed at school, he would often ask to go to the bathroom, whether or not he needed to. There he would take refuge in a stall, sometimes refusing to come back to class. His mother devised a unique strategy to use his interest as a way to provide a break when he needed one, especially from larger group activities. She collected Oreck catalogues, cut out pictures of vacuum cleaners, and organized them in a book she titled "Vinny's Happy Book." When he needed a break from large-group classroom activities, he could ask for the Happy Book and sit in a corner on a beanbag chair for a few minutes, examining photos of uprights and canisters, and refueling before he rejoined his classmates.

Some enthusiasms come and go as passing phases, and others last decades. Specific deep interests may have more obvious connections to future hobbies. Matt was passionate about everything related to time. When he was a young child and I visited his classroom as a school consultant, he would rush up to me and grab my arm to see my wristwatch. "Dr. Barry," he would say, without looking at me, "it's nine-fifteen in the morning!"

It was his entrée to a social connection. One December morning when he was just over five years old he was filled with excitement as he told me his latest discovery: "Dr. Barry, do you know what happens after eleven-fifty-nine p.m. on December thirty-first?"

"What?" I asked.

His body tensed as he raised himself up on tiptoe, hands flapping like wings on a bird. "The big ball comes down!" he said, his face lighting up with joy. "And it becomes the *next year!*" That was his enthusiasm, his way of having a conversation, of sharing what he knew and cared about. Years later, as a young adult, Matt remained enthusiastic about clocks and time, even preferring sports with a time element (such as hockey) over those without (such as baseball).

Nine-year-old Danny's enthusiasm was spices used in cooking. As a young boy he often watched his mother working in the kitchen. Without any kind of formal introduction, he took an interest in the seasonings she used. He made a habit of organizing the spices in alphabetical order and later took up watching cooking shows on TV and searching food websites. He became an expert in regional variations of barbecue, reeling off the differences among the styles from Texas,

Kentucky, Louisiana, and North Carolina. His parents couldn't identify what first piqued his interest in these topics or why they appealed
to him, but clearly he found them fulfilling. His mother imagined it
might lead Danny to attend a college for culinary arts and become a
chef. Far from wanting to redirect him, his parents took great pride
in Danny's expertise and found his enthusiasm infectious.

That's how I felt when I first met Brandon. I was visiting a classroom for a regular school consultation when one of the therapists introduced me to an adorable and wonderfully articulate four-year-old
who immediately told me his family had just relocated to the town.

"What state are you from?" he asked immediately.

I told him I lived in Rhode Island.

"Providence, Rhode Island?" he asked.

Just outside Providence, I told him.

"Providence is kind of a small city," he said. "Do you like big
cities?"

I told him I did, that I had grown up in New York City. Brandon's
eyes immediately lit up.

"You grew up in New York *City*?!" he asked. "My family likes to
visit New York City and I *love* New York City. We stay at the Mar-
riott Marquis in Times Square. We always stay on the sixteenth floor
because the sixteenth floor has the best views of all the signs in Times
Square." He went on to tell me the numbers of the various rooms
they had stayed in on recent visits and which ones had the best views.

I asked what he liked to look at from the hotel room windows. As
he answered, he got a distant look, as if he were running a video of
the scene in his mind. "There was a billboard for Nike with a picture
of Kobe Bryant over there," he began, pointing at the classroom wall,
then continued to describe the entire panorama in his mind's eye, as
if he was reliving the experience.

Using Interests to Build Connections

When a child or adult fixates on a topic, the way Brandon did on New York, and we join in, we can make the enthusiasm the basis for building relationships and trust. One significant reason many people on the spectrum focus on a particular topic is that it gives them a safe place to start a conversation. Even the most obscure, out-of-context, and seemingly irrelevant question ("What's your favorite dog breed?" "What kind of refrigerator do you have?") can be a strategy to connect. Whenever Brandon saw me, he seized the chance to talk to me about New York: "Did you live in Manhattan, or one of the other four boroughs? Brooklyn? Which part?"

That wasn't the end of the conversation, just the beginning. Often an enthusiasm offers the hook to engage a child, the lure for him to enter an activity or a conversation, taking pride in demonstrating his knowledge and even shared interests. Once he is engaged, we can gradually change or expand the subject to add more to the conversation. Of course how much is possible greatly depends on the individual's developmental abilities and interest in chatting. But with creativity, parents and teachers can use the child's passion for a topic to motivate social engagement in an enjoyable way, and to use communication to solve problems.

Matt, for example, was enrolled in an inclusive kindergarten class, but his teacher questioned whether he belonged there. One issue: he had trouble staying focused in group activities. He would participate in the class's morning meeting solely by chanting the days of the week when asked, but then tuned out the rest of the discussion, apparently lost in his thoughts.

Matt's mother knew what her five-year-old *did* pay attention to: Winnie the Pooh. Matt loved the Disney movie and talked endlessly about its characters. His mother brought the teacher a few packs of stickers with various Pooh characters. "If you can find a way to incorporate these into morning time," she said "maybe Matt will be more engaged."

The teacher introduced the stickers at the morning circle, assigning a character to each day of the week. Monday was Tigger day, Tuesday Roo day, Wednesday Eeyore day. That was enough to engage Matt far more than previously, and the other children in the class were happy to join him in using the character names for the days of the week.

Instead of considering Matt's fixation a detrimental factor that separated him from his peers, the teacher successfully used it as a way to connect him with his classmates and with the material she was teaching (days of the week, months of the year). He became more willing to participate with his peers than ever before and was less distracted because she provided a way to engage Matt so that he could continue to progress.

George, who was six, learned to tell jokes from a children's TV show, then began repeating them on Zoom meetings with his teacher and classmates. Concerned about whether that was appropriate, his mother considered discouraging him, but then one day sat and watched. His teacher and classmates so enjoyed his new talent that they started requesting George's latest material. ("Why did the Teddy bear say 'no' to dessert? Because he was stuffed!" "What do you get when you cross a vampire with a snowman? Frostbite!") His mother's concern disappeared as she saw George's pride and his classmate's delight in his new social sharing—and that joking helped him develop friendships. With the teacher's encouragement, George and his classmates then moved on to creating jokes of their own.

On the Uniquely Human podcast's "Enthusiasm of the Week" segment, my autistic co-host, Dave Finch, whose childhood enthusiasm was numbers, connected at length with eight-year-old Ryan, who had a similar enthusiasm and revealed his goal: to become a math teacher.

The same kind of growth and development can occur when families find ways to acknowledge and honor a child's particular interest, share it with family members and integrate it into family routines. Ryan's six-year- old sister's shared love of numbers and number games has led to hours of enjoyable shared playtime. I also saw this years ago when a father brought me to meet his teenage son, Hakeem, a twelve-year-old student at an international school in Kuwait, to offer advice about both his school and home life. Though the boy had many of the challenges common to autism, it was clear from observing him that he had far more flexibility and resilience than many such children. I soon learned that was largely thanks to his parents' very open approach to his enthusiasms.

When I visited their home, the first thing they shared with me was Hakeem's fascination with trains and, in particular, train schedules. They explained that they encouraged him to take an active role in planning the family's annual August vacation to Europe. The parents gave the boy a voice in choosing destinations, then they spent months researching the particulars, assembling maps, guidebooks, and all of the information necessary for the planning. Once the family had determined the general shape of the trip, it was up to Hakeem to figure out the particulars: which trains they would take, how many days they would stay in a city, when they would move on to the next destination.

Since this was before the internet, the planning required detailed and focused effort, but Hakeem was up to the challenge. They showed me scrapbooks they had assembled for each trip, with photographs and clippings from brochures and maps. Each section of the book started with a train schedule—clearly emblematic of how the family celebrated Hakeem's interests. By acknowledging and honoring their son's focus on train schedules, they had helped him expand his efforts to become more engaged with his family and the world, with a healthy sense of pride in his accomplishments. Not only did Hakeem have a remarkable breadth of knowledge of European cities and landmarks, but he felt like a valued member of his family.

Enthusiasms Focused on People

Sometimes the child's focus isn't a topic but a person. Like many children, autistic people often become fascinated with certain movie stars, musicians, or athletes. Sometimes a child becomes focused on a peer, in the way teenagers develop romantic crushes on each other. The difference is that autistic children often don't intuitively understand the boundaries others perceive, so these enthusiasms can become awkward. A child on the autism spectrum might not understand that kids don't generally announce their strong feelings for another person to that person or to anyone else. Those situations can be troubling, but an intense interest in a peer is also an opportunity for a teacher or parent to teach about friendships and social boundaries.

Tyler was a kindergartner with diagnoses of Asperger's syndrome and ADHD whose fixation was the principal of his elementary school, and what she did each day. I had first seen Tyler as a consultant to his preschool, when he was an energetic youngster who would roll on the classroom floor instead of joining his classmates in circle time. Blond and compact, bright and chatty, in preschool Tyler was primarily focused on robots and Lego.

Just a few weeks into kindergarten, he developed his fascination with Ms. Anderson, the principal. Whenever he saw her, he would ask a rapid-fire series of questions: Where do you sit? What do you do? What's your job? Do you have kids? She reciprocated, taking a special interest in Tyler, and invited him to visit her office. Seeing an opportunity to use his deep interest to support his participation in school, she offered him a deal: If he could try his best to participate in classroom activities for a month, then she would let him join her as principal for a day. For Tyler that meant if he joined circle time rather than crawling under a desk, if he asked for help rather than getting upset, if he could improve in a few other areas, he would earn this special privilege.

That got Tyler's attention, and he immediately fell into line. With his teacher he reviewed his progress daily. He practiced asking for help or a break when needed, a strategy that helped him stay well-regulated emotionally. He became more attentive in the classroom; he did his best to participate appropriately. By the end of the month the principal sealed the deal and Tyler had his special day. The school documented the experience in a photo album: Tyler dressed in a suit and paisley tie, shadowed the principal on her rounds and in meetings, and sat at a small desk in the corner of her office. He was delighted, felt like an important part of the school, and had learned about his own ability to stay well regulated and seek support as needed in pursuit of something important to him.

When Enthusiasms Cause Trouble

There are times when the object of a child's attention is genuinely problematic. Gabriel's particular interest was in women's ankles. In another person that might have been considered a fetish, but for this teenager it was merely an object of fascination that he wanted to explore—close up. Occasionally in a mall or on the street, when he spotted a woman in high heels with bare ankles, Gabriel, who was over six feet tall, would squat down, trying to touch her ankles. Those who knew him understood he was a sweet, gentle soul, but certainly the women whose ankles got his attention didn't know how to respond. Innocent as his motivation was, his behavior could easily have been interpreted as lewd, threatening, or even dangerous. Given that Gabriel was Black, his behavior, unfortunately, was viewed by many through a different lens than if he were white (see Chapter 11 discussion on issues of autism and race).

In such situations it is important to help the individual understand the rules and expectations for acceptable behavior, but to do so at a level that is appropriate for that person's abilities without making the person feel badly about himself. For a person with a high level of understanding, it might be helpful to create a list of acceptable or expected behaviors in social situations and discuss how the other person might perceive the situation. For younger children or those with more limited understanding, it's important to state rules in a more straightforward manner, with an emphasis on what they should do rather than what they shouldn't do. For those at all levels of ability, it's useful to employ visual supports—such as photographs, drawings, or even videos—rather than rely on talking. The long-term goal is to help individuals develop a sense of the appropriate responses in different social situations and to be able to inhibit impulsive reactions and stay well regulated, even if it's related to a passion or interest. It's also important to help the person understand how their behavior is viewed by or affects other people.

Even when the focus of a child's deep interest is more acceptable, enthusiasms can pose challenges. The most common concern I hear from parents is that their child talks excessively about a topic—dinosaurs, trains, cartoons, elevators, driving directions—and won't stop. Even if parents and peers understand and respect the person's particular interest, they still might feel frustration that the individual doesn't seem to understand that it's not appropriate to talk about it nonstop, particularly when peers or adults indicate their displeasure or just stop listening.

We all have preferred topics, but we need to learn when we've shared too much. When I meet another New York Yankees fan, we might spend an hour reliving the highlights of last night's game. But someone else might be bored after a minute or two and wondering why I won't stop. If I'm fluent in reading social cues, I can tell the difference and change my behavior. But if I have trouble understanding those subtle indicators, I might continue with the pitch-by-pitch details of the ninth inning while you're desperately trying to escape.

Teaching "Time and Place"

In helping a person with this aspect of understanding, it's useful to use what I call a "time and place" strategy: sometimes other people might want to hear about the particular interest, but other times they're less interested. A parent, teacher, or job coach might explain to the person that there's nothing wrong with her enthusiasm for train schedules or breakfast cereals, and that her interests are even "cool," but it's not what should be spoken about during a math lesson, or dental appointment, or other social engagement. ("We're here eating brunch with our relatives, so everybody wants to hear about what you're doing in school. But at one o'clock, we can hear about the train schedule. Okay?") It's an opportunity to deepen the person's social understanding. It's helpful to work with the person to generate a list of places and times when it's appropriate to focus on an interest, those when it's not, and with whom it's okay to converse about them. Using visual supports, such as calendars and written time schedules, rather than simply talking can help to enhance understanding. Additional supports such as role-playing or reminders on a smart phone may facilitate understanding. The goal is not to squelch an enthusiasm; it is to help a person be seen as a desirable conversational or play partner.

The truth is that even with practice and support, people might still have problems "curbing their enthusiasms." Some people, whether children, teens, or adults, aren't yet developmentally at a place where they can understand social conventions and rules that help social interactions to be more fluid and successful. Some may understand but have difficulty monitoring themselves and inhibiting their impulses in the moment, considering somebody else's perspective, or repressing their desire to share information. Close family members can feel desperate to find a way to help the person to control the impulse to focus too much on a topic or interest. They worry that it accentuates how different the individual appears to peers. Some family members and others close to the person might be tired of hearing about the same themes over and over again. Many times I have heard the most patient of parents finally say, "We just need him to stop."

The problem with that response is that it focuses on the *behavior* without asking what is *motivating* it. It's essential to ask questions: Are there times the person focuses on this topic more than other times? Do you see patterns? Could it be when the child feels stress? What might be causing the stress? How can you alleviate the pressure and anxiety? Is the person using this kind of talk to calm himself down? If it works for him, is it really a priority to eliminate this kind of talk? Is the person aware of his own behavior? How can we help him to be more aware?

In other words, it's not as simple as just stopping behavior. In fact, that should not be the primary goal. As always, the first step is asking what is underlying and motivating the behavior, and if possible, what are the emotions the person is experiencing.

It's also important to remember that if someone consistently opens a conversation by talking about his own interest, that's often because it's a comfortable place to start. For an autistic person, social interactions can provoke anxiety and confusion because they have no fixed structure and one can't always predict what another person will say. So an autistic person will try to create predictability and comfort in conversation by limiting the topics to areas in which he has mastery.

When a child or teenager needs help developing or refining conversational skills, groups focusing on social understanding and related social competencies can provide help, offering a safe and supportive space in which to gain awareness of how to negotiate a conversation and listen to and show interest in others. Instead of reprimanding a child and damaging her self-esteem, it's preferable to offer more positive options, such as activities or games that provide opportunities to practice conversational skills or role-playing everyday interactions in a manner that is enjoyable for all involved. Corrections, no matter how well intended, can sometimes make a more sensitive individual feel that they just can't get it right—so why even try?

Building on Strengths

Though they may come with challenges, enthusiasms often represent the greatest potential for autistic people. What begins as a strong interest or passion can become a way to connect with others with similar interests, a lifelong hobby, or, in many cases, a career. Remember Michael, the child who had a passion for music and the uncanny ability to hear a song for the first time and then sit down and pluck it out on the piano? Now in his forties and living semi-independently, he plays organ at his church and sings in a choir.

When Matt Savage was young, he was so hypersensitive to sound that if his mother played piano, he would cover his ears and run away screaming. With therapy he overcame that challenge and began displaying exceptional musical ability. When I met Matt he was only eleven, and already jazz legends such as Dave Brubeck and Chick Corea were hailing his remarkable piano talent. Now in his twenties, Matt has become an internationally known jazz pianist, composer, and recording artist with a generous spirit and infectious personality. He finds time to teach music to autistic children, performs at charitable events, and graciously provides his music for "Uniquely Human: The Podcast."

When Justin Canha (see Chapter 10) was a toddler, he was not yet speaking but loved watching animated movies and cartoons and showed an early talent for drawing. Now, as an adult, he displays his work in New York galleries, works as a storyboard artist, teaches art to young children, and designs and decorates birthday cakes for bakeries. Justin "brings a sense of humor, he brings a sense of peace, and sometimes a sense of wonder," to his work, says Randall Rossilli Jr, who runs a New Jersey video-production company where Justin had an internship. "He has inspired the artists he works with to become better artists and better people."

One of my favorite enthusiasm stories is of Stanford James, an autistic young man who was raised by a determined single mother in the housing projects of Chicago. From the time he was young, he had a passion for trains and loved to stand at the window of his grandmother's apartment, watching the elevated trains pass by.

"I don't know what the trains did for him," his mother, Dorothy, told a reporter for the *Chicago Tribune*. "But they sure got him." *

Though she was young, living in poverty, and knew little about autism, Dorothy fought for her son. She encouraged Stanford's interest and watched him use his remarkable ability to master the routes and schedules of Chicago's extensive transportation system, committing much of it to memory. In his early twenties he landed a job with Chicago's Regional Transit Authority, helping customers find the routes and schedules to match their needs.

Not only was he a natural for the job, but he showed such dedication, focus, and responsibility that the RTA named him Employee of the Year. "He comes to work no matter the weather and he's polite all the time," his supervisor told the newspaper. "He's thorough, and that's what the customers want."

More important, Stanford felt like an important and valued member of his community. When he was young, his mother wondered what would become of him. After he helps a customer, Stanford says with great pride, "I congratulate myself in my imagination, saying, 'Stanford, you are the best man who can do everything!' " Stanford is a testament to where following an enthusiasm can lead.

CHAPTER 4

Trust, Fear, and Control

A FTER just a few minutes with Derek, I could tell that
something was bothering him, but I wasn't sure precisely
what it was.*

For years I had visited Derek a few times annually at his parents'
request to offer guidance and advice. I would observe him at school
and at home, then meet with his parents and the school team. My
fall visit had always been in September, a few weeks into the school
year. But the year he turned eight, I arrived a few weeks later on the
calendar. In the past Derek had always greeted me enthusiastically—
or at least with a low-key smile. This time, though, he seemed
anxious and disconnected from the moment I arrived, repeatedly
resisting my attempts to engage him. After a while I asked him why.
"Is something wrong?" I asked. "You seem a little uncomfortable
with me."

He did not hesitate to reply. "Dr. Barry, you always first come in
September," he said. "Why are you here in October?"

It was only two weeks later than he typically saw me, but it was

---

*Some of the ideas and insights in this chapter first appeared in *Autism Spectrum
Quarterly* in 2009.

a different month on the calendar, and in his mind that made a big difference. Without discussing it, Derek had internalized the rhythm of my periodic visits. Since nobody realized that, no one had made the effort to explain to him that I would be coming later than in the past. So it was left to Derek to figure out why this violation had occurred in the order of his universe.

Without knowing it, I had breached his trust. Derek had developed an understanding of how things should happen based on how they had always happened, or at least how he remembered them. Now he had reason to wonder whether he could rely on me—or on the world he thought he had understood.

A Disability of Trust

Derek's reaction highlights a central challenge of autism: for the vast majority of people on the spectrum, autism can be best understood as a disability of trust. Because of their neurological challenges, autistic people face tremendous obstacles of three kinds: trusting their body, trusting the world around them, and—most challenging of all—trusting other people.

Daniel Tammet, the author of *Born on a Blue Day*, is known for feats of memory such as recalling more than twenty-two thousand digits of pi and learning a language in a week. Interviewed on *60 Minutes* he described how difficult it had been for him as a child to fit in socially. He felt uncomfortable among other children, whose behavior he found difficult to predict. He was baffled by the nuances of social interactions. So he found solace in math. "Numbers were my friends and they never changed," he said. "They were reliable. I could trust them."

My friend Michael John Carley, an adult with Asperger's who is a leader in the self-advocacy movement for autistic people, once put it this way: "The opposite of anxiety isn't calm, it's trust."

That insight helps to explain much of what makes all of us anxious, not just those on the spectrum, and why we react with fear and often seek ways to control our lives, surroundings, and relationships. These tendencies are even more pronounced in autistic people.

Trust in the Body

If a neurotypical person wakes up with a common cold, it's a minor inconvenience. Since you've most likely come down with a cold before, you have the perspective and experience to understand that your cough and runny nose are likely to last just a few days before you begin feeling like yourself again. But when a person on the autism spectrum experiences those same physical symptoms, she might react with anxiety and fear: What's happening to me? Why can't I breathe normally? Will this last forever?

That response isn't so different from the way most of us react to more severe illness. Some years ago I developed severe carpal tunnel syndrome. Years of splitting wood to heat our home had taken its toll. I had played drums since childhood, but now when I played, my hands went numb and I couldn't grip the drumsticks. When I tried to hold up a newspaper to read, needles of pain shot through my fingers. My arms and wrists didn't feel or act the way I had always relied on them to. Suddenly I *couldn't trust my body*. I felt upset and worried about the future course of my condition. Fortunately successful surgery on both wrists alleviated the symptoms. The tingling was gone; the numbness abated. I could trust my hands and play drums again.

Cancer patients often experience similar challenges. In some ways cancer can be thought of as one's body attacking itself. Much of the stress of the disease comes from the physical changes that occur, the uncertainty of the future course, and that same question: Will I ever be able to trust my body again?

A large proportion of autistic people cope with motor and movement disturbances, often including involuntary movement in various parts of their body. Martin expressed to his mother his bewilderment at the way his jaw would move, his arms would thrust out, and the other unpredictable tics he experienced, particularly when he felt dysregulated. "Am I going crazy?" he asked.

"What makes you think that?" she replied.

Martin's answer: "My body does things I can't control."

Similarly, nonspeaking autistic people often report that they struggle with producing intelligible speech due to motor and movement disturbances. When I met with members of the Tribe, a group of nonspeaking autistic people at the University of Virginia who use letter boards and keyboards to communicate, many noted how difficult it was to control their bodies in everyday activities. Ian Nordling, who had been considered intellectually disabled and severely aggressive as a child, said he had worked on bodily control and could communicate well by spelling words on a letter board by his early twenties. "It was not until my crazy body was taught how to work that I made progress," he said. "I have learned to control my body through the letter boards and practicing purposeful motor work. It started with spelling and now has morphed into work on whole-body control." Through hard work, Ian has become a fluent communicator through augmentative and alternative communication (AAC) and has greater control and trust in his body—and is working on adding speech to his multiple means of communicating. (See Chapter 11 for further discussion of nonspeakers on the autism spectrum.)

Colin, a third-grader with Asperger's, once showed me two elaborately detailed diagrams he had created: a map of his own brain and another he labeled a "normal" brain. The normal brain was a tidy grid, with symmetrical rows and columns drawn across the whole cerebral cortex—an image of orderliness and organization. The map of Colin's brain was a frenetic, chaotic mess, divided into uneven sections of various shapes and sizes. It included a video theater, which he described as the source of the virtual movies that constantly preoccupied him. He labeled his spinal cord the source of "cramps" he suffered. The largest section of the brain he labeled "Crazy Part," the part he blamed when he couldn't control his own thoughts or behavior.

Clearly Colin was trying to express that he couldn't trust his own brain.

Trust in the World

Even if you can trust your own body, it's hard to trust the world surrounding us. I often ask parents of young autistic children. "What does your child find most upsetting?" Often the source of frustration is a mechanical plaything that stops functioning as it once did. The batteries might run out on a toy car, or an iPad freezes, triggering a full-blown meltdown. Parents often find this baffling: the reaction seems far out of proportion to the problem. But take the child's perspective: his sense of order—of how things work—has been violated. He's come up against a world he can't trust.

Children manifest that experience in more subtle ways as well. Sharon noticed that her six-year-old's behavior took a marked turn for the worse in a particular week in the fall, though the change seemed unrelated to anything going on at home or in school. Dmitri would become so upset that he was practically inconsolable, and he wouldn't eat dinner. Then she identified the trigger: The change happened just after the switch from Daylight Savings Time to Standard Time. Dmitri's routine had been undermined. For months the family had eaten dinner when it was still light outside. Now, suddenly, he was expected to eat when it was dark. "It's like he can't trust what a day is," Sharon said, "or when the meal is supposed to be." As he saw it, his parents had changed the rules without any warning. Is it any wonder he was upset? For similar reasons, many parents dread school vacations—the very time other families eagerly anticipate—because the change in routine so upsets their children autistic children.

Matthew, fifteen, experienced a different sort of breach of trust in his physical surroundings. When I visited his home, he excitedly told me that the family had recently visited New York City.

"How did you enjoy the trip?" I asked.

"It was fine," he said, "except we got delayed for four minutes near Exit 87 on Route 95, and then we got delayed for three minutes near Exit 54," and on and on, listing every delay and detour the family had encountered, until his mother was able to stop him. What Matthew remembered about the three-day trip was the unexpected, the times things didn't happen the way they were supposed to—the times he discovered that he couldn't trust the world.

When I was a counselor at a summer camp serving children with developmental disabilities, one of my favorite campers was Dennis, a large, energetic twelve-year-old on the spectrum who had curly hair and rosy cheeks. One Monday morning our group set out by bus to an amusement park. Dennis loved roller coasters and Ferris wheels, and he had fixated on talking about this field trip for days. As our bus arrived at the park, though, I was chagrined to see that the parking lot was empty. The driver stepped on the brakes and, without bothering to consult with me, blurted out the bad news: "Sorry kids. The park is closed!"

Dennis's response was explosive. He rushed over to me screaming, "No, no, *no!*" His gaze averted upward and away, he suddenly began pounding on me with his fists. As I tried to fend him off—and at the same time keep us both safe—he ripped my shirt off and in his flailing frenzy he dug his nails into my arms and chest, causing deep scratches. It was heartbreaking and frightening to see this normally delightful child in this out-of-control state.

With help I was able to move Dennis to a seat, where he buried his head in a pillow and rocked, obviously perplexed and in shock about what had just happened. When well regulated, he was a happy and sweet boy who brought smiles to everyone around him. But when he experienced heightened anxiety, fear, or confusion, leading to a meltdown, he often went after the people to whom he felt closest. Why? In this instance, it was because the world had breached his trust. It was as if he had been pounded with a sledgehammer. We had made a promise about that day, and we had disappointed him. His expectation was violated—suddenly and abruptly.

Fortunately I was able to redeem the situation with what seemed like divine intervention. Once Dennis was safe and I had gathered myself, I stood up and explained that the park was closed. Then words mysteriously came to me and I heard myself say, "But we're going to go on a magical mystery tour!" (This was in 1970, just a couple of years after the Beatles album came out.) Dennis immediately looked up, showed interest, then repeated, "Magical mystery tour?," then "Magical mystery tour! Magical mystery tour!"

We counselors scurried to hatch a new plan. I quietly asked the driver if there were any other destinations nearby, and we patched together a morning stop at a small zoo, followed by miniature golf. When we shared the plan with the children, Dennis adjusted, and he ended up enjoying the day—and we promised to reschedule the amusement park trip.

I understood that Dennis's outburst was completely beyond his control, and even his awareness. The unexpected event triggered an extreme reaction in him because of his neurologically based disability. But I never forgot the lessons from that day: that some autistic people can go from zero to sixty without warning; that when severely dysregulated they may take out their frustration and confusion on the people they trust most; and that breaches of trust come in many forms.

One such disruption that affected people across the board was the onset of the Covid-19 pandemic, a stark demonstration of the anxiety that comes when we cannot trust the world and the routines we have established to navigate our daily lives. With health and safety becoming the highest priorities, most of us experienced an unnerving loss of predictability. Would school be in person or virtual? Did we dare get on an airplane for the vacation we so needed? Religious services, weddings, funerals and other important events that rely on interpersonal connection were cancelled or moved online. Would the vaccines prove effective? It's no wonder there was also an epidemic of anxiety disorders and other mental health challenges across the population, not just for those with neurodevelopmental differences.

Trust in People

The most significant trust-related challenge for autistic people is trusting others. Most of us are neurologically hardwired with the ability to predict the behavior of others—to read body language intuitively and make subconscious judgments based on how relaxed a person's body is, on how a person looks at other people, or by the social context. That is how we determine a person's intentions, whether they wish to engage, and even whether they are safe to be around. But that is often more difficult for people on the spectrum. Ros Blackburn explains that she lives every day trying to understand people's intentions when they approach her. "Because I find it so difficult to predict the behavior of other people" who aren't on the spectrum, Ros explains, "what they do often comes across as very sudden and threatening to me."

Ros's insight helps explain the defensive reaction I saw in Christopher. A teenager, he was a multimodal communicator using a low-tech picture communication system that involved pointing to pictures on a communication board, using his iPad with speech output, echoing phrases, or by uttering a single word at a time. If a peer or teacher in the high school hallway suddenly said, "Hi Chris!," he would instinctively recoil, ducking and looking startled, as if the person had jumped out and pulled a knife on him.

Not knowing whom to trust or what a person might do next means living in a constant state of vigilance, like the soldiers who work on bomb-disposal teams. Imagine going through life in that heightened, hypervigilant state of alert, wary of every person, every object. If your neurological system is constantly on heightened alert, how can you pay attention to anything else? It's exhausting. It becomes difficult to function. All of your energy is focused on merely keeping your defenses up.

Some autistic people have almost the opposite challenge. These individuals may move and react more slowly than others, appearing less alert and seemingly oblivious to the people and events around them. Their feelings are often more difficult to read because their facial expressions do not vary much. Being in a low state of arousal is like walking around in a nonfocused, drowsy condition. Professionals refer to these individuals as having a "low arousal bias." Because they display fewer problem behaviors, they appear to be better regulated and are often thought of as being "good kids" or "not a problem" because they appear so well-behaved. Does that mean they don't experience anxiety? Not necessarily. When they feel dysregulated, these individuals tend to internalize their anxiety rather than directing their behavior outward. The anxious feelings build over time, with few observable, or only very subtle, signs of anxiety or dysregulation, so outbursts or meltdowns can be difficult to predict.

The Role of Fear

We all face situations in which we feel uncertain or threatened. When we sense danger or risk, our natural reaction is to feel fear—and to fight or flee. Autistic people have a similar innate response, but the reaction threshold is far lower, especially for those with hyperreactive profiles. It takes less to trigger a strong emotional response. The source of anxiety doesn't have to be a lion or a fire or a man with a gun. When trust is broken, when the order a person depends on is breached, that triggers fear.

Temple Grandin is probably the world's best-known autistic person. A professor of animal science, she is an accomplished speaker who conveys self-confidence and poise. But she often describes her emotional life this way: "My primary emotion is, and always has been, fear." Most of her fears are rooted in her sensory sensitivities.

While thunder has little effect on her, for instance, the high-pitched alarm of a truck backing up can make her heart race. Unexpected changes in routine are also major anxiety triggers for her.

That fear is often what I observe in my first encounters with children on the spectrum; it is in their eyes and in their body language. When they face situations in which they feel insecure, when they're exposed to the sensory overload of a crowded, bustling school cafeteria or a noisy gymnasium, I see fear.

I saw that look in the eyes of Jeremy, a second-grader who one spring began displaying extreme anxiety around recess. When it was time for his class to go out to the play yard, he was deeply resistant, protesting and refusing to go at just the time the other children were excited and happy for the break.

The reason eventually became clear: The shrubbery bordering the playground attracted butterflies, and Jeremy was terrified of them. Why would a child be afraid of butterflies, creatures most children find beautiful and fascinating? They don't bite or sting or even make a sound. What scared Jeremy was that they were out of his control: he couldn't predict what they would do. Maybe he had once had a butterfly land on his arm or face, frightening him, and he hadn't been able to shoo it away. He didn't understand butterflies. They seemed to emerge from nowhere, whiz by unpredictably, and surprise him. At Jeremy's developmental stage, he wasn't able to reason through and consider that even if a butterfly landed on his nose, it wouldn't hurt him. He had very limited communication skills, so a stranger might conclude that he was irrational and deeply disturbed. But his behavior made sense: on a very primal level, he was trying to stay safe.

To help him, I suggested that his teacher give Jeremy a sense of control by spending time with pretend, paper butterflies, allowing them to "fly" close and then having Jeremy wave them off, saying, "Bye-bye butterflies!" He also spent time looking through books about butterflies to understand that they are harmless. This reframing over time helped him overcome his anxiety.

Lily had her own unique fear: she was afraid of statues. When she was seven, her class was strolling in a park at lunchtime when she spotted a sculpture of a man on a horse. A look of terror crossed her face. Why would a child be afraid of a bronze figure that doesn't move? Because it defied logic. It *looked* like a person, and it *looked* like a horse, but the rule she knew and understood was that people and animals move. The statue in the park shattered Lily's conception of what people are and what animals are, so she felt unsettled, anxious, and afraid. I have seen similar reactions when autistic children spot street fair performers acting like statues or robots—living things behaving as if they're not.

Helping Kids Overcome Fear

When that kind of fear grips an autistic person it can be difficult to overcome. Ned, a fifth-grader at a New York City school, grew terrified when his teacher announced an upcoming field trip on the Staten Island Ferry. The idea of it seemed to capture the imagination of his classmates. Filled with excitement, one girl asked about the waves they might encounter out on the water. A boy wanted to know if they might see any whales from the ferry. Ned fixated on something else: a boat accident that he'd heard about on the news. Then he mentioned another disaster: the sinking of the *Titanic*. Those associations meant that, for him, the Staten Island Ferry was out of the question. He stubbornly refused even to consider joining his class on the trip.

As the date of the field trip neared, Ned became increasingly preoccupied with the *Titanic*. He wanted to look at photographs of the disaster and the movie and repeatedly asked his teachers and parents what it would be like to be at the bottom of the ocean, with fish swimming all around. Clearly it would be difficult to get him to participate in the field trip.

When I met with his teachers and parents, who had sought my

advice, we discussed the challenge: Ned didn't feel safe. We agreed that the priority should be to reassure him, to provide information to make him confident that he would be safe. Together we explained to him that on the ferry he would be protected by a lifejacket, and lifeboats would be available in case of a problem. He was listening calmly, until he heard the word *problem*. Then he suddenly blurted out, "What kind of *PROBLEM*!?," becoming more anxious and nervous rather than less.

To try to calm him down and encourage him, we focused on two solutions: First, we tried to create a positive emotional connection by describing the excitement of boarding the ferry with his friends, spotting the colorful flags he might see in Battery Park, and some of the other highlights he would experience. Second, I introduced the concept of courage. "Being brave means that you try to do something even though it's scary," I said, "and that you trust the people you are with."

What we didn't do was force him to go. Ned was frightened. His fear was causing his dysregulation. Imposing the field trip on him against his will would only have served to make things worse. It would have also broken the trust he felt in the adults around him. It was essential that Ned feel that going on the trip was his choice. So after consulting with his parents, we told him that he had the option to be brave—to face his fears. But we also gave him the choice to stay home with his mother that day. We gave him until a few days before the trip to decide.

When the day arrived, he made his decision: "I'm going to be brave."

Ned went on the field trip and had a wonderful time with his classmates. When I saw him at our next appointment, a month later, he proudly told me, "Dr. Barry, I went on the ferry. I was a little scared when the boat rocked, but I was brave!" I could sense his pride—and so could his parents. He owned his success. After that, he frequently embraced the idea of being brave to help him face the sorts of challenging situations he would have avoided in the past. And he knew he could trust others if he needed extra support.

Ned's anxiety is a reminder that what most people might consider a treat can instill fear in autistic children and adults. I once helped plan a holiday party for a group of young autistic children. The idea was to create a special experience for children for whom it was impossible, or at least very difficult, to attend a typical holiday party. We wanted parents to be able to relax and not worry about explaining or apologizing for their children's behavior. The teachers, parents, and volunteers who helped in the planning were careful to create a tranquil atmosphere with low stimulation, in which the children would be comfortable and happy. We brought in toys the children were familiar with, created visual supports to help them choose favorite activities, and integrated familiar rituals from the preschool program to make the children feel comfortable.

Everything was going beautifully—until Santa arrived. The volunteer who had offered to play St. Nick was a colleague of one of the fathers but apparently was not well acquainted with autism. After a sudden, loud knock on the door, he came bounding into the room in his bright red suit, shouting "Ho, ho, ho!" His abrupt appearance so startled the children that they scattered, some screaming or dropping to the floor, others fleeing to the corners of the room, to their parents, or into the coat closet. Santa was a sensory tsunami, and against the background of an event that was already unfamiliar and full of excitement, they couldn't handle it. No matter how much you prepare, there are always surprises. And many autistic people do not do well with surprises. We did our best to manage the situation and help the children recover.

Autistic people have a range of responses when unexpected events trigger fear and anxiety: they flee; they panic; sometimes they shut down and become still, like deer in the headlights. Fainting goats are a breed with *myotonia congenita*, a condition that causes their leg muscles to become tense when they feel excited or threatened; they freeze in place and fall to the ground. That's similar to what happens to many autistic people. When they feel overwhelmed, anxious, or frightened, they abruptly stop in place. Sometimes they close their eyes and cover their ears, trying to shut out the world or bolt away in fear. As Ros Blackburn has shared, first responders and others who work in highly anxiety arousing situations receive extensive training to manage their reactions and stay emotionally grounded, but autistic people receive no such training.

Such reactions often make parents and others close to these individuals wonder about an apparent irony: Why do they often seem so frightened of ordinary, harmless things like butterflies and statues, when they're *not* afraid of so many other things they *should* be afraid of? Why will a boy who's terrified of statues dart into traffic or climb precariously high on the roof or try to stand up while riding a roller coaster seemingly without fear?

It's important to understand that children and some adults who seem fearless in such situations truly are; that is, they don't feel fear. When an autistic six-year-old climbs onto a roof, she's not assessing the situation and then considering what the potential outcome might be. She acts instinctively: *Maybe I'll climb up there because then I can see things that I wouldn't be able to see otherwise.* She's not weighing the risk because she doesn't perceive it. She doesn't feel fear in her body and putting herself in that position may actually provoke excitement or pleasure. Her brain isn't sending signals that warn that this could be dangerous, and her mind isn't predicting the potential dangerous consequence of her actions. She might feel frightened of a butterfly because she can't control it, but the prospect of falling twenty-five feet to the ground doesn't enter her thoughts. Focused on the sensation of the moment, she doesn't worry about possible harmful outcomes. To address these concerns, many programs for autistic people emphasize issues of safety to help them understand when situations may pose dangers or be harmful.

While those efforts are crucial to helping autistic people understand how to react to police or other first responders, it's a two-way street. Law-enforcement authorities who know little about autism might be physically intrusive or speak in a loud voice, triggering high anxiety in autistic people, who may react by pulling or running away, or not complying with directions. Police can interpret these reactions as indications of guilt, resulting in more extreme approaches. Recognizing these problems, many law-enforcement agencies now conduct extensive training about autism. Some municipalities now dispatch trained mental-health professionals rather than police as first responders to assess a situation and provide support when there is no imminent danger.

Control: A Natural Response to Fear and Anxiety

When our sense of trust is challenged and we feel frightened and anxious, our natural response is to try to exert control. Some autism professionals speak of control in negative terms. "Oh, she's being controlling again," they'll say, or "He's trying to control the conversation." But when you understand the underlying motivations, it becomes clear that many of these behaviors represent strategies to cope with anxiety or dysregulation. Some professionals work hard to seize control from autistic people, but when they do, they're not helping; they're causing *increased* dysregulation by interfering with their strategy to stay well-regulated.

Talking incessantly about a deep interest—trains or dinosaurs or automobiles—is one way of exerting control (see Chapter 3). A child might feel uncomfortable and anxious in social situations, unable to predict what another person might say or ask of him. But when he fills the silence with lengthy monologues about his area of interest, he feels that he has some control. Speaking wards off anxiety about the unknown and stifles the unpredictability of open-ended conversation.

While some children react to anxiety with excessive talking, others retreat into the protection of silence. Grace, eleven, had just transferred to a new school. She participated capably, making her way through the school cafeteria, sitting with classmates, and playing games with a therapist. But she never spoke—and never smiled. It wasn't that she was incapable of speaking. Grace had spoken at her previous school. But in the context of the new school, she had become silent, instead using gestures to make her needs known. In seven weeks, the staff reported, they had heard her whisper only a single word, on one occasion: "Cheese."

Her mother reported that Grace did talk at home—though much of her speaking was echoing—and that she could read aloud. In home videos her mother shared, Grace also readily smiled and laughed. The mother urged the staff not to pressure her daughter to speak, fearing that such efforts would increase her anxiety and do more damage than good. Observing as a consultant for the district, I agreed that it was more important to build trusting relationships with Grace, encouraging her active participation in activities and her communication (albeit nonverbal) rather than trying to force the girl to speak against her will.

Some professionals might have labeled Grace's behavior "controlling" or "withholding"—willfully and stubbornly refusing to speak. What I saw, though, was an alert, intelligent, and capable girl who was anxious about her new surroundings and did not yet know whom or what to trust. Not speaking was her way of coping, of exerting control and giving herself a chance to adjust and become comfortable in her new landscape. She was displaying a variation of selective (or elective) mutism, which is also seen in children who aren't on the autism spectrum. It is not primarily a speech and language problem but rather a reflection of significant anxiety.

Over time the teachers and therapist working with her built trusting relationships with Grace. When she was comfortable and felt ready, she began to read aloud at school and eventually grew more willing to speak and interact playfully with her classmates—and smile and laugh. Trust had been established—and her mother's instinct not to force her proved correct.

How People Exert Control

Some individuals try to gain a sense of control in unobservable ways, creating rules in their head to make sense of the world, trying to make it behave according to their logic. One was a second-grader named Jose, who was involved in planning his eighth birthday party. But in considering the guest list, Jose decided he would invite only one group: the boys in his class. His parents and teachers suggested that it would be nice to include the girls too, as well as other children from school and other parts of his life. But Jose was insistent: only boys, and only those from his class. It wasn't that he didn't like other children. He showed great interest in a variety of children in his life, but for some reason he had narrowed the birthday list to one category.

During my monthly consult at his elementary school, I met with his mother, teachers, and one of the therapists who worked with him to discuss how best to help him approach the party. Many of the adults wondered aloud why Jose seemed so stuck and stubbornly insistent about who would be included. Was he being insensitive or exclusionary? I didn't think so. I suspected he simply felt overwhelmed. Jose had never planned an event like this, and it surely felt overwhelming to consider the entire universe of people in his life. His way of exerting some control was to create a rule, however random it seemed, that narrowed the overwhelming array of possibilities. That kept things simple and calmed his anxiety.

His parents wanted to encourage Jose to open the party to more children, but I knew we couldn't accomplish that by appealing to his logic with lengthy explanations or by imposing a rule that didn't make sense to him. We knew that Jose loved board games, so we created a game-like grid, with various categories of children he knew: cousins, classmates, baseball teammates, boys, girls, and more. The teacher and a therapist suggested some new rules for the "birthday party game": choose at least one child for each box on the grid, a boy from his class, a girl from his class, a boy cousin, a girl cousin, and so on. Since this was a game with rules he understood, Jose was happy to play. After he had chosen at least one child to fill each box, he could select other children to put in boxes as he desired. The categories made sense to him, the process felt logical, predictable, and fun. Most importantly, the structure helped simplify what had been an intimidating set of decisions. In short, Jose felt a sense of control and ownership. We hadn't imposed a more varied group of children for him to invite, we just created a context in which he felt more comfortable doing so himself.

The need to feel control also helps to explain one of the more perplexing challenges related to autism: diet. Parents often wonder why their autistic children are such picky eaters. Some choose to eat only foods of a certain color (often beige) or won't eat the broccoli if it has touched the chicken on their plate. In a preschool program for autistic children where I worked, every child expressed a different preference in sandwiches, and most of the children scrutinized the contents of their sandwiches every day at lunchtime so they could be certain that no objectionable ingredients had infiltrated. One boy, Brian, didn't eat cheese, so if he found even the smallest trace his mom had snuck in, he would carefully remove it.

Often these preferences are related to sensory challenges. Children might be bothered by the texture of a particular food or its temperature, smell, or taste. Their choices of foods, how they are served, and the rituals surrounding eating are all ways of asserting control, efforts to make the world feel safer and more dependable.

In fact, nonspeaking autistic people often communicate loudly through their food preferences. That was true of Ron, a fifteen-year-old I met during my second summer camp job, when I was only nineteen. He was a large, barrel-chested teenager who didn't speak and rarely made a sound except a high-pitched babbling-like sound when he was delighted or distressed. He wore black, unlaced army boots, even with shorts on hot August days. Ron maintained many small rituals to keep himself grounded. On the way from the cabin to the dining hall, he always lumbered off the fieldstone path and stopped to rub the bark of a particular maple tree while making repetitive, chirping-like vocalizations. He also loved to wiggle his fingers to the side of his eyes while enjoying his own happy, high-frequency sounds. I was taken by Ron's quiet dignity and his attention to the details of his daily routine.

On my first day on the job, a counselor who knew Ron instructed me *never, ever* to give Ron anything with mayonnaise. At lunch the next day, I was doing my best in the new routine, trying to distribute lunch quickly, and not thinking. I placed a bowl of potato salad in front of Ron, then turned around. Suddenly I felt something moist and slimy drop on my head. Ron had dumped the potato salad on me! In my haste it hadn't struck me that it contained mayonnaise. It wasn't a violent or aggressive act; he was reminding me of his preference, asserting his sense of control and personhood by refusing what I had given him. It was his way of saying "I'm Ron, and welcome to camp!"

Control in Relationships

That effort to achieve control in the face of a confusing or overwhelming world often extends to relationships as well. Miguel and William were kindergartners, both on the spectrum, who seemed to gravitate toward each other and enjoy each other's company. But then their teacher expressed concern that Miguel had begun displaying disturbing behavior, following William around the classroom and playground so closely that he was practically clinging to him. "Sometimes he orders William to sit down next to him," she told me. "And now William is pushing him away—he doesn't want to be around him."

It's always worth asking "Why?" So when I met with the teacher in my advisory role with the school, I inquired whether anything had changed recently for Miguel—perhaps something unusual was going on at home. In fact something was: Miguel's father had broken his leg in a ski accident, landing him in the hospital for several days. Miguel faced a sudden interruption in his home routine. His father wasn't around, and his mother needed to leave him in the care of a babysitter when she visited the hospital. As he perceived it, things had changed dramatically, and the people he counted on every day weren't reliable. Was it any wonder that he was trying to exert control where he could, literally clinging to the relationship he thought he could count on?

Building Trust

Jonah's teachers reported that he was having great difficulty since starting middle school and was becoming increasingly disengaged from peers and educators. He had no real friends and often sat in class with his head down on the desk. He was a bright, articulate boy, who had experienced some success in elementary school. When he agreed to speak with me in my role consulting for the school, Jonah told me that he frequently felt sad. He didn't like his teachers, and the classmates who had once seemed to enjoy discussing his interests—dinosaurs, baseball, and video games—no longer did.

"Is there anyone in the school you can trust?" I asked.

"Not a chance!" he said.

I asked him what he thought it would take for him to make a new friend he could trust.

He answered, "A year of knowing someone, and at least four visits at my house and the other person's house."

Like many individuals on the spectrum, Jonah struggled with trust, which made it difficult to forge relationships. In my experience, developing trusting relationships is the key to helping autistic people cope with a world they perceive as confusing, unpredictable, and overwhelming. Many people on the spectrum routinely experience misunderstandings: they misinterpret the actions of others, and their own behavior is regularly misunderstood by peers, educators, strangers, and even those close to them. The more often such misunderstanding occurs, the less the individual trusts people and the more likely he will shut down and disconnect, feeling *Why should I even try?* In times of change, such as moving from elementary to middle school, where schedules involve many changes and relationships become more complex, it's difficult to know what or whom to trust.

That is why it is essential for the other people in their lives—parents, educators, peers, job coaches, other mentors and employers—to make the extra effort to build trusting relationships. What I have learned from my years of experience, and from valued friends on the spectrum, is that rather than demanding or pressuring an autistic person to change, we must change first. When we change in a manner that provides appropriate support, the autistic person changes too, due to a growing foundation of trust.

Too often, though, the opposite happens: the people around an autistic person serve to increase anxiety and fear instead of alleviating stress.

By persistently giving the message "You must change," we are inadvertently communicating "You're not getting it right. You're screwing up." Thus we quash self-esteem and, ultimately, trust. The child cannot trust other people to offer understanding and support. The child cannot trust that the world is a safe place—or the autistic adult may feel she is not respected and is being treated like a young child. As a result, anxiety, and in some cases anger, mounts. This situation may be exacerbated for nonspeaking or minimally speaking individuals. Too often people assume they are less aware or intelligent and therefore more in need of being controlled—violating their trust even more.

What can we do to help autistic people foster trusting relationships?

Acknowledge attempts to communicate. One of the core elements of a trusting relationship is feeling that another person hears you. Autistic people often communicate without speaking, using idiosyncratic speech, or by using natural gestures or other more sophisticated forms of augmentative alternative communication. It's crucial for those around them to strive to listen, acknowledge, and, whenever possible, respond. This may require great patience as nonspeakers may require more time to formulate and express what they wish to say, and speaking individuals may have issues retrieving the words to express thoughts and feelings, especially when dysregulated. With patience, we provide the foundation for the kind of progress that cannot otherwise occur.

Practice shared control to build self-determination. Think of a marriage or any intimate relationship: if one partner feels that the other is constantly trying to be the boss, directing the other partner, the victim is trust. Instead of imposing external control, it is essential to offer choices, to give the autistic person a voice in planning schedules, activities, and significant aspects of his life. When she feels respected and feels a sense of power over her own life, she feels more trusting of the people around her.

Acknowledge the individual's emotional state. When autistic people are emotionally dysregulated, they sometimes engage in behavior that appears inappropriate, disruptive, or unsafe. Instead of blaming them, we should pause and ask ourselves, "What must this person be feeling now? And what can I do to lessen the anxiety?" If we respond accordingly, we alleviate rather than exacerbate stress and, in turn, build trust.

Be dependable, reliable, and clear. Autistic people can find social situations confusing and can find it difficult to read the nuances of others' behavior in social encounters. We need to take the time and effort to explain social rules and expectations and why they exist. It is not enough merely to state the rules, especially for people who understand language at a high level. If rules don't make sense to an autistic individual, she may feel resentful and resist following them. However, when we take the time to discuss why rules exist and that we are all expected to follow them, we show greater respect. When we're clear about our intentions and we're consistent, we help to instill a sense of trust. And always remember: if we don't model in our own behavior what we are trying to teach, we really are teaching something else.

Celebrate successes. Too often those who work with autistic people—as well as some parents—pay excessive attention to what is going wrong, what is challenging and difficult. It's hard to trust a person who consistently responds to you with prohibitions, negative comments and criticism or who is constantly trying to change or fix you. Life is challenging enough without being reminded what you can't do or what you do wrong. When we focus on successes, we build self-esteem and enhance the person's ability to trust us, others, and the world.

CHAPTER 5

——

Emotional Memory

I ONCE paid a visit to the school in Buffalo where, a dozen years earlier, I had worked as a graduate student with several autistic children. Walking the familiar halls, I thought of the children I had so enjoyed, wondering what had become of them. As I entered one of the classrooms equipped with a small kitchen, some of the teens and young adults were working together to make breakfast. One of the students—around eighteen, over six feet tall, bursting with energy—eyed me from across the room and seemed immediately to recognize me. He smiled, jumping on his toes, then rocking and speaking excitedly, as he looked toward me.

Noticing his reaction, the teacher approached me. "I know you used to work here," she said. "Did you know Bernie?"

In fact I had worked with a boy named Bernie there. At the time he had been just six or seven years old.

The teacher called to the young man across the room. "Bernie, come over here. I want you to meet somebody."

Smiling again, he came bounding toward me, full of excitement. Clearly he recognized me, but his greeting was anything but typical. "It's Barry!" he said, embracing me in a tight hug. "Now let's sit down so we can tie our shoes!"

The memories flooded back: I had worked in Bernie's classroom years earlier. One of my tasks had been to teach him, over many weeks, how to tie his shoelaces.

"Let's sit down so we can tie our shoes," he repeated. As he did, he seemed to be not so much recalling those days as reliving them. A huge grin lit up his face, and I could hear the excitement and joy in his voice as he repeated the sentence. "Now let's sit down so we can tie our shoes!"

Another story: Louis contacted me because he and his wife were baffled by a mysterious habit of their four-year-old son, Julio. Every time they stopped their car at a particular stop sign, the child, who didn't speak, went into a panic, suddenly screaming and then pounding on his own head with his fists. "It's so upsetting to us," Louis told me. "What could cause that?"

I was baffled myself. "Can you avoid that intersection?" I asked, presuming that there was something about that location that triggered his extreme distress.

"No," Louis said. The crossing was along a route he and his wife regularly traveled, so it wouldn't be easy to stay away from it entirely.

I didn't have a specific hypothesis, but I reminded him that we often have to play the role of detective. I suggested that he keep his mind open to any possible connections.

Three days later Louis called again. "I think we figured it out," he said. He told me that when Julio had been much younger, the boy had experienced a dangerously high fever and become severely dehydrated. His parents had taken him to a medical clinic, where he had reacted with overwhelming fear and panic when staffers had to hold him down to insert an intravenous tube to replace his fluids.

Then Louis made the connection: at the intersection where Julio had experienced the screaming fits, there was a white stucco building that bore a striking resemblance to the clinic where Julio had been given the IV. Perhaps he had such powerful memories of that early experience that just seeing a similar building triggered the traumatic memory.

Just as Bernie had been transported back to the happy experience of learning to tie his shoes, Julio suddenly found himself recalling his moments of panic and sharp pain, as if he were experiencing a flashback. Seeing the white stucco building was enough to trigger a full-blown panic attack.

The Impact of Emotional Memory

These two stories—one of happy recollections, one of traumatic ones—demonstrate the powerful impact of *emotional memory* on autistic people. When we think about memory, we often think of facts—objective, neutral information about experiences we have had, people we have met or know about, or places we have been. Beyond the facts, though, we have memories of our feelings about things. In our minds we subconsciously tag memories with certain emotions: happy, sad, painful, frustrating, joyous, stressful, traumatic.

We all experience this to varying degrees. When I hear the song "Moon River," I become overwhelmed with melancholy. It was the favorite tune of my mother, who passed away when I was just twelve years old. I can hear her singing it to this day, more than fifty years later. A more common experience is attending a high school reunion and seeing a classmate whose name you can't recall, but you do recall strongly whether you liked or disliked him. Facts may be elusive, but the feelings associated with them remain powerfully embedded. We all function this way. If we have positive memories of people or places or activities, we're drawn to them. If we have negative, stress-filled memories, we avoid them, and just the thought of them can provoke uncomfortable feelings.

All of this is magnified in autistic people, for whom remembering is often a strength. Only a small proportion of autistic individuals possess the sorts of savant skills familiar from movies like *Rain Man*, or in well-known people like Daniel Tammet, but many parents and teachers marvel at their children's and students' remarkable feats of memory. Often these children have great memories for birthdays or geography or events in their own lives. What is less frequently discussed but important to understand in helping autistic people is the significant impact of *emotional* memories, both good and bad.

It's a perfect storm: a child has a powerful ability to remember the past, and because of neurological challenges, she also has accumulated more stressful experiences than typical peers because of the confusion, social misunderstandings, and sensory issues that come with autism. That's why a seemingly small association—seeing a white building or the face of an old teacher—can trigger what seems to be a disproportionately dramatic reaction. (Unfortunately, we *all* remember and recall stressful and even traumatic memories more accurately and for longer periods of time than positive memories.)

How Memories Explain Behavior

When we find a person's behavior baffling or inexplicable, it's often because the person standing right in front of us is caught up in a memory so intense and vivid that it's as if the events are happening all over again. When Bernie delighted in our shared experience of tying shoes, he wasn't reminiscing about the distant past; the memories were so intense and overpowering that it seemed as if he were there, in that place and time.

When a child or adult has a sudden meltdown or goes into an extreme panic with no warning or apparent cause, one reason might be unrecognized negative traumatic emotional memories, like Julio's. Surely he didn't *want* to be thrust back to those painful moments in the health clinic, but there he was: screaming with pain, beside himself, full of dread because of the sight of a white stucco building. Often there is no warning, nothing that is observable in the person's behavior that signals the increase in anxiety or fear so that someone might step in and offer support before things boiled over. Emotional memory doesn't work that way. Julio couldn't perceive that his visit to the medical clinic was years earlier, under different circumstances, and that this was a different place and time. The visual image triggered the memory, fear flooded his mind, and there was no easy way for him to turn it off.

The trigger can be something as simple as a name. Miguel was an eleven-year-old on the spectrum who had only limited ability to communicate by speaking. But when his single mother, Leslie, told him she was hiring a new aide named Jennifer to help him at school and at home, his reaction was quick and vocal: "No Jennifer!" he told her. "*No Jennifer!*"

He hadn't even met the woman, so his mother couldn't figure out why he was reacting so strongly. Sometime later Leslie realized what had triggered the outburst. When Miguel was a toddler, he'd had a babysitter named Jennifer. Leslie had been unhappy with her, as when she returned home from work, Miguel often was distraught and dysregulated, so she eventually let Jennifer go, and found another aide. When his mother asked, "Why no Jennifer?," with great effort Miguel blurted out that she had been physically abusive: "Jennifer hit Miguel. Jennifer hurt Miguel!" Although the new Jennifer was a completely different person, that didn't matter. Miguel heard the name, it triggered an emotional memory, and he couldn't escape it.

In my work I routinely experience how a single word can prove traumatizing to an autistic child. When some children hear me referred to as "Dr. Barry," they become quite anxious—not because of anything I've done but rather because of the word *doctor*.

I once paid a home visit to Billy, an autistic eight-year-old. As I waited in the living room, his father called to him, "Dr. Barry is here!"

Instead of coming to greet me, the boy shouted in protest, "No needles! *No needles!* No Dr. Barry! No Dr. Barry!"

Billy hadn't met me before, but merely hearing the word *doctor* had triggered negative emotional memories of visits to his pediatrician's office. I tried to reassure him that everything would be okay, but he was so upset that he fled to a bathroom, locking the door behind him. Through the door we could hear him screaming, then whimpering, "I don't want a shot! I don't want a *shot!*"

His father tried to talk him down: "Honey, Dr. Barry isn't a needle doctor. He's a play doctor." It took about ten minutes for the boy to calm down enough to listen and take in the information. We could hear him calming himself by repeating aloud: "Dr. Barry isn't a needle doctor! He's a *play* doctor!" Eventually he emerged from the bathroom and we spent a pleasant session together.

What if Billy had been a child who didn't speak—or if, instead of "No needles!," he had used words that had meaning to him but not to his father or me? His sudden, fearful response to my arrival would have been a mystery. Figuring it out would have taken more detective work.

The truth is that emotional memories don't require words at all. Naomi, a speech-language pathologist, could not get eight-year-old Max to come into her office at his school. She knew exactly why: for one of his early therapy sessions, she had gone to pick up Max from his classroom. It was a chilly winter day, and because the boy had certain sensory challenges, he had been allowed to navigate the school in sandals or in stocking feet. Together they made their way down the carpeted hallway—she walked, he shuffled—to the office, where she asked Max to open the door. When he reached for the knob—*zap!*— he was startled to receive a jolt of static electricity. Nothing dangerous, but still an unpleasant surprise.

For weeks after that, Max wouldn't come anywhere near her office. When he had to pass by in the hallway, he would press his body against the opposite wall. It was as if the doorknob had come alive and bitten him. It took her three months to help him overcome that negative emotional memory and come to her office for his therapy.

Why couldn't she reason with him? For autistic individuals, emotional memory responses are visceral and primal. Often they have limited ability to reason through a situation, to remind themselves that just because something happened once doesn't mean it will happen again. Another child would probably be able to place the experience in context: *Oh, I got a shock. That's happened before, but it won't happen again, and even if it does it's not that bad.* He might even want to provoke the electric shock as part of exploring his world. But for an autistic person, a memory lodges itself in the mind and often can't be shaken.

That happened to Steven, who was making steady progress getting used to a new school one autumn until one unfortunate event: a fire drill happened at the very moment he was standing under the alarm bell. Steven had sensory challenges and was particularly sensitive to loud noises, so it took a number of weeks before he could enter the school building again without experiencing significant stress.

Anything Can Be a Trigger

As most parents of autistic children know, it's difficult to predict what might be a trigger. Often we say something with the best of intentions and unwittingly provoke an instinctive, powerful response. As part of a school visit to observe Scott, then seven, I watched him run laps in the gymnasium. At one point, as he ran past me, I instinctively smiled and said, "Good job, Scott!"

He paused in his tracks and glared at me, looking displeased. "No 'Good job'!" he said sternly. "Don't say 'Good job'!"

Was he just being defiant? Did he not want to be the center of attention? Or was he asserting control in a distinctive way?

The next time he came around, I restrained myself and remained silent, but on the next lap I gave him a silent thumbs-up sign. Scott stopped in his tracks and glared at me again. "That means 'Good job'!" he said, then repeated: "No 'Good job'! No 'Good job'!"

Later I learned why Scott was disturbed by my innocent attempts to cheer him on. He had worked the previous year with a behavior therapist who relied on a traditional approach of sitting at a table for long periods and conducting teaching drills. She had rewarded successful efforts with praise and tangible rewards. "Good job!" had been her mantra, but he had come to detest those teaching sessions, understandably feeling controlled and manipulated. When I had said "Good job" in the gym, I meant it as a friendly gesture, but for Scott it sent him back to those difficult sessions and his unhappiness and discomfort. If I was going to be a "Good job!" person—or even a thumbs-up person—that was not going to work for him, and he wanted me to know that.

Children can't always make such clear efforts to communicate what's bothering them. Early in the school year, a second-grade teacher wondered why her student Alice habitually began crying and became despondent nearly every morning around eleven-thirty. Alice didn't speak, and no one could figure out what was causing her to be so upset. Thinking she might be hungry, the teacher offered her a snack. That didn't help. The teacher tried to adjust activities in the classroom, but still Alice got upset, every day. It was baffling.

Asked to help solve this mystery, I spoke to Alice's instructor from the previous year and described Alice's struggles. Almost immediately the teacher had an insight. "Last year, at eleven-thirty every day we took Alice outside to the playground and gave her time on the swing," she told me. It was a way to help her regulate and feel more comfortable toward the end of the long mornings. If it was raining or snowing outside, someone would take her to a swing in the gym, but every day at eleven-thirty she had her swing time.

Mystery solved. Alice had no way to communicate it, but she had powerful positive emotional memories of that activity. Despite the interval of a summer vacation and the change to a new classroom and teacher, she associated that time of the school day with the positive, regulating sensation of being on the swing. Whether or not she was aware of the connection to the previous year's schedule, it showed the significant role that emotional memory can play.

I also witnessed that in Michael, the young son of a colleague, who often engaged in "self-talk"—speaking to himself in various ways. One afternoon I was driving Michael to the roller-skating rink, and there in the passenger seat he began a rather one-sided conversation with a particular doctor. "Dr. Boyer, good to see you!" he said to nobody in particular. "How are you, Dr. Boyer? What are we going to do today, Dr. Boyer?"

I happened to know that the doctor he was talking about was deceased. So I asked, "Michael, is Dr. Boyer here?"

"No, Dr. Barry," he said, smiling. "I'm *pretending* that I'm talking to him because Dr. Boyer is a very nice man."

It wasn't so different from the way anyone might recall a pleasant experience with a person who has passed away. Michael didn't have inhibitions or concerns about what another person might think, so he carried on the conversation aloud, and I had the privilege of witnessing his very positive associations. Such positive memories help explain the comforting wish often shared with a person who has lost a loved one, "May her memory be a blessing."

The Lessons of PTSD

While we all experience emotional memory, for most of us it's rare for those memories to overwhelm us or significantly intrude on our lives and our ability to function. So when parents, teachers, and caregivers witness the extreme reactions their children or family members have to negative emotional memories, they sometimes wonder whether the person might actually be experiencing some form of Posttraumatic Stress Disorder. PTSD is an extreme form of negative emotional memory and the unfortunate outcome when a person experiences severe trauma: witnessing or enduring a violent episode, suffering from physical or sexual abuse, or surviving a frightening car accident. Single intense events may be the source of trauma, but repeated stressful events over time can result in "developmental trauma." For example, a person who is bullied repeatedly may experience school as a traumatic setting not because of one incident but due to the cumulative impact of repeated encounters.

There are differences between negative emotional memories and PTSD, but there is also overlap. PTSD is diagnosed when memories are persistently intrusive or incapacitating. Brain research shows that the brain processes emotional memories in the amygdala, part of the limbic system that is responsible for functions of memory and emotion. Situations that remind a person of traumatic events can trigger the release of stress hormones. This overactivates the amygdala, which sets off the release of still more of the hormones. The result: severe emotional distress in the form of racing thoughts, anger, and hypervigilance beyond a person's control or even conscious awareness.

That's why a soldier returning from war can find himself thrust back to his most painful moments, feeling that he is reliving the events, not that he is remembering from afar. We might see the person at home, in his living room, but in his mind, he's back in Baghdad.

For autistic people, emotional memories rarely prove as debilitating or intrusive as PTSD can be. But they are often responsible for the sudden and dramatic changes in behavior that mystify parents and teachers. And research on PTSD has led to valuable lessons about how parents and professionals can help autistic people to cope with and manage negative emotional memories. One significant insight: once you have a traumatic memory, you can't erase it; it lingers in the brain, in long-term memory. To use a computer analogy, you can't delete it from the hard drive. And it can be triggered by an associated word, image, smell, or even person.

In recent years, understanding the impact of trauma has become an important focus in autism. According to Autism Awareness Australia, "trauma is the result of singular or repetitive exposure to a deeply distressing or disturbing experience or event. Typical memories are reconstructions of past events and so they change and fade as time passes but traumatic memories do not follow this same pattern. Traumatic memories remain as horrible and vivid as when they were formed. Traumatized individuals regularly report the sense of reliving these past experiences."

But experience suggests we can slowly chip away at traumatic memories. Immediately after you experience a traumatic collision with a red Volvo SUV, the sight of any red SUV approaching might trigger high anxiety. But after months of seeing red SUVs pass without incident, you begin feeling more secure and the panicky feeling abates over time. That doesn't mean the memory is gone; it's just become less easily triggered, the intensity is diminished and even replaced by more positive or at least neutral memories. In the same way, a person's positive memories can dampen or even override more painful and difficult ones, but not eliminate them.

Sometimes parents and others can help create the positive emotional memories. Anna was a preschooler who was terrified of the bathroom. Serious gastrointestinal issues had caused her great pain and discomfort. During her regimented toilet training at home, sitting on her potty seat at specified times, in discomfort, had made her miserable. Eventually dietary changes helped her overcome her GI issues, but not her fear of the bathroom. To help with that, her parents began playing her favorite music in the bathroom, sang songs with her there, and let Anna enjoy some of her favorite books. In time that strategy worked to override her painful memories with pleasant ones.

How Can You Tell Whether Emotional Memory Is the Issue?

How can you know when negative emotional memories are the root of a person's behavior? It's not always easy. As is often the case, getting to the root of what's underlying behavior takes some detective work. There are three significant clues:

- The behavioral reaction does not seem related to something you can observe.
- The child or adult consistently expresses fear or anxiety in relation to a particular person, place, or activity.
- The child or adult engages in echolalia, repeating words or phrases linked to the stress experienced in relation to a person, place, or activity.

Managing Emotional Memories: How to Help

The most important factor in helping an autistic person cope with negative emotional memories is to acknowledge and validate her experience and provide supports for emotional regulation. Often parents and teachers—with the best of intentions—have the opposite instinct. Some ignore the issue, hoping it will just go away. Others try to minimize the child's experience with reassuring statements: "Oh, you don't need to worry about that."

However, those approaches aren't respectful of the person, they don't take the challenges seriously, they don't take the stressful feelings away, and they do not teach the person strategies to stay emotionally well regulated. On a practical level they just don't work. Instead of feeling understood and supported, the person feels dismissed—and possibly even more anxious.

Once we understand the negative memories that are troubling the person, it's helpful to avoid the triggers, to steer clear of situations or people who cause the problem. It seems like a simple strategy, but it can be extremely helpful. If you know that noisy rooms cause anxiety in a child, be sensitive to that. If you've seen that the sound of a particular electronic toy provokes a little girl to cover her ears at the mere sight of it, then put it away. And let her know even before the issue comes up that the toy is not around.

If particular topics cause stress, it may be best to alert listeners in advance about what will be discussed, giving them permission not to be present when the subjects come up. It's become common at conferences attended by autistic adults to provide "trigger warnings" at the start of sessions about sensitive topics such as physical or sexual abuse, or discussions of "therapies" experienced as traumatic. This forewarns attendees of the emotionally laden content and gives them permission to step out if they feel overwhelmed. When we did an episode of "Uniquely Human: The Podcast" on the topic of autism and encounters with the criminal justice system, we began with such a trigger warning in case listeners had personal traumatic experiences related to the topic.

Often the source of anxiety isn't avoidable. When that's the case, the best approach is to be respectful of the person and not to force things. George and Holly lived in an area with many theme parks. They had an autistic daughter, Amy, as well as three neuro-typical children. The other three children loved visiting the parks and went often, but Amy was afraid of visiting as she was easily overwhelmed by the sensory intrusions—the loud noises and people screaming on the roller coaster, the excited children darting around with no warning. What could have been an enjoyable activity for the entire family instead divided them.

Instead of forcing Amy to go, her parents gave her a sense of control. They offered her the option to come along without going on any rides. Before going, they showed her pictures of the carousel and the food court, two things she typically liked. They brought the same noise-dampening headphones that her school used. They showed her the quiet area provided by the park for children with sensory issues. When they saw her becoming anxious, her mother said, "Do you need your headphones? Do you need a break in the quiet area? Do you need to leave, Amy? Are you finished for today?" If Amy said she was finished, they honored that request. When they next returned, they let her bring a favorite stuffed animal, and they bought her a favorite snack. The visits were on her terms, not imposed on her.

They did this over five or six visits, never forcing Amy, always giving her a sense of control. When she understood that she was acting out of her own volition and not having anything forced on her, she relaxed and went willingly.

This gradual, empowering approach can apply to all kinds of experiences that people on the spectrum might find overwhelming: crowded cafeterias, classrooms, bowling alleys—basically anywhere they've had difficult moments before. For individuals who benefit from visual supports, it's often helpful to use cards or a tablet computer to offer choices to support emotional regulation. In my experience, forcing the issue only serves to create new fears and anxieties, and violates any sense of trust.

Creating Positive Emotional Memories

Another helpful approach is working strategically to turn a negative into a positive—to find ways to make places or activities associated with negative emotional memories more welcoming and comfortable. For autistic people, and for many neurotypicals, a dental visit, for example, is often rife with challenges: the unfamiliar noises of the drills and other equipment; the intense lights shining in their eyes; the need to remain still while dental tools are inserted in the mouths; the difficulty predicting what's going to happen next. And previous visits might have involved painful procedures. A neurotypical person may be able place the experience in context, understanding that despite those factors, the dentist is highly skilled and wouldn't intentionally hurt a patient, and dental care is an important part of staying healthy. We can reassure ourselves that we're safe, and we can cope by closing our eyes or tightly gripping the arms of the chair or sending our thoughts elsewhere.

When an autistic person becomes dysregulated, though, she may not be able to instinctively calm herself in the same way. She may have a *fight* response or a *flight* response: either she struggles to protect herself, or she avoids the situation altogether or tries to flee.

Two different approaches to coping with dental visits offer lessons for helping autistic people manage the inherent stress of these visits.

Marquis was an autistic fourteen-year-old who generally spoke in one- to three-word utterances and also used pictures to communicate. His visits to the dentist always triggered such severe anxiety that his mother had a difficult time even getting him through the office door. But over time, she developed strategies to give her son the support he needed. She donated a rocking chair for the dentist's waiting room, so that Marquis—and others who shared his needs—could rock to provide calming sensory input himself as he waited. She also brought music and headphones for him. And he brought along one of his favorite toys, a Shrek figure he could fidget with while he waited. Finally she met with the dentist to coach him on how to act, move slowly, and use positive language when telling Marquis what was coming next, so that things were more predictable. Marquis's mom knew that they couldn't avoid seeing the dentist, but instead of merely forcing him to go, she helped transform the dentist's office into a safe place where he could feel regulated and calm.

More and more dental practices and other health care providers are now integrating supports and strategies to lessen or eliminate stressful factors for vulnerable people. The mother of one autistic child, for example, not only advocated for these kinds of supportive settings, but helped create one. A dental hygienist, she combined forces with another mother, also a hygienist, and a dentist to open a practice specifically aimed at children with particular fears or sensitivities related to conditions such as autism or sensory-processing disorders. Their first strategy was to reduce uncertainty about visits by posting photos and videos on a website showing the office, the people who worked there, and, with step-by-step photos of some of the procedures a patient might undergo. For one afternoon each week, instead of scheduling appointments they opened the office, put out toys, and welcomed patients and their families to come play and meet the dental staff. In short, they reduced uncertainty and created positive emotional memories in a place that could easily be a trigger for the opposite.

Stressful memories may be associated with many different settings. Therapists who work in schools often meet children who are resistant to engaging and seem overly anxious. Sometimes the problem is the space. The child might have worked in the same office or at the same desk with another therapist or teacher and found the encounters to be a source of stress rather than help. When it's time for a session, the child protests—"No! No! No!"—and drops to the floor.

The solution: create positive emotional memories. Before anything else, give the child a choice of two favorite toys. Spend the first five or ten minutes just having fun. Follow the child's lead and let her enjoy the time and the space so that she begins to associate more positive feelings with it. Make it a joyful experience, and only gradually add more challenging material.

An even simpler approach, especially for young children: don't call it "work." Too many therapists and teachers label their time with a child that way: *It's time to work. We can't play now—time for work.* Sometimes we're projecting our own concerns about how challenging the session will be for the child. The child hears *work* or senses our tone, and it triggers a flood of negative memories. Instead why not lighten the emotional tone and create a more positive, welcoming atmosphere? For our music and expressive arts sessions on Zoom for the Miracle Project–New England, we give participants fun songs to learn, and in some cases, to help write at home. I suggested to the team that rather than calling the assignment "homework," we should call it "homefun," because that's what it was.

Parents can take the same approach at home. One mother complained it had become a struggle to get her five-year-old, Judah, to join the family dinner each night. The problem: he so enjoyed being on his backyard swing that when she called him, he ignored her. I suggested she think about it from his perspective. When the child heard, "Judah! Time for dinner!," what he experienced was being taken from an activity he loved, that made him feel good (swinging), to one that was more challenging (sitting, listening, staying at the dinner table).

"Is there anything he likes about dinner?" I asked.

His mother told me that Judah savored his Flintstones vitamins.

"Tomorrow," I said, "when you call him, hold up the bottle of vitamins."

The next week she reported that the visual cue had worked. When she simultaneously called Judah and held up the Flintstones vitamins, he ran right past her and into the house, repeating, "Time for dinner!," and sat in his place. Some might call that a bribe, but it wasn't. It was a visual cue that linked dinner with a positive association. And that began a series of positive memories, making the dinner table a more desired and welcoming place for Judah.

Of course that's the most helpful strategy of all: creating a life full of positive memories. As parents and professionals, we help to do that whenever we offer choices instead of exerting control; whenever we foster the child's interests and honor the child's strengths rather than redirecting; whenever we make learning, work, and life fun and joyful. When we do those things, our children, teens, and adults on the autism spectrum will have far fewer negative emotional memories to cope with, making them more open to the joys and pleasures that life offers.

CHAPTER 6

Social Understanding

NEARLY every parent of an autistic child who speaks has a version of this story: Philip's fifth-grade class was in the midst of studying the human body. He had worked hard to pay attention to the discussions on diet, exercise, and the many ways we can take care of our body. That same week his parents took him to the movies. They arrived at the theater only to discover a long line of people waiting for tickets. Excited, Philip took the opportunity to demonstrate his newfound knowledge. Pacing up and down the line, he pointed at each person and announced in a loud voice, "That's a fat man! There's a skinny man! That woman's very short! That man is obese and he might die soon!"

By the time Philip's parents shared this story, they recounted his social insensitivity with amusement. But they weren't laughing when it happened.

Then there was Eli, a teenager who had just entered high school and was struggling to learn how to engage in conversations. Like many autistic people, he had a tendency to speak in detail about the topics he cared about, but he rarely bothered to ask others what they were interested in. I made some suggestions about asking questions and listening to clues about what the other person might want to discuss, but I could see from his facial expressions that he was feeling increasingly confused and frustrated. "Other people can do that," Eli finally said, "but it's not easy for me."

"Why not?" I asked.

"Well," he said, "other people can read each other's minds."

That was how Eli made sense of the social world, where he was extremely aware that friends and strangers were interacting with little difficulty in ways he could not comprehend. The only way he could explain how easy it seemed to them was to assume that neurotypical people must be imbued with telepathy, a power he lacked. What else could account for his struggles?

In a sense those two experiences—Philip in the movie line, Eli's assumption about mind reading—illustrate two extremes of how some autistic people relate to the neurotypical social world, with its hidden rules, unspoken expectations, and often nuanced use of language. Nearly every autistic person has some degree of difficulty navigating the social world. Some, like Philip, are so oblivious to social convention that they aren't aware of their own blunders and pay little attention to how others perceive their actions. Others, like Eli, struggle in a different way: they are all too cognizant that social rules and expectations exist, but since they don't intuitively understand them, they often feel anxious and their self-esteem may suffer as they struggle to negotiate a world of social conventions that seem to defy their grasp. Always worrying "Am I getting it right or wrong?" can arouse anxiety and even be paralyzing. For others who have become acutely aware of neurotypical social expectations, such as making polite "small talk" with strangers, these expectations may seem to serve no purpose.

The Challenge of Learning Social Rules

For all groups—those who are blissfully unaware, those who worry excessively, and those who view neurotypical social conventions as being without logical purpose—the challenge is rooted in the same issues. Human beings are hardwired to be socially intuitive, but the neurological differences in autism poses challenges to developing that intuition.

Consider the organic way we learn language. A mother doesn't sit her toddler down and explain the parts of speech or how to conjugate a verb. We learn by being exposed to language and immersed in it. We listen and observe in order to construct our own knowledge of language. In the jargon of language-development research, we *induce* the rules of language, and as a result we learn the meanings of words and how to use them in phrases and conversation to express complex ideas.

The same is true of neurotypical social rules. Typically people *induce* the often subtle, invisible conventions of social interaction. They learn by a process of immersion and osmosis, monitoring the social landscape with periodic coaching as needed ("Please do not interrupt while Mommy's talking to Grandpa."). But for autistic people, the nature of their disability makes it very difficult to survey the social landscape and induce those rules. They can learn them, but it's like learning a second language as an adult, when it's much harder to achieve the same fluency and comfort as native speakers. What comes naturally and effortlessly to others always requires some degree of conscious effort, and one is constantly reminded of the struggle. For those who are more successful, such social learning is not intuitive, it occurs through analysis and logic. Interestingly, many autistic self-advocates who socialize with other autistic people report how much more comfortable they feel because there are shared expectations, almost as if they are entering a different culture with different rules of communicating and socializing.

I first met Philip when I was doing a home consultation for his four-year-old autistic son. Philip was a successful investment banker in his forties and was diagnosed as an adult with Asperger's syndrome. He had graduated with honors from a prestigious MBA program, but he told me that achievement was nothing compared to grappling with learning and understanding the rules of the neurotypical social world. "Learning economics and finance was like breathing air to me," he said. "But to this day I have to read books and study the behavior of people to help me understand them—their facial expressions and how they carry on conversations with all the social nuance and innuendo."

Imagine walking into an unfamiliar cafeteria for the first time. There are different types of cafeterias: in some, customers pay a cashier first, then pick up a tray and select food from various stations; in others you choose the foods you'll eat, put them on your tray, and then pay at the end of the line. Where does one pick up the cutlery, the condiments, the beverages? It's different at every cafeteria.

When you enter a cafeteria for the first time, how do you learn the social rules and expectations? *You watch people.* You discover the unwritten rules of the cafeteria by observing how other customers make their way through the line, how they act, what food they get, and where they get it.

If you were on the autism spectrum, though, you probably wouldn't instinctively watch people in that situation. You might just head directly to get the food you want—possibly by cutting the line, as getting food is your goal, after all. As an autistic person, you might have some awareness that rules need to be followed, but because you don't know what they are, you might feel disoriented and lost, or you might look around for clues, bewildered. And it's unlikely that your first impulse would be to learn by observing other people's behavior, by surveying the social landscape to guide what you do by what you see.

That's how the social world can feel to an autistic person: like an unfamiliar cafeteria, with rules that all the other diners apparently already know but that seem nearly impossible to learn, especially in busier and noisier settings.

Of course autistic people can learn the rules—with support. Another cafeteria analogy is helpful. On a visit to Denver I once dined in a salad-bar restaurant with its own unique arrangement. When customers entered, they were immediately directed to the salad bar, and after making a salad, they paid a cashier. Next came another area for soup, sandwiches, and desserts, all included in the fixed price. How was a newcomer to understand the proper sequence of steps? Someone had considered that question and developed visual supports to teach the rules, probably after bewildered customers were confused about how to proceed! The restaurant posted signs with visual diagrams breaking down the process for novices: start with the salad line, then pay, then help yourself to soup and dessert. It was as if every customer was autistic, and the restaurant was accommodating us by providing a sequence of steps so we could understand. We call these executive-function supports, as they help a person to stay focused and follow the necessary steps to reach an end goal.

In the real social world, many autistic people are usually left to fend for themselves, navigating a reality that seems to make sense to everyone but themselves. It's no wonder Ros Blackburn is fond of offering a candid statement: "That's why I don't do social." Another young autistic adult, Justin Canha (see Chapter 10), offered his own charmingly blunt assessment. Told by a friend—also on the autism spectrum—that he needed to practice his manners, Justin smiled and replied, "Manners suck."

Another social factor we consider, usually without deliberately thinking about it, is the cultural context in which we find ourselves. When I travel internationally I am reminded of how many of the rules governing social interactions are specific to our own society. On a trip to mainland China, I paid a visit to a large, crowded retail store in Guangzhou to get a feel for the local culture. I was waiting in line at the cashier when a woman behind me abruptly pushed me, apparently to join someone in front of me in line. As she passed, without warning she grabbed my shoulder and roughly shoved me aside, never pausing to excuse herself or apologize. If someone had done that to me in my local Target, it would have been grounds for confronting her. But I had learned that in China, where large crowds are common, such behavior is acceptable and socially appropriate. I was

able to put it in context and (shaken as I was!) react appropriately—
which is to say, not at all. And of course, the Covid-19 pandemic
brought the need for an entirely new set of social rules we all had to
learn regarding social distance, mask wearing, and handwashing that
cut across all cultures.

Difficulty Reading Social Situations

When autistic people display behavior that others may interpret as
abrupt or rude, or when they simply seem oblivious, it is often because their neurological wiring makes it difficult to weigh the many
subliminal factors that help us read and react appropriately, according to social expectations, in social situations. This lack of innate
understanding manifests itself in all kinds of ways. Michael's family
occasionally held Sunday barbeques for the twelve-year-old child's
team, the professionals and teachers who worked with their son. In
the midst of these gatherings, Michael would sometimes begin gig-
gling to himself, sitting at the table but clearly occupied by his own
thoughts. Even after one of his parents asked him to stop, he would
continue. When it happened while I was visiting, I seized the opportunity to gain some insight into his behavior. "Michael," I said,
"could you explain what's so funny to you?"

He pointed at one of the therapists across the table. "It's *Susie*!"
he said. "She has such a high, squeaky voice. It makes my body feel
funny."

The young woman blushed, embarrassed. "Well, I guess I'm going
to have to adjust my voice to a lower register during our therapy sessions," she told him.

Michael was unaware that he had caused embarrassment. He was
answering my question with an objective fact: she *did* have a high,
squeaky voice. He didn't understand the social rule that it's best not to
say anything about a person in public if it's not positive. How would
any child learn that? A parent would likely provide some coaching

for a younger child, but by age twelve most children would have had multiple experiences in surveying the social landscape, a process that leads to a fuller understanding of the unspoken rules of politeness.

Luke was another child whose social challenges showed up early, when his kindergarten teacher complained that he didn't know how to play with other children. Instead of playing the way other children played in his inclusive class, Luke would grab other kids and try to tackle them. Luke was a sweet child who had never been aggressive, and he was generally a happy youngster. In fact he flashed a broad smile while dragging kids to the ground, so it wasn't immediately clear why he was being so physical. As a consultant, I met with his parents and the team of educators who worked with Luke, and his mother offered an explanation. Luke had two older brothers, and their play at home tended to be physical: lots of jumping on each other and tackling. So at four and a half Luke had taken that concept of play to school. He wasn't able to discern from the children's body language or facial expressions that they weren't enjoying his physical play. Nor did he intuitively understand that different rules applied at home and at school.

In one of our Miracle Project New England expressive arts sessions on Zoom, participants were having such a fun time that we were not aware of going past the scheduled 6 pm end time. Just minutes earlier, Pedro, 26, had been quite engaged, but suddenly said sternly, "It's 6:05 pm and we really need to end!" In another context, others would likely perceive such behavior as rude, but we knew that his intentions were good—he simply felt stressed by the break in routine.

The Limitations of Teaching Social Rules

Schools are full of explicit rules, and autistic children often excel at following them, especially when a rule is explained and makes sense. In fact many autistic individuals become the rule keepers, pointing out when other children violate the tenets of acceptable behavior. It's the unspoken, subtle rules that are more challenging. Ned, a ten-year-old I worked with, always got excited when his teacher asked questions in class, especially about his favorite subjects. When he knew the answer, he would blurt it out. Why not demonstrate how interested and smart he was? He loved geography, so when the teacher displayed a map of Africa and asked the children to identify the countries, he shouted the name of one country after another without pausing: "Kenya! Tanzania! Tunisia!"

In his social skills group, the speech-language pathologist offered Ned instructions about the importance of raising his hand in class. "If you raise your hand," she explained, "it will make your teacher happy, and it will make your friends happy, because then everyone will have a chance to answer questions." The rule he was taught was this: If I raise my hand, the teacher will call on me.

The problem, of course, was that she didn't *always* call on him. Ned would raise his hand with great excitement and anticipation, struggling not to blurt out the answer, but the teacher sometimes seemed to ignore him. He had learned the rule but not the exceptions, so when he raised his hand and the teacher didn't call on him, Ned's mood quickly shifted, and he grew anxious and upset. In the next session of his social skills group, the therapist made sure Ned understood the rule more precisely from his perspective: If I raise my hand, *sometimes* the teacher will call on me, but sometimes she may call on my friends.

After he had practiced for a few weeks, I visited the classroom. I wasn't sure he was even aware I was there, until the teacher posed a question to the class. Ned immediately thrust his hand in the air to respond, then turned around and called out to me, "Dr. Barry! Just because I'm raising my hand it doesn't mean the teacher will call on me!"

To his credit, Ned was making great efforts to understand rules that made no logical sense to him: Why raise your hand at all? If you do, why doesn't the teacher call on you? And if she doesn't, why not state the rule aloud to explain why you are not being called on?

Ned's experience shows the limitations inherent in teaching the rules of the social world and the challenges we face when we try. We teach one rule, only to have the child encounter its exceptions. We teach the exceptions but forget to mention that generally *people don't talk about the rules, they just follow them.* The child wants so badly to get it right, but sometimes entering the world of social rules only brings more misunderstandings—sometimes comically.

Following Rules Can Be Confusing

Early in my career I supervised a student clinician to help Michael learn the proper ways to address people. We were living in a small midwestern town in the early 1980s, and manners mattered. So we taught Michael to assess his relationship to the person quickly, and then use a corresponding term: "buddy" for a peer, "ma'am" for a woman, and "sir" for a man.

All of this was challenging for Michael because he wasn't just memorizing words. The process involved a central challenge: considering specific characteristics of people, such as gender and age, and where these individuals fit into his life. One afternoon my student working with him was delighted with how much progress Michael had made. Shown a picture of a woman, Michael would practice by saying, "Hi Ma'am"; shown a picture of another boy, he would say "Hi Buddy," and so forth with perfect accuracy. So at the session's end he asked Michael to show off his new skills for me. Michael looked at me, smiled, and, overcome by confusion but with full enthusiasm, blurted out, "Hi Doctor buddy-ma'am-sir!"

Michael had learned the rules, but at the first opportunity to apply them, he was too excited and overwhelmed to do so. But what was even more evident was how hard he was trying, how challenging this was, and how much he truly wanted to connect with me. To this day I cherish that moniker, Doctor buddy-ma'am-sir.

Language can be a barrier to social understanding because autistic people tend to interpret language literally, and neurotypicals often do not say what we mean. That's why metaphors, sarcasm, and other nonliteral uses of language are endlessly confounding for many autistic individuals.

Helen noticed that her son Zeke, who was nine, seemed particularly upset after school one day, so she asked him why.

"I don't want Mrs. Milstein to die!" he said.

Curious about what was ailing Zeke's fourth-grade teacher, Helen asked him to explain.

"I heard her tell Mrs. O'Connor, 'If it rains one more day this week, I'm going to kill myself.'"

Sandra went shopping with her daughter Lisa, who was seven, for a birthday present for Lisa's brother. Lisa chose a baseball. On their way home Sandra reminded Lisa that birthday presents are a secret until the big day: "You need to keep this under your hat." Later that day, when Lisa's father was in her bedroom, he noticed a beach hat on a bookshelf, out of its usual place. When he reached to move it, Lisa cried out, "No! Don't touch! It's a secret!"

Even simple exchanges can cause unexpected problems. A child answers the telephone, and when the caller asks, "Is your mother home?," the child says "Yes," and promptly hangs up. A child accidentally knocks over a can of paint, spilling it all over the floor. When the teacher responds sarcastically, "That's just wonderful!," the child thinks he's done well.

The Importance of Clarity and Directness

To avoid such problems, parents and teachers should be as clear and direct as possible in their communication with autistic people. In fact, that is exactly what many adults on the spectrum say that is most helpful for them. It's also helpful to use "comprehension checks"— that is, to ask the person if he understands what is being said rather than assuming he does, and, if necessary, offer an explanation. And direct requests always work better than subtle hints. "Those cookies look good" might be the polite way to imply to a neurotypical person that you want one, but with a person on the spectrum, "Please give me a cookie" works much better.

We also need to be clear about the meanings of specific words we use. Nicholas's parents taught him to dial 911 when there is an emergency, which they described as when something very bad happens to you or someone else. The next day, when he asked for more dessert after dinner, and his mother said no, he called 911, telling the operator, "It's an emergency! My mom won't give me more dessert!" In this case it would have helped if his parents listed specific examples of emergencies: a fire, a car accident, or a bad injury.

For some autistic people it may be necessary to explain the concept of nonliteral language and to teach the specific meanings of words and phrases (such as idioms) that aren't transparent or obvious. The implied meanings of "That's a piece of cake" or "Break a leg" can be quite confusing, but the meaning of such expressions can be taught directly, like words from another language translated into English. Many autistic people keep lists of words or phrases that are confusing to them and review them with therapists, parents, or teachers. It's important to remember that this issue varies greatly depending on a person's age, abilities in language, and social experiences. The best way to deal with these challenges is for all parties to take some responsibility—for neurotypicals to adjust their language to be less confusing and for autistic people to learn about common expressions that should not be taken literally and what they really mean.

When Honesty Isn't the Best Policy

The social world is infinitely complex, with no end of unwritten rules, exceptions, and variables. No matter how much effort parents and professionals put into preparing a child, we can never anticipate every possible misstep, even when we (or our autistic children or family members) have the best of intentions. Consider Ricky, an autistic teenager who was a talented pianist. Ricky once volunteered to entertain the residents of an assisted-living center. He had never visited such a facility, but his parents told him what a lovely, caring gesture it would be. They also informed him that some of the elderly people he would see had terminal illnesses and other challenges, so surely his music would help to lift their spirits. On the day of his performance, a few dozen residents gathered in a recreation room to listen. Before he sat down to play, Ricky introduced himself, said how happy he was to be there, and added this: "I'm very sorry that some of you are going to die soon."

Ricky had an appropriate sense of compassion for the elderly people he was meeting but couldn't yet discern that it might be considered insensitive to remind them so bluntly that they were at death's door!

We could also sum up Ricky's mistake another way: he was honest. As much as our culture purports to value truth and candor, interacting with autistic people can make us realize how truly deceptive and at times outright dishonest the social world requires us to be.

Donald, who was in his twenties, worked for a pharmacy chain stocking shelves and helping customers. "My manager tells me I'm a very valued employee," he told me when we met, "but my immediate supervisor doesn't like me very much. He calls me an asshole."

I asked why. He told me that an elderly woman had come to the store in search of a particular kind of battery. Within earshot of his supervisor, Donald suggested that even though the store stocked the battery, she would be better off buying it at the hardware store a block away, where the selection and prices were better.

Even as he recounted the story, he seemed not to grasp what had displeased his supervisor. "My manager tells us that our job as customer service employees is to be trustworthy so that customers think of this as their friendly neighborhood store," he said. "So why would my supervisor call me an asshole for doing just that?"

Why indeed? It's no wonder Eli assumed that other people could secretly read each other's minds. For many autistic people, trying to comprehend the social world can mean living in an almost constant state of confusion, bewilderment, frustration, and even anger.

The Stress of Misunderstanding

I have met countless autistic children and adults who misread social situations and behavior, and even after someone tries explaining what they hadn't grasped, they still may not understand. Enduring that experience again and again takes its toll. Knowing *I'm supposed to understand this, but no matter how hard I try, I can't* causes frustration, unhappiness, and anxiety. Many react by shutting down in the face of social encounters or simply avoiding them. Some turn inward and experience depression. Self-esteem suffers as they ask, "Why don't I understand this? What's wrong with me? Am I *stupid?*"

Social understanding is only one kind of being smart. You can be brilliant in many other ways and still struggle with grasping facial expressions and other subtle cues in social situations. Social understanding requires what Howard Gardner, famous for his theory of multiple intelligences, called interpersonal intelligence. A person with strengths in this area can assess the emotions, desires, and intentions of others across different social situations. Of course someone who struggles with interpersonal intelligence can demonstrate intelligence in, for example, music, math, or solving complex puzzles.

Aware of their difficulty, many autistic people apologize for themselves, almost habitually—even without understanding what they're apologizing for. They may understand social rules in extremes of black and white. They may have been told by insensitive partners for years that they are rude and can't get it right and coached to say "I'm sorry" endlessly. They're making every effort to get it right, and if they suspect they haven't said the right thing or acted the right way, their instinct is to blurt out "Sorry! Sorry!" No matter how many times parents or teachers reassure them, they come to expect that they will make mistakes, so they automatically apologize.

Living in a state of constant confusion about even ordinary social interactions can mean that when situations arise that are unanticipated or truly unfamiliar, it's likely the child will react in unexpected or extreme ways. To an observer the behavior can look rash, sudden, or inexplicable, but it's often the result of frustration and anxiety that has been building in the person for some time.

Most neurotypical people create emotional boundaries, knowing that if another person is experiencing strong emotions, it is that person's experience. We may feel sympathy or even empathy, but we do not feel the same intense feeling resulting in significant dysregulation for us. In my experience, that is not the case for many autistic people. Benny, a thirteen-year-old, rarely initiated communication. He was struggling in his public middle school classes and often became irritable in the middle of the school day because of the stress and demands of his morning classes. He also had a difficult time when he was around people expressing negative emotions. When some autistic people encounter strong emotions in other people—happiness, sadness, excitement, nervousness—they become confused and even dysregulated themselves. It's as if they are absorbing the intensity of the emotions, without understanding why they feel as they do.

A fire alarm at school rang at just the time of day when Benny typically became anxious and impatient. As he and his classmates filed out of their classroom and outside, Benny witnessed two boys roughhousing, ignoring the instructions of their teacher. When the principal spotted them, she became irate, stepped between Benny and the boys, and gave them a harsh reprimand, wagging a finger in their faces and firmly ordering them to join their classmates immediately.

Benny's reaction was sudden and unexpected: he reached over to the principal and shoved her, knocking her to the ground. It didn't help that he was a fairly large boy and she was just over five feet tall. The principal got up and dusted herself off. Fortunately she was unhurt, though shaken. Later that day, following school policy, she suspended Benny from school until school staff had a chance to review the incident.

Soon afterward I met with her in my role as consultant for the district. "Barry, I'll admit that I'm still learning about autism," she said, "but we can't have that kind of behavior in our school—and we have policies on how to proceed when such incidents occur." She was concerned not only about herself but about how Benny's classmates might perceive his behavior.

I tried to explain my understanding of the incident as the result of a series of snowballing events invisible to everyone but Benny. Even before the alarm, he had already been feeling unusually anxious. The noise and surprise of the fire drill had thrown him off even more. Then came the principal's harsh reprimand, which he found confusing and emotionally overwhelming. It upset and dysregulated him to see her so angry and to observe what he might have perceived as an aggressive act, so he reacted impulsively. The anxiety was building within him and the fire drill—and her confrontation with the boys—were simply the triggers that set him off.

There was no easy solution. It was impossible to anticipate every situation that might cause Benny anxiety. Middle school is full of situations that can be confusing and anxiety-inducing. What we could do was to make sure the school made every effort to help Benny communicate his anxiety, that staff were primed to notice the first hints of dysregulation, and that supports were in place so that when the unexpected happened—when Benny was pushed to his limit— someone could intervene. As part of his emotional regulation plan, his team put an extra break in his schedule just at the time he typically became irritable and shifted an aide to his classroom to help Benny to cope and adjust.

Social Understanding and School

To her credit, Benny's principal made an effort to understand his behavior rather than merely dismissing his misconduct as naked aggression. Autistic people often act in ways that appear confusing and open to misinterpretation. When I work with various schools, it is common for me to hear teachers complain that a student is aggressive or noncompliant or manipulative, and then later discover the real issue: the teacher doesn't understand the student and unobservable factors are often at play. Often that is because the child lacks a degree of social understanding, and the teacher misinterprets his behavior as intentional. ("He knows exactly what he's doing.")

Consider it this way: In most academic settings, most students feel innately motivated to please the teacher—to answer the question correctly, to earn an A on the exam, to succeed at the science fair, to behave in accordance with classroom and school rules. Many students also aim to make their parents proud. But an autistic person might lack those motivations. A boy might have so mastered an algebra unit that he can produce the correct answer to an assigned problem, but if the teacher asks him to describe the steps he went through to get to that answer, he might refuse. He's not being noncompliant; he just doesn't understand the social expectation of explaining his thinking. *I know how I did it, and I got the right answer*, he thinks. *Why should I have to tell you how I got it?*

Teachers are accustomed to pupils aiming to please, or at least understanding that they should. So if they lack proper training about autism, they naturally find it confusing when they deal with students like Jason, a bright, verbal autistic fifth-grader with whom I worked. One day his art teacher asked each student to write down the names of two favorite animals. Jason wrote "horse" and "eagle."

"Now," the teacher said, "I'd like you to use your imagination and create a picture of an animal that combines the features of the two animals you selected."

From the back of the classroom, Jason responded immediately in a loud, stern voice, "I will not do that."

One of the classroom aides approached him and explained the assignment again.

"I will not do that!" Jason repeated.

"But Jason," the aide said, "that's our assignment today. Everyone in the class is doing it."

"I will not do that!"

Seeing that his anxiety was rising and hoping to prevent any further escalation, the aide asked if he needed a break. She took him for a walk outside, trying to help him calm himself and reiterating along the way that all the students were participating in the same project. When they returned to the classroom, the instructor asked Jason, who seemed better regulated, if he was ready to create his picture.

"I will not do that!" he repeated, to her surprise.

It struck me that nobody had asked the most important question. I approached him slowly. "Jason," I asked, "*why* don't you want to make the picture the teacher is asking you to make?"

"There's no such *thing* as an animal that's part eagle and part horse," he replied. "I will not do that. It's stupid."

Jason wasn't being intentionally defiant or disobedient. The assignment didn't make sense to him; it defied his sense of logic. It didn't matter to him that the unwritten social rule said he should do the assignment to please the teacher, that part of his job as a student was to go along with what was asked of him, whether or not he wanted to. That sense of social obligation wasn't part of his consciousness. And even if he knew that his teacher wanted him to cooperate—and that he should—in the heat of the moment, the challenge of dealing with subject matter that so violated his sense of the world triggered his instinctive refusal.

As in Jason's case, the way a child responds to a school assignment can provide unique insight into how the child processes information and understands the social world. Sherise was in third grade when, for Martin Luther King Jr. Day, her teacher assigned a worksheet about Dr. King. Like so many autistic individuals, Sherise had an impressive capacity for memorizing dates and information and could reel off the dates of significant events in Dr. King's life better than anyone in the class. What she sometimes lacked was a sense of how to put all of the information in a social and cultural context.

One question on the sheet asked the student to list Dr. King's positive traits. Sherise wrote, "He likes dogs. He can read books." She continued in a similar vein:

Describe what you like best about Dr. King. "He helps me. He cleans my room."

Tell me one thing Dr. King has taught you. "He taught me how to write long and short vowel sounds."

Compare yourself to Dr. King. "Dr. King has a tie. I do not have a tie."

Explain why you think Dr. King is a good role model. "Because Martin Luther King Jr.'s birthday is a holiday."

Again, this was not a child who was being intentionally defiant. Sherise was a bright girl who astounded her teachers and others with her remarkable memory. But she couldn't grasp the intent of the assignment or the individual questions. Others might have intuited that the questions were about how Dr. King changed society and the way people live. But the assignment didn't explicitly state that. When the sheet asked for "positive traits," Sherise thought of *her own* positive traits. When it asked what Dr. King taught, she simply thought of something *she* had learned, albeit unrelated to the assignment. The assignment required deeper social understanding than Sherise had developed due to her social disability. It was almost like asking a child with a physical disability to compete successfully in the sixty-yard dash.

Teachers puzzling over responses like Sherise's might well slap their foreheads in frustration. Instead they should take heart and applaud the student's sincere efforts. Frustrating or baffling as the assignment might have been, Sherise didn't say, "I can't do it. I don't understand." She put in a full effort. And her lack of insight as a third-grader certainly didn't mean she would never grasp these social concepts. Social and emotional understanding, like so much else, develops over time. Different children move through various developmental stages at different rates, often only after considerable experience and with direct support. What was best for Sherise wasn't to be scolded for not cooperating but to be praised for her efforts and given extra support to understand the assignment. Not to put her self-esteem at risk, but to support her desire to succeed in a task that was challenging due to her neurological differences.

Understanding Emotions

If it's difficult for some individuals on the spectrum to comprehend the subtle, hidden rules of social interaction, it can be even more challenging to gain an understanding of emotions—their own and those of others. In 1989, the first time Oprah Winfrey interviewed Temple Grandin, Oprah asked, "What are your feelings like?" Temple answered by describing how uncomfortable she was in "scratchy" wool sweaters. By "feelings," Winfrey meant emotions, the complex world of our inner lives. But Temple assumed she was talking about sensory experiences—in particular, the sense of touch.

Or maybe she didn't want to answer the question. Emotions are abstract, intangible, and difficult to grasp, and autistic people often find it challenging to communicate about such matters, especially when doing so requires self-reflection. In the past some professionals and others have mistakenly believed that this difficulty and discomfort talking about feelings meant that people on the autism spectrum somehow lacked emotion. Of course that's not true. They experience the same full range of human emotions we all do. If anything, autistic people tell us that theirs may be magnified. The challenge for many autistic people is understanding and expressing their own emotions and reading the emotion in others.

Alvin was ten, a student who spoke fluently but struggled with anxiety and sensory issues. One day his special education teacher showed him a photograph of a baby crying and posed a number of questions: How does the baby feel? Why does the baby feel this way? Alvin was able to explain that the baby was crying because he felt sad. The teacher followed up with another question: "Alvin, what makes you feel sad?"

"What makes me feel *sad*?" he said. "What makes me feel ill? Yellow cheese." Somehow Alvin had transformed *sad* into *ill*, perhaps because it was a negative feeling that was more visceral, easier to grasp.

The teacher tried again: "What makes you feel *sad*?"

"What makes me feel *bad*? Diarrhea."

Alvin could easily identify an emotion in the baby, sadness, but couldn't yet relate it to his own internal experience. Surely he felt sad sometimes, but at age ten he couldn't explain his own emotional experience in words. The exchange reveals how an individual might have the ability to identify emotions in another person but lack the capacity to express his own emotions—which requires reflecting on one's own feelings.

Another child, Eric, who was thirteen, struggled with a similar challenge. To help Eric and his class learn about emotions, his teacher had the children spin an "emotion wheel," a sort of roulette wheel with the names of various emotions (happy, confused, angry) placed around the wheel, and then answer questions about the particular emotion the pointer landed on. Eric's word was *jealous*. The discussion went like this:

Teacher: How are you feeling today, Eric?
Eric: I feel jealous.
Teacher: Can you tell us why?

Eric: 'Cause I'm so jealous.

Teacher: And why are you feeling jealous?

Eric: Because . . . Indiana will play LSU.

Teacher: Why does that make you feel jealous?

Eric: 'Cause feeling jealous makes me feel beautiful. (Eric looks away, confused)

The conversation continued, with Eric clearly not grasping the term.

Teacher: Do you understand what it is to be jealous?

Eric: What it is to be jealous?

Teacher: If Darrell has a brand new watch and I think it's the nicest watch I've ever seen, and I want it, then I'm jealous because Darrell has a better watch than I do.

Eric: Yeah.

Teacher: Okay, do you understand that?

Eric: 'Cause Darrell has a new watch.

Teacher: And I want it.

Eric: And you would want it. . . .

Teacher: So, do you feel jealous today?

Eric: Yes.

Teacher: Why?

Eric: 'Cause Darrell wants a new watch.

Teacher: No.

Eric: 'Cause you have a new watch.

Teacher: Why does Eric feel jealous?

Eric: 'Cause I have a watch at home.

Teacher: Would you please pick another feeling?

Eric: No. I picked jealous!

Eric was doing his best to get it right, and to his credit he wouldn't quit, even when his teacher suggested he do so. But his concrete thinking style made him struggle with an abstract notion.

How Not to Teach Emotions

Too often educators think they're teaching autistic people how to express their emotions when what they are actually teaching is emotional *recognition*—how to label pictures of people expressing emotions. Using language to describe one's emotional state—that is, emotional *expression*—is among the most abstract tasks autistic children and some adults face. It's one thing to recognize an apple or a table and identify it; conveying how you feel or how someone else might feel is far more complex. Emotions involve both cognitive and physiological reactions. We not only feel; we reflect on how we are feeling and why. We also experience emotions in our body.

Such reactions are dynamic and intangible. But some therapists recommend attempting to teach emotions to autistic children by having them identify facial expressions in diagrams: happy, sad, excited, angry, surprised, confused. Ros Blackburn pointed out to me the problem with this approach. "For years, people tried to teach me emotions by having me label happy and frowny faces," she said. "The only problem is that people do not look like that." These teachers aren't teaching emotion; they're teaching picture recognition. And they're certainly not teaching the child to express and understand why he is feeling a particular emotion.

A more effective approach is introducing a label—happy, silly, frustrated, anxious—at the moment the person is experiencing that feeling. (For some people it's more appropriate to make the connection between a visual image such as a photograph and the person's feeling.) That way, he learns to express and communicate a cognitive-emotional experience, not just a facial expression. Learning to understand different emotions, and the language we use to express them develops over time. We feel emotions in our heads and our bodies, and we learn to associate categories of experiences connected to those feelings. We also hear or see the words that other people provide for us to express those feelings.

Teaching Social: What's the Goal?

In the same way, adults often emphasize teaching what are called "social skills" over teaching *social understanding* and *social thinking.** And they often teach the skills that are deemed important in a rote manner, with the goal of making a child appear "normal." This doesn't help a child to make good decisions when interacting with others, read social situations, or understand other people's perspective, emotional experience, or point of view, and may cause considerable stress for the child.

Eye contact is a prime example. Many autistic people avoid looking directly at other people's faces, perhaps because it increases anxiety, so they find it uncomfortable, perhaps because it takes focus and energy to do so, detracting from their ability to think clearly about what they want to say.

But since American culture values looking people in the eye, the late behavioral psychologist Ivar Lovaas developed approaches to "train" autistic children with the goal of making them "indistinguishable" from their peers. He felt it was essential to train eye contact before moving on to other skills. For years a hallmark of his treatment approach was his claim—not supported by scientific evidence—that the ability to make eye contact on command was a prerequisite for learning other skills. He eventually retracted this position, but unfortunately many practitioners still engage in "eye contact training."

If you listen to autistic people, they send a clear message: looking others in the eye can be extremely difficult. It makes them feel anxious. They resist efforts to force them to do so. They're more comfortable, more regulated when they're *not* looking directly at other people or are doing so intermittently. Neurotypical people develop the habit of looking directly at people from an early age, but gaze aversion

---

*Michelle Garcia Winner addresses this issue in detail in her book *Why Teach Social Thinking?* (San Jose, CA: Think Social, 2014).

serves a purpose as well. Conversations typically involve looking at the person you're talking to as well as moments of looking *away* from the person. That gives us a chance to gather our thoughts, to relax, to regulate ourselves.

I once taught a group of graduate students who came from Ghana to study at the university where I worked. During office hours I had a meeting with several of them. They were exceedingly polite, but I felt uneasy that none of them would look me in the eye, not even for a brief glance, while we spoke. Finally I raised the issue with them. "Is something wrong?" I asked. "I feel uncomfortable that you keep looking down, and not at me."

"I'm sorry sir," one of them replied, "but in our culture, it is considered a sign of disrespect to look at a person of higher status when you're speaking to them, and you are our professor."

It was a reminder that many of the social traits and practices we consider important, even crucial, aren't inherent human behaviors but rather rules that can vary widely from one culture to another.

They also differ from person to person. When I was responsible for overseeing a department in a teaching hospital I noticed that one of my newly hired employees, a speech-language pathologist, spent her entire first department meeting doodling on a pad, almost never looking at me when I spoke. At the second meeting she did the same thing. I found it so disconcerting that I confronted her. "I don't understand why you aren't paying attention to me in our meetings," I told her.

She apologized for not disclosing it earlier, then explained that she had a learning disability that made it difficult to look at a person and simultaneously process what the person was saying. I had made inaccurate assumptions about my colleague's level of interest and attention in meetings based on the messages she was sending with her body and facial language.

Many autistic people say that it is often easier to focus on what a person is saying without the extra burden and stress of watching the person's face. Seasoned teachers know that certain students may be listening and learning even though they may not be watching the instructor during a lesson.

Still, autistic people can learn the unspoken obligation to let someone know you're listening. Taking a "social understanding" or "social thinking" approach, parents, teachers, and therapists can help an individual understand that he can indicate he's paying attention by looking at another person, even for brief moments during a conversation, or by saying "Uh-huh" and nodding. Some children find looking another person in the eye so difficult that it causes discomfort. In that case they can be taught to offer an explanation so the person they're with doesn't assume that they're bored or inattentive. ("Please understand that I'm paying attention, even when I may not be looking at you.") Doing so is similar to what neurotypicals do when they know they will have to exit a meeting or lecture early because of another commitment: it's polite to inform the speaker in advance in order to avoid having their behavior misconstrued and to show sensitivity to the speaker's feelings.

Sharing that kind of information is an act of self-advocacy. It's what an autistic author did when he interviewed me on Zoom for a book he was working on. Following some of my responses to his questions, there were long pauses as he looked off to the side, followed by hesitations and halting speech when he spoke again. He felt the need to inform me that he was understanding and agreeing with everything I was saying, but was so excited about the conversation that his speech fluency was affected, and he needed to look away from the screen. By explaining why he was behaving that way, he made sure I did not misinterpret his behavior.

The Role of Unspoken Assumptions

We all make assumptions about each other's behavior that usually go unspoken but that nevertheless have great impact on our interactions. Often autistic people don't perceive the need to communicate what's bothering them—or sometimes they find unorthodox ways to do so.

An elementary school principal once showed me a collection of drawings a fourth-grader with Asperger's syndrome named Enrique had begun routinely leaving on her desk. Each depicted a devilish character with horns and a pointed tail. On each page the boy had written the principal's name, followed by her new title, "The Evil Principal."

"That's me," she said with a smile. "Whenever this student finds something he doesn't like in the school, he blames me." When Enrique was unhappy with the new ketchup in the cafeteria, he would leave a devil picture. If he didn't think a rule was fair, he'd leave another. To her credit, the principal welcomed this unique form of expression, respected his attempt to express his feelings, and eventually helped Enrique find more conventional ways to come in and discuss his grievances.

Others don't have the instinct to communicate their displeasure. Bud, a bright autistic thirteen-year-old was showing signs of severe depression. Instead of participating in his middle school classes, he would slump at his desk, face down, eyes closed, with his head resting in his arms. His teachers were baffled about how to deal with his melancholy, so they asked me to intervene.

At our first meeting Bud didn't hesitate to share. "I hate being in school," he told me, "because all my teachers hate me."

His teachers hadn't expressed any negative feelings about Bud to me, only bewilderment about how to help him. I asked Bud why he thought his teachers didn't like him.

"Because," he said, "in all my classes, they try to teach me things I'm not interested in."

Bud made an assumption that his teachers, acting out of some kind of animus, had schemed to assign him exactly the material that would most annoy and bore him. What else would explain his difficulties?

"Do your teachers ever ask what you're interested in?" I asked.

"No, they *hate* me. Why would they ask that?" he replied.

I suggested to him that when I was his age, I too was required to take classes I didn't enjoy and that I was sure many of his classmates didn't like all of their classes all the time. What seemed like common knowledge to me seemed to be new information to Bud. A neurotypical teenager would have understood that a student might not like every class and that part of being a student was learning to live with that. But to Bud the only explanation was that the teachers hated him.

After our conversation I suggested that Bud participate in a group with other students in which he could learn why people behave the way they do and say what they do, and all the possible ways to interpret their actions. There he learned things that other students understood more readily: sometimes you like your classes, sometimes you don't; if you are having difficulty, you can ask the teacher, who will be happy to help. Nobody had taken the time to explain these things to him because no one perceived how he misunderstood. The school also made an effort to integrate his interests—heavy metal music, video games—into his program. We didn't solve all of his challenges but asking him what was bothering him revealed that most of his unhappiness came from his own misunderstandings. We also emphasized that he should not feel shameful for his misunderstandings. All it took was asking him to explain, for us to listen respectfully, and then finding creative ways to integrate his interests in his daily school programming.

When we work on enhancing social understanding, the goal is not to make autistic people into neurotypical-like social clones. To do so would be disrespectful of the uniqueness of each individual and their neurology, with the risk of making the individual feel terrible about herself. The goal is to improve social competence, self-esteem, and confidence in order to lessen the misunderstandings and stress that all partners—autistic and neurotypical—experience in shared relationships. Ideally, we want to work on what the autistic individual identifies as most helpful. If that is not possible, we should strive to lessen challenges that are obvious barriers to positive and joyful social experiences. Most autistic people want to be accepted for who they are, even if that means being more comfortable on the less social end of the continuum of social engagement, which varies across all people. Most of all, we must understand that one of the highest priorities for the autistic self-advocate community is to be able to live their lives being their authentic selves.

PART TWO

Living on the Autism Spectrum

CHAPTER 7

What It Takes to "Get It"

I LEARN some of my most significant lessons just from observing, and I learned a lot from observing Paul.

Paul was a classroom aide who had been assigned to Denise, a sixteen-year-old autistic student who had recently transferred to a new school. She had felt so frustrated at her previous school—and was so frequently dysregulated—that she often attempted to hit teachers and had been identified as aggressive. In this new classroom setting, Denise often indulged in repetitive rituals. For instance, she would pull baggies full of CDs she liked to listen to from her backpack, then line them up in precise sequence across the desktop—a process that seemed to calm her. She rarely spoke, only occasionally uttering two or three words at low volume. Still, while she appeared cautious and edgy, Denise showed no obvious signs of aggression or anger.

When I observed her in familiar school routines as part of my work with the school, I immediately noticed how remarkably effective her classroom aide was. With his shaved head and large earring, Paul, who was in his twenties, reminded me of Mr. Clean, the face of the household-cleaning product. Paul would make sure Denise had the materials she needed for whatever work she was assigned and helped her get organized, but then he would back off and give her space.

He kept a close eye on her from across the room, and whenever she became frustrated, agitated, or distracted, Paul would draw closer to her, moving slowly so as not to startle her. I noticed that each time he did so, she would calm down and relax. He was extraordinarily able to observe the most subtle sign that she was becoming dysregulated, and he knew the right thing to say or do to decrease her anxiety or frustration. Sometimes he did so from a few feet away, in barely noticeable ways, giving her a reassuring head nod, pointing, or saying a few words. It was as if they had a magical, silent, symbiotic connection. Whenever I suspected that Denise was becoming tense and anxious and might need assistance, he would help her stay composed and engaged.

I wondered how he had devised a method that worked so well to help this girl stay regulated, especially since she had struggled elsewhere. I wanted to learn from whatever strategy he was using, so I asked Paul to chat for a few minutes. I mentioned what I had noticed and told him how impressed I was that he was so readily able to read the girl's signals and intervene so appropriately. "Can you talk to me about what you were doing or what you were noticing?" I asked.

He shrugged his shoulders, seeming almost baffled by my question. His answer was brief: "I just pay attention."

I just pay attention. He made it sound so simple. But those four words said so much. Paul was effective in providing exactly the support this teenager needed not because he had mastered a particular kind of therapy, followed steps in a behavior plan, or dispensed the right "reinforcers." What enabled him to provide exactly the support Denise needed was that he had the instinct and ability to watch, to listen, and to be sensitive to her needs. In doing so he earned her trust.

Where are the Pauls of the world? One of the most challenging aspects of raising an autistic child or supporting an adult on the spectrum is finding the helpers—doctors, therapists, educators, mentors, and others—who are most effective, who best connect with the person, and who inspire the most progress. Particularly when parents are dealing with autism, or the possibility of autism, for the first time, it can be difficult to know whom to trust, whose advice is worthwhile, which teacher or therapist might be the best match for the child and the family.

My perspective on this question was forever changed when I met Dr. Jill Calder, a physician who is also the mother of an autistic son. Speaking in a packed lecture hall at the University of British Columbia in Vancouver, I asked the audience if they had ever encountered people like Paul, individuals who are naturals with their child or family member not because of specific training but because of an instinctual ability.

About twenty rows back, Jill stood up. "In my family," she said, "we call it the 'It Factor.'" She explained that she had watched for years as various professionals interacted with her son. She noticed that when the school assigned a new aide to her son, the boy would often return home even more anxious and unhappy than before. But on other occasions the new person was able to make an immediate connection with the boy, and her son was noticeably more composed and happier.

What made the difference? Jill explained that some people are just naturals: within five or ten minutes they would know how to interact with her son and he would relax with them; there was a chemistry. "We say those people have 'got It,'" she said. No matter their title, no matter their training, they connect.

Next she described a second tier of people she called "It-like." These individuals may lack the natural, intuitive ability to connect with autistic people; they may even be nervous, hesitant, or uncomfortable. But they are eager to learn, and they seek support and advice from a parent or someone else who knows the person well. Jill explained that this included many professionals she met and that she was always happy to meet such people—people who are enthusiastic about working with autistic people, willing to learn and grow, and open to taking direction from the people who know the individual best.

Jill also identified a third group: those who seem unable to connect and often are the source of a person's dysregulation. These people are less open to learning from the autistic person or family and come with their own preconceived (often inaccurate) notions. They lack the ability, either intuitive or learned, to get through to the person. In many cases they focus on discipline and consequences without asking the "why" question. Their goal is to be in total control, they're often insensitive to—or minimize the impact of—sensory issues, other autism-related challenges, and especially their own behavior as they impose their own goals.

"Oh," I chimed in, "you mean the 'It-less' people." Jill and the audience nodded knowingly.

She mentioned that on more than a few occasions, an adult had entered her son's life, only to cause him increased stress and anxiety. She paused, took a deep breath, gathered her emotions, and said, "And I will *never* allow that to happen again." That triggered a torrent of comments, as others in the audience described teachers or other service providers who didn't understand their kids or family members, therapists who were stuck on an approach that was insensitive to an individual's emotional state, and doctors who focused on the behaviors, not the whole person.

I'll never forget the father of an older autistic teenager who spoke up at the annual parent-retreat weekend I help facilitate. He kicked off a discussion session on the topic of parent-professional relationships with this bold statement: "I just want to tell all of you who are parents of young kids that you can't trust professionals as far as you can throw them."

Those kinds of strong feelings emerge from having too many encounters with "It-less" professionals, those who can't seem to connect with an autistic person and who therefore lose (or never gain) the trust of the parents or caregivers. Parents rarely begin the journey wary of professionals; they're usually eager for help, desperate to meet people with the experience and perspective to provide assistance. What makes them jaded and suspicious is repeatedly encountering people who are supposed to help but instead let them down.

So what are the ingredients that make a difference? What are the factors that enable a person really to "get It"? What should a parent look for in a professional or educator? What can you do to help a promising professional become more "It-like"?

Being a person who "gets It" is not about having a particular graduate degree or a certain number of years of training or experience in the field. I have met individuals with impressive résumés and stellar credentials who nevertheless lack the basic human qualities that enable others to connect with autistic children or adults, and their families. Many others, like Paul, lack advanced training but forge real human connections, intuitively sense the needs of people they support, and help facilitate meaningful progress.

In my experience those who "get It" share a number of significant traits and instincts. Among the most important are these:

- **Empathy.** They try to understand how an autistic person comprehends and experiences the world. Rather than generalizing from their own experiences or from those of other autistic people or others with disabilities, these people pay close attention to the individual, always reading and making sense of the person's behavior, and then respond in a supportive manner.

- **The human factor.** They perceive the person's behavior as *human* behavior, resisting the temptation to explain every behavior and reaction as stemming from autism. They ask "Why?" They don't simply label a child's resistance as "noncompliant" or "attention-seeking" behavior, as if that explains why a child hesitates, refuses, or reacts in a specific manner. It's easy to say a child is "stimming" and to call that "autistic behavior" without asking questions such as "Why at this time, and not at others?" "Could it be that this is helpful to this person?" A person who's "got It" will make the extra effort to explore what's underlying the behavior and what the person's experience is, rather than starting with preconceived opinions.

- **Sensitivity.** They're attuned to the person's emotional state, including the sometimes subtle signals indicating varying degrees of regulation and dysregulation. Like most human beings, autistic people often give outward signs of their inner feelings through the subtleties of body language and facial expression. A sensitive person who "gets It" recognizes that when a child averts her gaze in a certain way or when her body tenses, she is sending a signal that she is upset or is becoming overwhelmed; that when a child rocks his body it means he is feeling unsettled. The same person might notice that when a speaking child becomes argumentative or refuses to participate in a conversation, it is likely a sign that she feels dysregulated.

- **Shared control.** They don't feel a need to exert control over the autistic person. Too many educators and therapists see their role as pushing a certain agenda or structure to keep the autistic person within certain bounds of behavior. Compliance is the goal. Instead parents and professionals should *share control* with the person, help her feel empowered, and provide support and guidance as needed. That approach is more respectful of the individual and her sense of autonomy and self. Just as important, giving the autistic person control in a variety of situations and settings ultimately leads to greater independence, self-sufficiency, and self-determination, all the necessary ingredients that lead to a strong sense of purpose and identity.

- **Humor.** They don't take things too seriously and don't view autism as a tragedy. Life can be rife with challenges for autistic people and their families, and sometimes professionals, educators, relatives, and others only make things worse by overly emphasizing the negative, seeming to view every difficult incident through a tragic lens. It's much more helpful for both the autistic individual and the family when those around them maintain a sense of humor (a respectful sense of humor, to be sure) and a healthy perspective about situations the person confronts or what she says or does. Whenever appropriate, creating lighter moments by finding the humor in a situation helps to lift and lighten the emotional tone even under difficult circumstances.

- **Trust.** They focus on forging a positive relationship and building trust. As in any relationship, the best way to build trust is to listen, to try to understand the other person's experience, and consider that person's needs and desires rather than imposing an external agenda. Professionals often forget the importance of building trust from the outset and spend the remainder of the relationship trying to make up for that. That's why it is essential to begin by listening and showing respect for the autistic individual and by partnering with the family rather than arriving with preconceived notions about what would be most helpful for a person and her family.

- **Flexibility.** They adapt to the situation rather than stubbornly sticking to a fixed agenda or a prescribed program or plan that does not reflect the needs of the individual it is designed to help. Too often therapists pay more attention to the program they are given to follow than to the person they are supposed to be helping or guiding. Some approaches are so detailed in prescribing responses or consequences that they don't leave room for the professional (or even a parent) to try to feel what the person is feeling and to understand what's underlying a behavioral reaction. When observing professionals or support personnel during a consultation, I may disagree with—or don't understand—a particular choice the person has made in reacting to an autistic individual. When I raise the matter, the response often is "I agree with you, but I'm following the behavior plan." A plan needs to be flexible enough to be responsive to the person. It's important to recognize when Plan A isn't working and it's time to shift to Plan B. It's a mistake to impose a one-size-fits-all approach when it may not be appropriate for an individual. When a professional asks parents to implement behavior plans that the parents don't see as respectful or helpful, the request may cause great stress for them. This is especially true when caregivers do not feel heard, and the plan directs them to ignore their intuition about what would be most helpful for their child or family member. Ultimately, the result may be a loss of trust in the professional.

• **Willingness to learn from autistic individuals.** People who "get It" value and seek out the insights and teachings of autistic people. The contributions and insights provided by autistic people have motivated the most dramatic and positive changes in education, treatment, and support for autistic people in recent years, and have helped to redefine what true progress is. Based on their lived experience, autistic people have debunked many harmful myths about autism and have provided invaluable direction about the most effective and respectful ways autistic people should be understood and supported.

The "It Factor" in Action

Though I have been working in the autism field for five decades, I often learn the most from people with little formal training—people who just "get It."

Sometimes the simplest things can make a difference. Carlos, who was relatively new to his school, had had some significant outbursts and meltdowns in his seventh-grade class. Various teachers reported on how aggressive and unpredictable he could be, but one person had developed a relationship with him: the principal.

As an advisor to the school district, I paid a visit to the principal to ask how she had been able to connect with Carlos. She explained that after a particularly disruptive classroom episode, she had invited the boy to her office. Instead of reprimanding him or disciplining him, she tried something else: she shared an orange with him. He so enjoyed it that she told him if he could follow classroom rules and manage himself appropriately, she would invite him back. She also observed Carlos in his class so he could see how invested she was in his success, and made some helpful suggestions to his young teacher.

That became a routine for the two of them. I asked her how it worked.

"It's very simple," she said. "We sit down together, we peel oranges, and we enjoy eating the oranges."

The principal understood that it wasn't going to help this particular boy for yet another adult to tell him that he was behaving poorly or that he needed to settle down. What he needed was to have a connection with a person, a trustworthy adult he could depend on in the school. Her actions communicated to Carlos that she wanted him to be successful in school—and believed that he could be.

It's often small rituals like peeling oranges that are the basis of close bonds—and growth. People who have "got It" understand that: that the significant relationships autistic people develop often bear little resemblance to the relationships other people might have.

Denise Melucci is a skilled artist who worked with Justin Canha, a talented autistic artist (see Chapter 10), when he was young. Justin had displayed emerging talent as an artist, and when his parents asked Denise if she would tutor him, she was enthusiastic, though she lacked any formal training in autism and had never worked with an autistic child.

Justin was insistent on drawing cartoon characters—Mickey Mouse, Homer Simpson, Bambi—and resisted her suggestions that he move beyond that. Seeing his ability, she wanted to expand his repertoire and help him learn that he could enjoy and excel at creating other kinds of pictures as well. At first Justin stubbornly refused.

How did she coax him to expand beyond cartoons?

She meowed.

Denise knew that Justin's greatest passion besides animated characters was animals. He routinely visited zoos and enthusiastically greeted dogs and cats. In order to motivate him, she offered him a deal: every time Justin made an effort to draw something outside his repertoire of cartoon characters—a landscape, say, or a still life— Denise would meow like a cat. To her surprise, it worked. Not only did her novel strategy open Justin to exploring new areas of artistic expression, but it also helped inject fun into the experience and, most important, created the foundation for a trusting relationship between student and teacher.

Making a "meow" sound seems like a small thing, but what was significant was Denise's willingness to be flexible and creative in considering what might motivate her student. Another teacher might have resorted to making demands, offering snacks as reinforcers, or simply given up, but she saw a challenge and met it with imagination based on Justin's enthusiasms.

Joshua, a sixth-grader, benefited from the same kind of creative thinking when his gym teacher devised a way to motivate him to participate in his class's exercise program. Joshua's passion was U.S. presidents. At an early age he had memorized the presidents in chronological order. Now he spent long hours on the Internet and with books, accumulating and memorizing facts about various residents of the White House.

The teacher's creative solution: she made connections between various exercises and presidents. She connected President Lincoln, known for his height, with stretching. She connected George Washington, associated with the story of chopping down a cherry tree as a youth, with arm swings. President Obama played basketball, so she connected him with leaping as if the child were shooting a jump shot.

Instead of forcing the matter, the teacher found a way to motivate Joshua by following his lead and incorporating his interests. It wasn't just for Joshua; the entire class participated. And the teacher often let Joshua decide which exercises the class would do on a given day. With creativity and flexibility and by paying attention to what excited Joshua, the teacher achieved multiple objectives: she motivated Joshua to get physical exercise, she engaged him by giving him a say in what he did in class, and she connected him socially to his classmates.

When teachers are resistant to such innovative strategies, it's not always because they lack creative impulses. Sometimes they fear that school administrators are not willing to support approaches that vary from the normal curriculum. In most schools the principal is the one to set the tone and determine priorities for the entire staff. When a principal "gets It," that can make all the difference for autistic students.

Nina was a petite first-grader whose mother liked to dress her in bright, flowery dresses. In preschool Nina was constantly in motion, spending much of the day rolling on the floor and crawling on tables. By first grade she had made great strides but still had difficulty with impulse control and awareness of her body. When her classmates would sit on the rug for their morning meeting and she wanted to join them, she would throw her body in the middle of the group instead of sitting as expected.

To help Nina have better control of her body, one of her therapists provided her with a small, circular rubber pad—a colorful disc, about twelve inches in diameter—to help Nina know where to sit. When the children were seated on the rug for an activity, the teacher would designate a spot for Nina and place the pad there. It was a simple solution to help her control her impulses, organize her movement, and understand where she should be.

Just as Joshua's classmates wanted to join in presidential calisthenics, all of Nina's classmates wanted colorful discs of their own. And the teacher complied, giving each child a circle with its own color and number. That helped to normalize what had been helpful to Nina. She wasn't the only one with a disc; she was just one of the kids.

The problem arose when the class moved to other parts of the school, in particular to the music room. The music teacher had her own traditional methods of classroom "behavior management" and wasn't open to change. When the therapist explained to her that Nina would be sitting on her colored disc in class, the music teacher rejected the idea, not wanting to offer any kind of special treatment. The girl needed to learn to sit, she said, despite her problems with body awareness and impulse control.

Of course Nina struggled to sit still in music class without the additional support. When the children sat on the floor, she rolled about, awkwardly trying to move her body into the group, causing havoc.

The matter came up at a meeting of the various educators and therapists working to support Nina. Everyone agreed that the disc had been beneficial, providing the key to helping Nina to organize her body and understand where to sit. Her team shared that Nina also appeared proud—with a beaming smile—when she could sit up like her classmates.

Finally the principal spoke up. "Are you convinced that this works?" he asked the group.

Everyone agreed that it did.

He pounded his fist on the table. "If this helps Nina, then *everyone* in the school will honor and respect that."

Some at the table doubted the music teacher would cooperate.

"It's not her decision," the principal responded. "This is a school decision. We support every student at the level they need to be supported to be successful."

That was a principal who "got It," who understood that it's essential to be creative, responsive, and flexible in supporting children of different abilities. When a principal takes such a stand, not only does it help individual children like Nina, but it also makes the teachers and therapists working with those children feel valued, supported, and validated. Knowing that they have that kind of support gives these educators the motivation and confidence to seek out the solutions that will best support their students, no matter how unorthodox they might seem.

Principals and other leaders who "get It" see it as their responsibility to ensure that families of children with disabilities feel welcomed. They visibly interact with students and their families, and when problems or challenges arise, they see it as their role to help devise creative and appropriate solutions. These leaders create compassionate, caring communities and earn the loyalty and respect of their staff.

In some school districts, particularly smaller districts, the special education director sets that tone, sometimes from the very beginning of a family's journey. Stacy, a special education director in Connecticut, made it her business to initiate contact with families in her district whose toddlers were in early intervention programs and would likely be enrolling in her district's special education programs. She visited the families at home to listen to their concerns and inform them of the ways her schools could help.

Some of Stacy's colleagues from other districts questioned the wisdom of these personal visits, wondering whether a busy district administrator was overly burdening herself by calling on every new family. But Stacy knew that the transition to school for such families is fraught with anxiety for both students and parents. She also understood that one of her most significant roles was building trusting relationships with families. When parents feel nurtured from the beginning of a child's educational journey, that serves to enhance that relationship for years to come.

Linda, a special education director in another district where I consulted, learned of a family in her district with twin girls approaching three years of age, both on the autism spectrum. Having learned from Stacy, I suggested we pay a visit to the twins and their parents. In their home, a cluttered trailer, Linda and I sat on the floor and played with the two girls while we answered questions from their parents. Over the course of ninety minutes, Linda helped ease the minds of these parents, who were relatively new to the challenges of autism and how the schools could help.

As the visit ended and we drove away together, I noticed Linda had a smile on her face and a tear in her eye. "That just felt so right," she said. "I am so proud of what we did." In that brief visit she had sent a message about her district's open and welcoming attitude toward families struggling with disabilities and planted the seeds of a trusting relationship with anxious, overwhelmed parents.

Teachers and Others Who "Get It"

Teachers and other service providers don't have to specialize in autism or special education to understand the challenges, strengths, and needs of autistic students. Visiting a school I consulted for in Virginia, I watched one elementary school music teacher show remarkable skill in his efforts to include three autistic students seamlessly with their twenty neurotypical classmates.

One of the children, an eight-year-old boy, sang a part from the opera *Aida* in Italian. The teacher explained later that the boy had perfect pitch and had demonstrated the ability to memorize nearly any piece of music. Another boy played piano, leading the rest of the class in a song. When the teacher used a SMART Board to display an animated musical staff as part of a lesson in reading music, the autistic children were just as actively engaged, motivated, and focused as any of their classmates.

When I asked the teacher later about his approach, he explained that he always sought to find the strengths and talents within each student, including those on the autism spectrum, and to put them on display. "These children have so many obvious challenges," he told me. "I'm not doing my job unless I make sure that all of the students participate and that all of the students see the abilities of their classmates."

Other educators stand out by creating innovative ways to engage and motivate students. At a middle school on Cape Cod, I once observed a speech-language pathologist leading a group of neurodivergent students as they shared the process of baking chocolate chip cookies. After the children had completed the work and distributed the cookies onto plates, the therapist eagerly announced, "Okay, now it's time for the rest of our activity!"

Together the children took to the halls of the school, each carrying a plate of cookies. Each took a turn knocking on a classroom door, the teacher's lounge, and various offices, then greeting the person who came to the door and engaging in a conversation.

"Welcome to our classroom! What kind of cookies did you bring today?"

"We made chocolate chip cookies."

"How many do you have?"

Clearly this had become part of the school's routine, a regular opportunity for the students to be active participants in the community of the school, to engage with teachers and other students, and to have a sense of giving back. (And who doesn't like cookies?)

Diane was an educator who worked with a number of middle school students on functional academics—that is, improving reading and mathematics skills in order to use them in practical, everyday ways. She also sought out ways to create opportunities for natural social interactions. Diane worked with her students to create a store in their school where they sold snacks and drinks to staff members and students.

It was a simple idea, but it magically drew other students into the room where the autistic students spent much of their time. Diane did not rely on programmed interactions based on a formal social skills curriculum; instead the store provided a space in which the children experienced natural interactions and learned in the process. Even the students with the greatest challenges had opportunities to contribute, and the school's typical kids didn't have to be coerced into artificial social connections with Diane's students; they came for the snacks and stayed for table games. Her creative approach offered opportunities and helped foster a sense of community for all.

Then there was the high-school gym teacher who took notice of Felipe, a burly, enthusiastic, and energetic student, and suggested he would make a great addition to the co-ed basketball cheerleading squad. The coach who oversaw the cheerleaders welcomed the suggestion, as did Felipe and his family. Felipe quickly became a crowd favorite and a valued member of the squad, helping to lead the cheers in front of a packed gym with the full support of his fellow cheerleaders. What he lacked in coordination, he made up for with his beaming smile and enthusiasm—he knew he belonged. Fortunately, his school was one that didn't just "talk the talk" of inclusion, but truly "walked the walk."

What these situations have in common is that creating inclusive opportunities was important, but only the first step. As my friend and colleague Shelly Christensen says, we must go beyond inclusion to create a sense of belonging so that a person feels valued as a member of a community.

Encountering It-less People

As much as an educator or therapist who "gets It" can make a positive difference for a student and a community, encountering someone in the "It-less" category can make a challenging situation even worse, whether the person is a teacher, a therapist, a neighbor, or the cashier at the local pharmacy. Unfortunately I have seen far too many school administrators, teachers, and therapists whose ignorance, stubbornness, and inflexibility create more problems than they solve.

They Have a "Deficit Checklist" Mentality

Some professionals and service providers view individuals solely as the sum of their challenges—taking what I first referred to in 1983 as a "deficit-checklist" approach. Instead, it is essential to take a more sensitive and valuable developmental approach by understanding each person's strengths and needs as they grow and evolve through stages over time. When goals and services focus mostly on a checklist of "problem behaviors" and what the person cannot do, they mistakenly emphasize some "normative" notion of how a person should behave and what they should learn rather than giving a more complete picture of the actual person. What is lost, or neglected, is a rich understanding of the unique, distinctive individual.

In most cases parents and caregivers know their child or family member better than anyone. And because diagnosing autism and assessing what an individual needs is a collaborative process, it is essential that mothers and fathers—and others who know the child well—be included. Professionals should communicate to parents that their observations are valid, respected, and important. Rather than simply delivering a verdict, the professional should look to the parents or other caregivers to validate (or correct) the professional's observations and conclusions, and reach a collaborative consensus.

It is now recognized that many people who are on the spectrum remain undiagnosed well into the teen or adult years or may be misdiagnosed with other conditions. In cases of late diagnosis these individuals should play an active role in the diagnostic and assessment process. Many self-diagnose and then self-refer in order to obtain an accurate diagnosis. And just as with early diagnosis, the emphasis should be on relative strengths, and what has worked and is working well for that individual, and not just challenges.

The most common mistake many professionals make in diagnosis, especially for children and those caregivers who are "new to it all," is providing a diagnostic label and casting diagnosis only in a negative light, but nothing beyond that. That is both irresponsible and insensitive. Professionals should also seek to identify relative strengths, especially those that can play an important part in a child's or adult's future. That helps parents and significant others understand that diagnosis represents only one step in a long journey. Receiving a diagnosis is often helpful and, in my opinion, essential, as it helps parents and caregivers move beyond uncertainty and confusion about their child. For later diagnosis in teens and adults, it can help to provide insight into challenges that have caused much stress over the years and eventually connect the person to the rapidly growing community of autistic people who have become an essential source of support (see Chapter 11 for further discussion on disclosure). The crucial question isn't what the person's label is but rather Where do we go from here? What is the best array of services or supports we can assemble to assure the individual the best possible future? For older individuals, we should always be asking. "What has already been helpful?"

Parents receiving a diagnosis for their young children usually have another question: What is the long-term prognosis? The answer: What's most important isn't where your child is now; it's the *trajectory of growth* the child demonstrates over time. In other words, the child's progress will tell us about her potential. Our job and obligation is to make sure that the right supports are in place, including the right people. Despite the fears some professionals instill, there is no limit on a person's potential. For all of us—including all autistic people—development is a lifelong process.

They Pay More Attention to a Plan Than to the Child

The parents of a child I had known as a preschooler asked me years later to visit the private autism school where their son, then twelve, had just been enrolled in middle school. Alex was a thin, gangly boy who did not speak due to a severe motor speech disorder; aware and intelligent, he was unable to coordinate and sequence the fine-motor movements to produce intelligible speech. He also had extreme sensory sensitivity and found certain noises torturous. Over time he had become self-injurious and had to wear a helmet for his protection.

At one point during my visit, an administrator told Alex it was time to go from his classroom to the gymnasium. I saw an expression of fear and anxiety flash across the child's face. The teacher mentioned that Alex often experienced difficulty with excessively noisy and busy rooms such as the gym, but the administrator, a strong, determined young man, was insistent.

"He doesn't have a choice," he said, then picked up Alex under his arms and dragged him up the stairs as I followed closely behind. It had been six years since I had seen Alex, but he looked at me, pleading with his eyes, and then reached out and grabbed my shirt, seeming to beg for support. The administrator dragged him all the way to the gym, where he threw him onto the mat, as if to show him who was in charge. "This is our intervention for noncompliance," he said. Alex was stunned, but not physically hurt. This happened suddenly, and as a visitor and guest, I felt powerless to do much to intervene, but my heart broke for him and I knew I needed to take action.

I informed his parents and another administrator of the abuse I had observed. To this day I am haunted by situations such as this and it fuels my passion for change. It is difficult to understand how it served any purpose to force a child into a setting that would certainly cause him emotional and physical pain. Unfortunately this wasn't an isolated incident but rather an extreme result of an approach predicated on controlling the child. The educator was blind to the boy in front of him and of the damage he was doing.

They Focus on the Child's Reputation, Not the Child's Potential

When students transfer to new schools, teachers and therapists appropriately familiarize themselves with the child's history and learn what challenges caused difficulty previously. The problem arises when they make assumptions about the present based on past and, in some cases, inaccurate accounts of the person.

One girl I knew had a history of lunging at therapists when she was particularly agitated. I observed that even newer therapists tended to be on guard with her, treating her as if they *expected* her to be aggressive. The one aide who was able to help her the most ignored what he had heard, treated her with respect, paid close attention, and expected the best from her.

As David Luterman, one of my mentors, teaches, people conform to expectations. Individuals often come with baggage: a label, a history of a particular kind of behavior, a reputation. While being familiar with history may be helpful, it should not be an obstacle to creating a new, more positive course by being open to an individual's potential growth and development.

They Try to Control Rather Than Support

When a student is assigned an aide or paraprofessional, the hope is that the individual will be well trained and sensitive to the child's needs, providing guidance and support when needed, and keeping a distance when that is more appropriate. Although many paraprofessionals fulfill their duties well, especially when part of a functioning team, sometimes the problem stems from an aide who lacks proper training. Allen had an aide who hovered within inches of his face and physically prompted him so frequently that her very proximity became a dysregulating factor. As time passed, Allen became more and more agitated—mostly because of the aide's behavior.

Some educational staff who work with autistic individuals have the misguided concept that to be effective, it's best to be in the person's face, or to use an overly physical hands-on approach, even to give positive support. But for an autistic child or adult who has social anxiety and sensory challenges, that can be scary and intimidating. It can also impede progress. The autistic person can't decipher the social intentions, so instead of perceiving a helpful, energetic person, they see only somebody hovering frighteningly close.

This aide also made the common mistake of forcing her agenda on the child. Instead of reading the child's signals, she put all of her energies into telling him what to do with a focus on getting him to comply, no matter what. That approach is disrespectful and often provokes resistance and anxiety.

They Are Insensitive to Parents' Hopes and Dreams

The Individualized Education Program (IEP) meeting was coming up for Josh, a seventh-grader I had followed for several years. Though he was bright and communicated effectively, the teachers and therapists who saw him regularly made it clear that he was falling behind academically and having significant challenges. He had been in an inclusive classroom alongside neurotypical peers, and it was clear to everyone that it was time for him to focus on more functional academic skills rather than struggling to stay at grade level in his academic subjects. Still, I knew that for his mother, Gloria, academic achievement was important, so it would be difficult to hear his educators recommending that he be moved off the standard academic track.

When I met with the administrator who would be managing Josh's IEP meeting, I raised this concern and suggested that she broach the topic first in a private meeting with Gloria, not the larger meeting. "She's at a fragile point and will take this as a symbol of failure," I said. But the administrator, who prided herself on running an efficient operation, assured me it would be fine.

When the day came, I watched around the long table as one member of the team after another reported on Josh's limited academic progress and suggested that his program be shifted to a more functional, life skills focus. With each report, Gloria's hopeful expression grew more and more despondent. By the time the fourth person spoke, the air in the room felt heavy, and Gloria burst into tears and bolted from the room.

The administrator had prioritized efficiency and standard operating procedure over sensitivity to the mother and what she needed to hear: that the team wasn't giving up on her son, just appropriately adjusting his program. As a result she not only caught Gloria off guard, but in doing so she lost her trust because she didn't take into account where Gloria was on her journey, and as a mother Gloria clearly was not respected as a collaborator in making decisions about her son's program.

By the nature of their work, teachers and other autism professionals deal with many families at once. But they need to treat each child, and each family, as unique and important. Being sensitive to the needs, hopes, and dreams of each child and parent is essential to building trust, working collaboratively, and serving the best interests of all.

The Importance of Knowing Your Role

One of the key ingredients of "getting It" is humility. The first time I taught a university course on autism, in 1979, one of my guest speakers was Terry Shepherd, then a professor at Southern Illinois University, who is the father of an autistic son. He told my students that life with his son was like living on a carousel, with each year representing another rotation. "Please understand that you will be getting on the merry-go-round with different families," he said. "You might be on my family's merry-go-round for one or two years before you get off. But please understand: we *live* on this merry-go-round."

I have heard that sentiment echoed again and again when I ask parents of autistic children or adults what are the most important qualities they seek in the people who work with their autistic family member. Perhaps the most eloquent answer came from the mother of a young man who was then in his twenties. "The people we valued most were the ones who never judged us," she said, "but joined us on the journey."

Nothing could better sum up what it means to "get It."

CHAPTER 8

Wisdom from the Circle

O NE weekend each year I sit in a circle of friends and acquaintances, old and new, and take in wisdom.

The ritual began more than two decades ago. My wife, Elaine, and I were on vacation, hiking in Olympic National Park, when we began discussing the value of what we were doing: getting away to enjoy nature and escape the stress of everyday life. We reflected on how rarely most parents caring for autistic children or family members had such chances to escape the constant demands of their daily routines. So we set about creating a way to offer that opportunity.

The result was a retreat, created in partnership with Community Autism Resources, a parent-founded and parent-run agency in New England that supports families of autistic children and adults. For one weekend each year, some sixty parents come together at a New England retreat center to step away from their pressures at home and connect with others who have the lived experience of autism by raising and caring for an autistic family member. Together they share their stories—joyful, humorous, frustrating, agonizing—in a place where compassionate moms, dads or other family members who share similar experiences will listen and understand.

Of all the places my career has taken me—workshops in St. Croix,

Singapore, or Sydney, classrooms across the country, living rooms and playgrounds and hospitals—this is where I have learned the most. In particular each year I am moved to tears at the closing circle, where the participants—some newcomers, some veterans, some parents of preschoolers, others of adults in their thirties—gather to reflect on the past two days and the past year, and begin to consider what they hope for the coming year. There are no rules, and each parent has the chance to share whatever they feel moved to say. We ask only that all be open and honest and to listen. Some parents bare their souls, many express their love and gratitude for their partners and children, and others reflect deeply on the messages shared by others.

The circle is where I heard a father of Muslim faith tell me that every night he watches his autistic son fall asleep and sees the face of God. The retreat is where a mother called her son, then in his twenties, "the best human being I know," and tearfully shared her frustration that employers wouldn't give him a fair chance. It's where I heard one father agonize over not finding an appropriate school for his child and another chuckle over his son's habit of approaching every young woman with long blonde hair at school and telling her that she looks just like Britney Spears. It's where one Black mother shared that while others may see her family—a blind husband and two daughters, one blind and the other autistic—as weird, especially by their white neighbors, she knows that they are really "hip" and that all the parents who have autistic children should know that they, too, are hip, because they really are.

Those raising or caring for an autistic child or sharing their lives with an autistic partner can gather information, advice, and fortitude from a variety of sources: therapists, doctors, educators, books, and websites. In my experience, however, the most valuable, useful, and empowering wisdom often comes from other parents, mothers and fathers who have already been down this path. Over the years these parents and their autistic family members have been my best teachers, and their messages continue to inform my work and my understanding of the autistic experience.

Parents, Family Members,
and Caregivers Are the Experts

It's natural to feel overwhelmed, confused, and even fearful about finding the best ways to help a child or family member on the spectrum. For many parents their instinct is to rely on the wisdom of others who seem better qualified and more knowledgeable. Here is the advice I have heard parents of older children and adults share: Those experts might know more about autism, but you're the expert on your own child or family member.

Nobody has the perspective, the sensitivity, or the ability to perceive the nuances of a child's or older person's behavior that a parent or family member possesses. No one knows what a subtle facial expression means or what a particular cry or moan or giggle means the way a mother or father does. A parent knows when a daughter needs a break, when a son might be open to connecting. One dad told me how much he cherishes reading stories to his son at bedtime, an hour when he can "get in deep." A sibling knows the best ways to keep their autistic brother or sister engaged in play. Parents and other family members are the ones who notice breakthroughs and milestones that even so-called experts might miss because they're just not as attuned to the individual. They are the ones from whom I've heard over and over again, "I was told my child would never (speak, have friends, get a job, drive, go to college, live on their own), but my son (or daughter) proved them wrong again!"

Of course some parents and siblings have their own significant challenges. All parents aim to be the best providers, the most understanding caregivers, and the greatest supports for their children or family members on the spectrum. But often circumstances make that difficult. When parents struggle financially or have their own medical or mental health difficulties, they face significant obstacles in raising children or caring for a family member—even more so when the autistic person has her own serious challenges. A brother or sister, due to their own developmental challenges, might go through phases of resenting having a sibling on the spectrum, perhaps triggered by occasions when their brother or sister's behavior might embarrass them at school, or if they feel left out as too much attention is given to their autistic family member.

When parents and family members are present, able, and well supported, though, it makes all the difference. Researchers studying child development have posed this question in various ways: Child-rearing practices vary so dramatically from one culture to another, how can parents and families in *all* of these cultures raise children who are emotionally healthy? In a developed country a stay-at-home parent might spend hours interacting with an infant or toddler, face-to-face, while in a developing country the mother might spend half the day in the fields with her child on a cradleboard on her back. What both mothers offer is responsive caregiving. Whether the mother is sitting on a playroom floor full of toys or in the field, when her child cries or fusses, she responds and calms the child. When the child is most alert and available, the parent seizes on the opportunity to teach and interact. In many families and across cultures, siblings, grandparents, and other caregivers fulfill the need for responsive care-giving, either part-time or full-time. The best predictor of emotion-ally healthy children is having highly responsive caregivers.

Autism can add a challenge to this scenario since it can be more difficult for a parent or caregiver to attend to a child's needs when the child's signals are difficult to read. But parents and familiar care-givers learn and adapt and are far better equipped to understand the child's or family member's communication and state of regulation than anyone else. Professionals can offer insight, support, resources, and guidance, but that doesn't replace or outweigh an attentive par-ent's or caregiver's perceptions, whether the child is three or thirty and whether the parent is new to autism or has decades of experience.

Natalie was one such mother, with a keen sense of her son Keith's abilities and challenges. When I first met Keith, he was five years old and not speaking. In addition to autism, he suffered from co-occurring medical conditions: a seizure disorder, severe food allergies, and gastrointestinal issues. Keith, with flushed skin and tense posture, often appeared to be in significant pain. As his medical issues were addressed with some success, he began speaking and he progressed socially, finding some degree of comfort and stability in his elementary school.

When Keith was in his last year at the elementary school, his mother sought my help. It was many months before Keith was to move up to middle school, but Natalie confided that she was already so worried about the prospect of that transition that she was losing sleep. She and her husband felt that it would be best for him to stay in the elementary school for another year rather than moving on with his classmates. They believed that the familiarity and stability would benefit him, and they valued that his current teachers were well acquainted with Keith and his complex medical history, were able to read his signals, and were in the best position to provide the support he needed. Natalie understood the district policy that students at a certain age progress to the next school, but her strong maternal instinct was that it would better serve her son to wait. Because of the severity of his disability due primarily to his medical challenges, he had made slow progress for many years, but important gains had accelerated in the past two years. Why take the risk of setting him back?

I trusted their hunch, and I agreed to advocate for their position in my role as a consultant for the district. It was extremely rare to hold students back, and Keith didn't meet all the criteria for doing so, but I suggested that in this case the educators should pay attention not to the policy but to the child and his parents. "These parents know their child," I said. "They're invested in him and his success in school, and they know what's right."

In the end the special education director and principal agreed and gave Keith another year in his elementary school. After that year he made a successful transition to middle school. The district also won the trust and appreciation of a pair of parents, grateful that their instincts about their son were honored and respected.

Trust Your Gut, Follow Your Instinct

Almost weekly I have an exchange of this sort: A mother or father asks me advice about a particular activity, a therapy, or some approach involving their children. When I reassure the parent that her own hunch is probably correct, the frequent reply is "That's what I thought, but my therapist (or doctor or teacher) disagreed."

Trust your gut.

David and Susan had two teenage boys, both nonspeaking and autistic. Though they lived in a beautiful part of New England, they hadn't been outdoor enthusiasts until after their boys were diagnosed. Spending time in a state park, they took a one-mile family hike and discovered that the boys not only enjoyed the activity but also found it calming and regulating. When the boys were in their early teens, David and Susan hatched a plan to tackle the rigorous nine-mile hike up Franconia Notch, the famous New Hampshire mountain pass.

When the boys' occupational therapist heard the plan, she warned against it, cautioning that the two lacked the physical conditioning and the stamina to make the hike. Besides that, the boys, like many autistic children and teens, had a tendency to wander.

In the end, though, David and Susan didn't share the therapist's concerns and made the trip. Not only did the boys handle the challenge of the trek; they thrived, enjoying the outdoors, the experience, and even the physical challenge.

As Susan explained, she heard so much about her sons' limitations that she rarely considered their potential. By following her own instinct instead she opened up a new world of possibilities for the boys and the entire family. For years Susan kept a photograph of Franconia Notch posted near her desk as a reminder of the rewards of her journey with her children. "It's my own visual reminder," she said, "that one fine day we accomplished a goal I'd always wanted not just in spite of autism but because of it." Now, with the boys as young adults, the family is achieving new goals each year as they meet new goals in climbing peaks throughout New England.

Find Community

When parents discover that a child is on the autism spectrum, it's natural for them to feel alone and isolated. Their social circles shift. Neighbors, friends, even relatives sometimes distance themselves, in many cases because they don't know what to say or how to interact with the autistic person. They're uncomfortable; they can't relate; their own children are on different paths, different trajectories, and they pull away. Even those close to the family who wish to help may not know how. Parents often describe this shift: people who had been in their lives previously, even those with emotional attachments, don't know what to say or do about this new reality. Those changes can be painful and disorienting for parents who are already dealing with the difficulties and uncertainty that come with the child's diagnosis.

It's essential for such families to connect with others, to find a community where they are understood, accepted, and welcomed, where they can be comfortable and don't need to explain themselves. Community can take many forms: groups of relatives; school support groups; churches, synagogues, or mosques; informal circles of friends. I have learned the importance of connecting with other parents and families from the instant community that forms each year at our parent retreat. I experienced it again when I partnered with members of my temple and an extraordinary rabbi to create a special Sabbath service as an alternative for families of children who felt overwhelmed in the main sanctuary. After all, shouldn't your place of worship be the welcoming place where you can find a supportive environment, as well as acceptance and nonjudgmental attitudes toward children and adults who may look or behave differently? (See Epilogue for a discussion of finding community.)

When parents and caregivers share time and stories with others who have experienced similar setbacks and achievements, who have struggled to support their autistic loved ones in the same ways, they form an almost instant bond. What had been painful—a child's meltdown, an adult's embarrassing public encounter—becomes the source of reflection, and even laughter and release. What had been isolating—disappointments with schools or friends or employers—becomes the basis of connection and shared experience with others. Newcomers to our retreat often tell me that they hadn't even realized how much they had been missing this vital connection until they discovered it at the retreat. Fathers in particular gain from hearing other fathers express the same emotions that they feel but rarely share. Parents who have returned again and again to the retreat say they feel much more deeply connected to other retreat parents, whom they see just once a year, than to people they see routinely at home.

That said, it's important to find the right community. Sometimes other parents under great stress want to vent and be heard, but aren't seeking support. And it's important to remember that autistic people fall on a broad spectrum of ages and abilities, so one family's experience may not bear much resemblance to another's. When there is a good match, the best community is the one that offers companionship, understanding without judgment, and support without needless criticism.

See the Cup as Half Full

It is also essential to seek out those who pursue and find the positive along the way. As one father at our retreat put it, "We've learned to avoid the doom-and-gloom crowd." He recounted how, feeling the need for connection and understanding, he and his wife had joined a local support group for parents of children on the autism spectrum. "All we heard about at that first meeting was how stressed out everybody was, their conflicts with the schools, what their kids couldn't do and the therapy they needed," he said. They had gone in search of sustenance, but the session had left them with a dark, hopeless feeling.

A mother explained the issue this way: "We know the difficulties twenty-four/seven. We want to hear some of the positives. We want people to celebrate with us."

That doesn't mean being Pollyannaish or avoiding the truth. It means surrounding yourself with people who can see—and help you see—your child or family member's beauty, wonder, and potential.

Parents face the same sorts of challenges in their encounters with professionals. Some physicians and therapists feel obligated to deliver diagnoses and opinions in the worst possible light, informing parents of the direst prognoses: what the child will never do or accomplish. Some teachers report only a child's struggles and problems, losing sight of the progress and unexpected achievements, however seemingly insignificant. Not only can this cast a negative pall on the child; it can also affect parents' perceptions of their children and shatter hopes for the future. When I hear of the negative ways some practitioners present information, I'm reminded of the Paul Simon song "Tenderness": "No, you don't have to lie to me. Just give me some tenderness beneath your honesty."

Parents who are veterans of the autism journey have put it this way: Many factors about your child and your child's or family member's disability are out of your direct control. But you *can* control your choices: with whom you and your family spend time, which professionals you pursue, whose advice you listen to. Why not choose the people who are capable of seeing the cup half-full and who give you tenderness with their honesty?

Have Faith

I once listened to Maria Teresa Canha, mother of Justin, the talented artist, tell her family's story to a rapt group of parents at the fundraising conference for our parent retreat. Afterward the audience peppered her with practical questions: How had she found an art tutor for her son? How had Justin learned to care for himself? How had he learned the social skills required for job interviews? How was Justin able to move from home and live in his own apartment? Then a mother in the front row raised her hand and asked how the Canhas could send their son from their home in New Jersey on public transportation to a job in New York City and eventually to live in his own apartment: "How do you deal with the fear?"

Maria Teresa did not hesitate to answer. "I have faith in God," she said, "and I have faith in Justin." Her faith led to Justin now being able to live on his own (with his cat)—a goal he and they had set for him as a teen.

Parents frequently express the importance of maintaining those two kinds of faith: in your child or family member and in something larger than yourself. Admittedly, as a young professional I held less stock in the role of faith, especially within organized religion, and placed more confidence in science and research, probably due to my own discomfort. But over time and in hundreds of encounters with families of all kinds, I have seen firsthand how important a strong sense of faith can be to families coping with the challenges presented by autism and by systems supposedly designed to be of help for autistic individuals and their families.

At a school meeting about her five-year-old son, a mother marveled at the progress the boy had achieved. Before age four he had been unable to speak; then, after considerable work with therapists, he had begun communicating with the help of a keyboard and, later, an iPad with a text-to-speech app. Before long that led to the beginnings of actual speech. The mother was clearly delighted. She had questioned whether he would ever be able to develop speech to communicate, so she was overjoyed that this ability had emerged so quickly.

"Well," I told her, "your son has done a lot of hard work."

The mom smiled and praised the teachers and therapists who had been working with her son. Then she told me that every night, she prayed for her son. "I see this as a collaborative team effort," she said, "between God, my son, and the school staff."

Faith can take many forms. Parents struggle to have spiritual faith and faith in their children but also to have faith in doctors, in therapists, in teachers, and in school districts, community-living agencies, and employers. Do they understand my daughter? Do they have my son's best interests in mind? Can they see how intelligent and unique she is? That's not always easy, and for some that faith is routinely shaken. But the parents I know who cope the best are those who find a way to have faith and trust and to keep moving forward.

Many parents see themselves in partnership with a higher power in raising a child. This brings comfort, a sense of shared responsibility and trust, and decreases anxiety. For others what is important is developing faith in their own ability to know what's best for their loved ones. When I see these issues raised in discussions with parents, I am always struck by that breadth of the continuum, from those who see a divine hand in the process to those who feel that they are on their own.

The common factor is hope. The late poet Maya Angelou once said, "In order to survive, a human being needs to live in a place furnished with hope." Of course the hope should be tempered by realism. Raising false hopes or expectations about a child's prospects serves neither the parents nor the child. Plenty of parents have come across quacks and charlatans who promise "cures" and "recovery," only to lose money, time, and ultimately some degree of faith. (See Chapter 11.) For many professionals it is a tricky balance to convey the real potential for lifelong meaningful growth for the individual without minimizing the significant potential challenges.

Hope can come from paying close attention to a person's achievements and celebrating progress, even in its most subtle forms. It also comes from meeting parents who are farther down the road on their journey and who can share their stories of unexpected progress. Research shows that when parents are more optimistic about their prospects, children are less likely to display problematic behaviors, which improves quality of life for all, and in turn, enhances hope.

Accept and Express Your Feelings

Being the parent, grandparent, or sibling of an autistic person brings most family members to uncharted emotional territory. Raising a child or advocating for a family member with challenges brings powerful feelings they may not have experienced previously in the same way: guilt, resentment, anxiety, anger. Fathers often describe feeling frustrated that they can't connect with their sons as they had hoped. A mother might share how her daughter's endless chatter about a particular topic or inflexible routines drives her crazy. And these feelings may be exacerbated by physical and emotional exhaustion. Then the parent often says with guilt, "I know I shouldn't feel this way."

Raising an autistic child doesn't mean you have to be a saint. We're all human. Our feelings are both natural and legitimate. Parents, siblings, and family members need not be hard on themselves. Nor should they try controlling what is beyond their control.

In some cases the troubling feelings aren't about the child but about other people close to the parents—relatives, close friends who mean to be helpful but aren't. An uncle might offer unsolicited advice about raising an autistic child, or the child's grandmother might criticize how the parents discipline their child—or don't. It's important to realize that challenges associated with autism can be disorienting and provoke anxiety in the extended family as well as in parents. This is especially true for children and adults with co-occurring medical issues and who often experience discomfort and dysregulation, and may therefore have greater challenges in developing loving and trusting relationships. In speaking with parents and family members, I often try to remind them that most often the comments and suggestions come from a place of caring and a desire to help in some way, judgmental as they can sometimes sound.

"We pretty much have this autism thing down and feel confident in supporting our daughter," one father said, "but our greatest challenges, by far, have to do with pushy, insensitive family members."

The parents who cope most successfully with such situations are those who are the most honest and direct. They express gratitude for the person's caring and interest, but then they draw the line: "We appreciate your concern. Please understand that we are doing things the way we feel is best for our family."

Be Appropriately Assertive, Not Aggressive (and Know the Difference)

Raising an autistic child or caring for an autistic family member means constantly acting as the person's advocate, working to secure the proper supports and services. Parents routinely find themselves making requests of school district administrators, teachers, therapists, insurance companies, and others. As one mother said, "I need to be the Warrior Mom."

Seeking and securing the best options for a child may feel like going to battle, but parents often tell me they experience a delicate balancing act: sometimes they're locked in conflict with the very people in whom they entrust the care of their child or family member. The instinct is to push and push, but if you push too much, and it becomes personal, you may damage relationships with those you rely on.

Here's the essential thing: Keep the autistic person front and center.

Many parents have described finding themselves in a clash of adults, a personal struggle between parents and educators or administrators. Those battles are unlikely to end well for anyone. Consider these encounters from the point of view of the teacher or other professional whose work entails serving multiple students and their families. If every meeting with a parent is a skirmish, if the parent makes contact primarily to complain and make demands, it hardly feels like teamwork. And to a professional who feels she is doing her best, it may cause confusion and dismay.

In some cases having a child or family member with a disability comes with so much anger, resentment, and disappointment that a parent needs a way to channel these feelings. Autism is a passionate affair, full of strong emotion, and we need to somehow direct and resolve that energy. Some find the answer in the battle, hiring lawyers or professional advocates—or threatening to—and issuing demands of all kinds. Of course sometimes that's unavoidable in situations of true injustice or violations of a person's legal and human rights, but more often, finding a positive way to channel the energy is more helpful to all. One important strategy for staying positive: Keep the focus on the autistic person. Some parents make a practice of always coming to IEP meetings and other conferences with a photo of their child. They place it on the table in front of them so that if things become contentious or difficult, they gesture to the photograph—a reminder that, while things might get testy, "this is about what's best for our son."

When parents keep the focus on solutions to help the child or adult rather than pointing the finger at administrators or teachers, it provides openings for the professionals to rise to the occasion. They see the parents or caregivers as human beings trying to do their best, and view the autistic person in the context of the larger family. In such circumstances, it is far easier for professionals to assure them that they are heard, and to work in collaboration with them to serve the person's best interests.

It's also appreciated when caregivers ask how they can help: Chaperoning the class field trip? Sorting books in the school library? Volunteering to assist at holiday parties or community outings? Co-teaching a science or shop class? When school or community living staff perceive caregivers as disengaged, heard from only when they have complaints or criticisms, that can undermine a collaborative, trusting relationship that is so important to the child's or adult's well-being. When teachers or service providers know that a caregiver is engaged and interested, they are generally more open to constructive criticism and collaboration.

Pick Your Battles

When a young child is newly diagnosed, parents who are new to it all can feel overwhelmed by the need to find schools, communicate with educators, and shuttle their child to various therapies. They may need to consider approaches to mitigate sensory challenges, special diets to address food sensitivities or allergies, or other ancillary approaches, always weighing which teachers, therapists, and administrators appear most trustworthy to engage as partners. And all of that is in addition to the routine details of life: attending to their other children, grandparents, or extended family members, the stresses of work, the demands of family life, and (for those in a relationship) care of the marriage or partnership. Some parents feel that it's their job to become superhuman, to take it all on and do it all well. And for a parent raising a child without a partner, the challenges and demands may feel insurmountable. Most often caregivers move the needs of the autistic child or family member to the top of the agenda out of fear that the child will not progress, could regress, or that, at the very least, opportunities will be missed. Too often, professionals amplify those fears, insisting that more is better.

One of the most common bits of advice more experienced parents share with newer ones is this: Pick your battles and prioritize where to direct your time, energy, and your emotional and fiscal resources.

That approach applies to dealings with schools and adult service agencies. Parents might disagree with a teacher's assessment of a child or the way the child's schedule is arranged. They might feel strongly that a child needs one-to-one support throughout the school day, while the school staff believes the child has made so much progress that less direct support and more independence with appropriate levels of monitoring is sufficient. Debates may ensue about the distinction between an appropriate versus an optimal level of support. When parents participate in decisions as part of the child's team, reasonable compromise is part of the process. It's important not to make life one big battle but to decide what's most important for the person and what's not.

This same mindset can be helpful in dealing with patterns of behavior at home or in the community. Others might express the opinion that a particular pattern of behavior poses problems and ought to be addressed. But parents might decide that it's not a significant priority, or even a problem to consider at that moment. Fifteen-year-old Flora vocalizes with glee and excitement when she first sees small dogs in the local park across the street from her school. School staff suggested a behavior plan to eliminate what they refer to as "screaming," but her parents never saw this as a problem and always delighted in her joy. Sometimes these decisions relate to what else is most important and worthwhile to address given the child and the family's time and energy. For young children, a developmental perspective says it's important to address concerns when it's developmentally appropriate to do so, for both the child and family, and to always ask: is this really a priority, or even a problem?

Even when there is clear concern, often a parent will admit, "I know we have established a detailed plan to address my son's very restricted diet, but my father has been in the hospital several times this month and I'm drained. I can't be consistent with that plan now."

Support plans are created to serve the autistic person and the family. There is no perfect plan, no boilerplate approach that works in every situation. And no one can decide what's important more accurately than caregivers can. Ideally, and when possible, the autistic person should be directly involved in the development of plan as well.

Find the Humor

Bob smiled when he told the story of accompanying his six-year-old son Nick to a fast-food restaurant. On their way to sit down, Nick approached a table of strangers, reached out, and grabbed a couple of French fries from a man's tray, and shoveled them into his mouth. "That's delicious!" Nick said.

Bob smiled, shrugged, sheepishly said "I'm sorry," and escorted his son away.

When their children act in unexpected and surprising ways in public, many parents feel embarrassed and humiliated, struggling with how much they need to explain their children.

Sometimes it's healthier for all just to laugh—but it's easier said than done.

Another family was shopping at Home Depot around the time the parents were working with their young autistic son on toilet training. He had made inconsistent progress, so they had worked on motivating the boy to spend more time in front of the toilet. In the middle of the Home Depot visit, the boy decided to test his new-found abilities—on a nonworking display toilet.

The parents glanced at each other, as if to say, "What do we do now?" Their quick decision: leave. They felt badly, but realized that their priority at the moment was to avoid the possibility of an un-comfortable confrontation that might have triggered a meltdown—and to escape.

Looking back, they could have laughed or cried. They chose to laugh.

Both stories also serve as a reminder of the importance of connect-ing with other parents of autistic children or family members. Such moments can feel embarrassing, difficult, and humiliating, but when we share similar stories with others who understand, they become the basis for laughter, comfort, and shared connections. At our weekend parent retreat, we share as much laughter and humorous stories as serious discussion about challenging issues. One of our most popu-lar discussion group topics that leads to boisterous laughter is: "You wouldn't believe it, but . . . !"

Finding humor is essential for professionals too. When I was a summer camp counselor, I was assigned to pay attention to Dennis, who was twelve, on an outing to a rodeo. As our group enjoyed the show, I suddenly heard a little girl behind us cry out, *"Daaady!"*

I turned to see Dennis, with his chubby rosy cheeks, happily chomping on a huge clump of pink cotton candy. When nobody was looking, he'd snatched it from the girl. Nervously I turned to apologize to her truck-driver-size dad, fearing the worst.

"Oh, let him enjoy it," he said, chuckling. "We'll get another one."

When visitors' day came, I shared the story with Dennis's parents. They both broke into broad smiles and laughed. "Welcome to our life!" they said in unison.

Finding humor also is helpful for my autistic friends, as they reflect on their own behavior and the behavior of neurotypical people. Some autistic people talk about criteria for diagnosing "NSD" or "Neurotypical Spectrum Disorder," with symptoms such as "Frequently engages in meaningless, small talk rather than more meaningful conversations," "Not always saying what they truly mean" and an "Uncontrollable compulsion to touch other human beings." Clearly, humor lightens the load and results in shared positive emotional connections.

Insist on Respect

When I first met Teddy, he practically tore my office apart. He was an energetic six-year-old who stopped speaking around age three, at the time his seizures began. His parents, Jack and Karen, had already taken him to countless specialists before they found their way to the children's hospital where I was providing outpatient evaluation services. As I tried to assess Teddy's abilities in social communication and emotional regulation, and hear about him from his parents, Teddy suddenly became so agitated that he bolted across the room and began throwing books and files from my shelves, escalating into a full-blown meltdown.

At the end of the appointment, after we had helped Teddy recover from his extreme dysregulation, his parents apologized, but I assured them that was unnecessary; I knew Teddy was extremely confused and upset, as I could see it in his eyes. Later they told me how much my response had comforted them. In earlier appointments they had met professionals who—perhaps not in words but in tone—seemed to question why they couldn't do a better job controlling their child.

I continued to see Teddy and his parents for decades, consulting to his school programs. He remained nonspeaking but learned to communicate effectively using first low-tech, and then high-tech assistive devices. Years later Karen told me that when they encountered teachers or therapists who they felt were being judgmental, they would flee. "There's enough guilt that goes along with this role—we don't need those looks and comments," she said.

Early in the journey of raising an autistic child, parents often feel disempowered and disoriented. Perplexed and confused by the child's behavior, they don't know where to turn or whom to trust. That is when Jack and Karen's advice is particularly pertinent. Some parents, particularly those with less experience with the medical establishment, school district bureaucracies, or adult service agencies assume that they don't have a choice, that dealing with professionals who are condescending or patronizing is a necessary part of raising a child or providing care for an autistic family member—that they just need to "bite the bullet."

They don't. Caregivers can insist on better treatment, and both they and their family member deserve better.

At our retreat's closing circle one year, a father echoed Karen's sentiment. "We're not asking a lot," he said. "When we deal with administrators and professionals and our relatives, all we want is to be respected as parents and for our children to be respected."

I can't remember a comment in that setting that so resonated. Looking around the circle, I saw nearly every head nodding. The good news is that caring, respectful, and responsive professionals are out there, and they want to help. Sometimes the challenge is in finding them.

Channel Your Energy

Not long after my dear friend Elaine Hall adopted her son Neal at twenty-three months, his challenges became clear: the toddler had trouble sleeping, spun in circles, opened and closed cabinet doors, pulled pictures off walls, and frequently had meltdowns. At three he was diagnosed with autism. Elaine surrounded her son with artists and actors, and Neal responded. With their creativity and energy, they were able to connect with him, and Elaine saw Neal engaging in ways she had never seen before.

Yet all around her Elaine saw other autistic children struggling, other parents perplexed, frustrated, and anxious about their children. So she created a program that would bring to others what had been so effective for Neal. In 2004 she launched the Miracle Project, a theater and arts program for children on the autism spectrum. Within a few years the program had grown from its base in Los Angeles to a national organization with affiliates in several cities and countries. It was featured in a 2012 Emmy award-winning HBO documentary, *Autism: The Musical,* followed by *Autism: The Sequel* in 2020. Elaine spoke at the United Nations on World Autism Awareness Day on multiple occasions, and Neal, who is nonspeaking, also presented at the UN and continues to present at conferences using his computer with speech output. As a young adult Neal worked on an organic farm and does professional modeling.

Inspired by Elaine's story and buoyed by our close friendship and Elaine's inspirational support, my colleagues and I at Brown University developed the Miracle Project–New England. And after many years of Elaine and I dreaming about the possibility of a play inspired by the initial publication of *Uniquely Human,* the autistic teens and young adults and their mentors in The Miracle Project, based in Los

Angeles, wrote and performed "Journey to Namuh" (human spelled backwards), an original feature length musical film that debuted in 2021. The film's major message is the importance of autistic people discovering their authentic selves and identities, and for society to accept and support autistic individuals as valuable and important members of our communities.

And it all began with one mom who was confused and perplexed but committed to change the world.

Raising an autistic child can require great quantities of emotional and physical energy. But again and again I have seen parents who not only rise to the task but actually change the course of their lives, as Elaine did, to help others facing the same challenges. It's easy to feel frustrated and angry, but instead of directing their anger at teachers or school administrators, these caregivers have channeled their energies in creative directions or opted for new career paths based on their parenting experiences.

Many parents initially direct their energy in adversarial ways, especially when facing barriers and perceived injustice, triggered by their instincts to fight for the most appropriate services and best supports for their child. This might result in personal battles with school administrators or legal action, sometimes justified, other times not, encouraged by the advice of lawyers or professional advocates. But later they often shift their efforts constructively as fundraisers, volunteers, and advocates for political and systemic change. Many pursue degrees in special education, counseling, or therapeutic fields.

A lawyer became an expert on government policy affecting autistic people. A father joined his local school board. A mother who was a registered nurse opened a practice focusing on co-occurring medical issues common in autism. The parents of three autistic children were spending so much time focused on autism that they eventually decided to make it the focus of their careers: the mother earned a nutrition degree and opened a practice focused on children with disabilities, and the father created a nonprofit organization offering community-based activities for children with various disabilities. Another mother started a foundation named for her son to raise funds for local services supporting autistic children and families. A father retiring from twenty years in a state corrections facility wants to be a classroom aide, so that he "can truly make a difference in people's lives." Another father, who composes music and teaches at a university, created a choral piece incorporating his young son's vocalizations and performed by a university choir to increase awareness and acceptance of autistic people.

None of these parents set out to change their careers or have their work transformed by the lived experience of autism. What they share is that they were open to seeing in their journey not just struggle but possibility. In the process each discovered the gratification and inspiration that comes from helping others, and sharing their expertise and talents to improve quality of life for autistic people and their families.

CHAPTER 9

The Real Experts

I N 1986 Temple Grandin forever altered public perceptions about autism when she published her first book, *Emergence: Labeled Autistic*. Here, for the first time, was an articulate, intelligent adult who could describe with insight and clarity the experience of living on the autism spectrum. She detailed her thinking processes, explained her sensory sensitivities, spoke of the different learning styles of autistic people, and recounted the numerous and varied challenges she had faced growing up.

Before Temple began writing and speaking publicly, our understanding (and misunderstanding) of autism had largely been based on research and the accounts of parents and other observers, some ill-informed. Much of what she said confirmed long-held beliefs; some of her insights contradicted them. But one thing was clear: autistic people have intact minds, strong opinions and great potential, and some have tremendous insight into their own experience.

Decades later Temple remains the most famous autistic person, but many others have emerged as articulate spokespeople and astute chroniclers of their own experience. My work has offered me the privilege of getting to know many of these people, some of whom have become valued friends and collaborators. The experiences of sharing time with them and their friends and families, listening to their accounts and writing and presenting workshops with them, has deeply informed my understanding of autism, providing insights and perspectives I would otherwise lack.

My podcast, inspired by this book and entitled "Uniquely Human: The Podcast," has provided me and my autistic co-host, Dave Finch, unique opportunities to have meaningful discussions with autistic people, family members, and thought leaders from around the world. With Dave being on the spectrum, he also adds personal insights during our dozens of episodes addressing a broad array of vital and cutting-edge issues.

Three of our guests who are valued long-time friends have truly enhanced my thinking and understanding, and their insights guide me almost every day in my work: Ros Blackburn, Michael John Carley, and Stephen Shore. Each has each helped me and countless others to understand the autistic experience and how best to help people on the spectrum lead fulfilling and meaningful lives.

When I mention such people, some express doubt about (or silently wonder) how these articulate individuals can accurately represent the experience of individuals who are nonspeaking or are otherwise more severely challenged. My response: If they can't, then who can? Who better to explain the experience of autism than an autistic person, those who experience life through an autistic lens every day? And in recent years, many who are nonspeaking, were once nonspeaking, or had more severe challenges themselves also have developed deep insights about being autistic that they are excited to be able to share after years of silence. (See Chapter 11.)

Let's begin with Ros, Michael, and Stephen, whom I have known for decades. I am eternally grateful to these three individuals because they explain things that no amount of research can reveal. I am happy to share some of what they have taught me.

Ros Blackburn: "I Don't Do Social"

I first met Ros Blackburn at an autism conference in Michigan, when my colleague Carol Gray, the well-known autism educational expert, beckoned me over to meet this young woman visiting from England who would be speaking about her experiences growing up autistic. We shook hands, and Ros, then in her mid-thirties, said something, that due to her rapid speech and British accent, sounded like "Wannameesteert?"

I had to ask her to repeat herself. It took a few repetitions before I heard clearly what she was asking: "Want to meet Stuart?"

I offered a blank face.

"Stuart," she said. "Stuart Little."

I nodded, and Ros—with an impish grin—pulled her hand from her coat pocket and revealed what she was holding: a tiny stuffed mouse, based on the character from the children's movie. "Barry, this is Stuart. Stuart, this is Barry," she said.

And that is Ros: playful, quirky, mischievous, unique—and full of surprises (not to mention passionate about the movies she loves).

Ros explains that this is her true self, her autistic self. She has also learned, over time, to present a different self to the world: restrained, polite, controlled.

That dichotomy originated in her childhood. She was diagnosed with autism as a child. Her parents clearly understood her challenges but taught her the social skills she would need to function in the world.

While they were compassionate, her mother and father were also demanding, never accepting autism as an excuse for inappropriate behavior. Their approach helped inform the advice she often shares: that parents should have high expectations of their autistic children, matched by equally high levels of support.

When she explains autism, Ros describes living with an almost constant feeling of anxiety and fear. She is fond of pointing out that people in the military, police officers, and firefighters are trained to be calm in the face of panic. Not so for autistic people: "We don't receive the same type of training, yet we experience this level of panic every day."

What most exacerbates that fear is being forced into social situations. She is comfortable and never experiences nervousness addressing large audiences, where she feels in control. But more informal social settings can terrify her because she cannot predict what others will say or do. "I don't do social," she likes to say.

I once met her in a hotel lobby where, nearby, a group of young children were chasing each other. One slid across a coffee table and nearly fell on her. A look of fright crossed her face. "See?" she said, a bit shaken. "That's why I don't like children!"

Despite her distaste for unpredictable social situations, she doesn't experience embarrassment because she doesn't worry about what others are thinking of her. Ros often says that her greatest ability—expressing herself verbally—is also her greatest disability. What she means is that people observing her assume that because she is an articulate, intelligent, and capable speaker, she must be a confident, comfortable person inside as well.

The truth is that Ros often finds the world overwhelming—a buzzing, confusing, out-of-control reality filled with unexpected events and baffling social rules. And when she has strong emotional reactions and panic attacks, which happen much less frequently than when she was younger, she loses the ability to communicate through speech and cannot tolerate being in social situations. Her advice to those with her when she becomes extremely dysregulated: "Make sure I am safe but support me in silence; support me with your presence." Given a few minutes, she says, she can usually pull herself together, but when others—even with good intentions—speak to her and touch her, it can be like throwing gasoline on the fire.

Ros has developed a wide repertoire of strategies to prevent and deal with dysregulation. One favorite regulating activity is jumping on a trampoline, an activity that brings release and even joy. When she travels, she always has a traveling companion, one of several young women she describes as "carers." When she feels fatigued, she avoids what she calls "doing social" which can cause, or add to, anxiety.

Once Ros attended a conference I helped organize, where I had the privilege of hosting the actress Sigourney Weaver. I welcomed Sigourney to spend time with Ros to prepare for her role in the movie *Snow Cake*, in which she plays an autistic woman. When the conference concluded, the two of them were to be among a group I was gathering for dinner at my home. But as our small group was discussing logistics, Ros abruptly interrupted. "Barry," she said, "I could really benefit from some trampolining right now."

Trampolining? It was early evening on a winter day in Rhode Island, with snow on the ground. I had no idea where to find a trampoline. Then Sue, a mom who was among our group, spoke up: "Barry, we have a trampoline in our backyard that my son uses. We just shoveled the snow off."

Ros smiled like a child hearing there's a second day of Christmas. "Can I go?"

Off they went, Ros and Sigourney Weaver, to bounce in their winter coats in a suburban backyard. Earlier Ros had given a fabulous two-hour presentation for more than five hundred parents and professionals, and graciously answered questions afterward. All day she had "done social" and as she says, "put on her act." Now she needed time to be Ros. (Based on this experience, Sigourney suggested the trampoline scene that director Marc Evans added to *Snow Cake*.)

One of my favorite moments during their visit was when Ros was teaching Sigourney how to act "autistic."

Sigourney: Ros, I noticed that when you get very excited, you lift up your hands to the side of your head and rock back and forth while flapping your hands close to your ears. *(Sigourney then demonstrated the action while sitting up straight.)*

Ros: No, actually, it is a bit more like this. *(Ros proceeded to lean her body to the right while performing the same action, correcting Sigourney's attempts. Sigourney imitated.)* Much better, you've got it!

Ros's other loves are figure skating and certain movies. After her first visit to Providence to speak at our conference, I invited her for a return visit, but she was hesitant. She could not understand why I would want to invite her back since she had already presented her story. Besides, travel makes her very anxious, and attending conferences forces her to be in social situations. (Ros's carers offer great support as they help her negotiate unfamiliar situations and places.) Finally she agreed to come when I offered to take her to New York City so she could skate at the Wollman Rink in Central Park, which she had seen in a favorite movie. During her visit, the same woman who had so dazzled audiences with her insights took great pleasure in gliding across the ice, Stuart Little in her pocket, and later posing Stuart for photos around Central Park.

On that same visit Ros and I went to a crowded Italian restaurant with four others. The host led us to a table in the middle of the room and was about to seat us when Ros started shaking her head anxiously. "Can't sit here," she said.

I couldn't see another option, but the seating host read Ros's signal and gestured toward another section of the restaurant he hadn't opened yet. Ros chose a table against the wall so she could sit with her back to the wall.

"I hate quadraphonic sound," she said, "and when there's too much movement in my peripheral visual field, I get very anxious." For all of her challenges, Ros's great strengths are her highly developed awareness of her own needs and limits and her ability to advocate for herself, especially in speaking up for her need to avoid dysregulating circumstances.

In contrast, Ros is blissfully unaware of things most people deem socially impressive and important. When we saw each other a few years after the trampoline episode, I asked her if she had been in touch with Sigourney Weaver lately. "Yes," she said, "she came to London last year, and we got together."

When I asked for specifics, she explained that Sigourney had invited her to the opening of "some movie," where they had walked down a red carpet together. Connecting the dots, I realized what she was telling me: Ros had attended the premier of *Avatar*, the highest grossing movie of all time, with one of its stars.

"Wow, what an experience!" I said. "How was it?"

Ros answered bluntly, "Really, really noisy and crowded."

Another challenge: being dishonest. "Lying is hard for me," she says. "For instance, saying 'It's very nice to meet you' when I'd rather be trampolining is still hard for me."

Still, her playful side is unrestrained. Ros often travels with favorite toys, such as a box of fidgets, including rubber lizards she shares with her audiences. As a sort of practical joke, she carries mirrors with her on airplane trips. Why? She uses them to reflect sunlight into the eyes of fellow passengers, endlessly amusing herself by watching their annoyed reactions.

After one of Ros's talks, I asked a mother in the audience for her reaction. The woman told me that she simultaneously loved and hated Ros's presentation. She loved the window Ros offered into how the woman's son experienced the world but hated how painful Ros's experience of life sounded.

I knew just what she meant. Perhaps more than anyone I have known, Ros has made me understand the challenges faced by autistic individuals who find the world overwhelming and anxiety-producing. When I look into the eyes of a three-year-old who can't communicate through speech and is being forced into a noisy, chaotic room, I think of Ros and realize this youngster is not being noncompliant or uncooperative. The child is terrified.

On a Uniquely Human podcast episode, almost fifteen years after I first met her, I reunited Ros and Sigourney Weaver to reflect on their shared experiences years earlier. Sigourney expressed deep grati-tude for Ros's honesty, for teaching her that playing is not just for children, and for renewing her fascination and sensitivity for the sen-sory world. I will forever be grateful to Ros, whose neurology makes her so vulnerable to our social and sensory world and who is a model of bravery in stepping forward to confront her challenges and share her experiences—all in service to helping countless others.

Michael John Carley:
"We Need to Hear About What We Can Do"

When Michael John Carley was thirty-six years old, his four-year-old son was diagnosed with Asperger's syndrome. After delivering the diagnosis, the clinician turned to Michael. "Now," she said. "Let's talk about you."

Within a few days, Michael too had an Asperger's diagnosis.

His first response was shock. How had he lived three and a half decades without realizing he was on the autism spectrum? He was happily married and had maintained a successful career as a diplo-mat, traveling to such hotspots as Bosnia and Iraq. He was also an accomplished playwright, a star baseball pitcher, a talented guitarist, and a host on a local NPR station.

At first he hid his diagnosis. But the more he reflected on his life, the more it made sense to him. He had always felt that he did not connect with people. In his buttoned-down private high school, he was such a misfit that teachers perceived him as a kid with behav-ioral problems and suspected he might have serious psychological problems. Eventually he transferred to a charter school with a more flexible, alternative orientation. There he flourished.

Still, as he went through life, many experiences and encounters left him baffled. He didn't understand why people engaged in small talk and had never been able to fathom the hidden rules of flirt-ing. When an acquaintance asked him his opinion on a subject—

politics or something in the news—he would launch into a reply so detailed and lengthy that listeners were rolling their eyes. Friends would abruptly cut off relationships with him, often after Michael said things that offended them. Afterward he still didn't understand what he had done wrong.

The initial shock of diagnosis gave way to relief—and eventually pride. The diagnosis became not a burden but a revelation.

Always passionate and micro-focused about his work and virtually anything he took on, Michael gradually reconfigured his life to direct his energy and focus into advocating for people on the autism spectrum. In 2003 he founded GRASP, the Global and Regional Asperger Syndrome Partnership, and as its executive director helped it become the nation's largest membership organization consisting of adults on the autism spectrum. He designed GRASP to particularly focus on adolescents and adults, populations he knew at the time were underserved and largely misunderstood. He published an important and acclaimed book, *Asperger's from the Inside Out*, part autobiography, part self-help guide for people on the autism spectrum. And he went on to found and direct the Asperger Syndrome Training and Employment Partnership, which worked with large companies to help train managers either to better manage existing employees who are the autism spectrum or to increase their confidence in hiring new ones.

Michael was an outspoken critic when, in 2012, the American Psychiatric Association was considering eliminating Asperger's Disorder as an official diagnosis, a change it ultimately made. He was concerned that the change would make accurate diagnosis more difficult and diminish public understanding of people with an Asperger's profile. He also felt strongly that people on the spectrum should have a direct voice in developing policies that affect them.

I first met Michael years ago when I invited him to address our fundraising symposium. I was struck immediately by how articulate, intensely energetic, and focused he was. You might not guess that he was autistic until he begins speaking about something he is excited about. He speaks quickly. His laughter is boisterous and contagious. His handshakes are extraordinarily firm. He gives extremely tight hugs. In conversation he stands unusually close and his gaze is intense and direct. When you are engaged with Michael, it is a riveting experience.

When I learned that he had once represented a veteran's organization, Veterans for Peace, at the United Nations, I was astounded that a person with Asperger's had found success as a diplomat. One would think it would take great social savvy, flexibility, and interpersonal sensitivity to conduct oneself properly—greeting dignitaries in proper fashion, standing in the right place, saying the appropriate thing. But Michael explained to me that diplomatic protocol is so laden with rigid, documented rules that once he had mastered them all, it was actually much easier for him to conduct himself in that world than in less formal social settings, where social engagement is fluid, less structured, less predictable, and where social rules are unwritten.

His considerable professional success made it easier for him to cope with his son's diagnosis than it might have been for other parents. While others might pray for a bright future for their children, he has said, "I had the advantage of evidence-based conviction." That is, his own life was a testimony to both the struggles and the potential of a person with an autism spectrum diagnosis.

Serious and driven, he also has an enviable sense of humor about himself. I once spent time with him at his vacation cabin, where I spotted a guitar. Knowing of his talent, I asked him to play a bit. Michael picked up the guitar and began finger-picking a blues progression. "Okay, but you're about to listen to twelve straight minutes of blues," he said, smiling. "Remember, I have Asperger's and need to have a sense of completion—I don't stop in the middle of songs."

A committed father and husband, he has coached his two sons' baseball teams. He is especially determined to be a positive role model for his son with Asperger's and frequently speaks of the importance of exposing young people on the spectrum to autistic adults who have managed to build successful lives, families, and careers.

Among Michael's great insights is this: an autistic teen or adult is more a product of his life's experiences than of his autism. Michael is very concerned about many of the serious mental-health, substance-abuse, and addiction issues some autistic people develop due to their misunderstandings of social situations and being misinterpreted—and in extreme cases abused—by others. While others may be tempted to point to autism as the primary cause of every struggle or setback, he says that, with proper support, many people can build emotionally healthy, productive, and successful lives.

He is also a spokesperson, able to explain with insight and intelligence the experience of being on the autism spectrum. His central focus is the importance of developing trusting relationships and the many factors that make doing so difficult for people on the spectrum. In particular, Michael explains the many painful experiences autistic people endure that neurotypical people might not perceive as unpleasant or difficult. To an autistic person, for instance, being restrained can be the equivalent of being physically and psychologically pummeled. For someone very sensitive to certain sounds, a high-pitched noise or even a shout can induce pain. The constant barrage of such aversive experiences can lead to considerable challenges. Michael's other main commitment is to supporting the many autistic people who lack family support and whose lives are filled with anxiety, stress, and fear, leading many of them to alcoholism and drug addiction. GRASP runs support groups in many cities, in person and online, to connect people who share the same challenges and struggles. He has also written books and presents on other critical quality-of-life issues such as employment for autistic adults and leading happy and positive sexual lives.

He is determined to share with others on the spectrum the insight that so transformed his outlook when he received his own diagnosis: that many of the painful experiences they have endured in life have an explanation that is not rooted in their character but rather in their neurological wiring and others' unhelpful and even harmful reactions.

That is the message he brought to Capitol Hill in November 2012 when the U.S. House Committee on Oversight and Government Reform conducted historic hearings about the dramatic rise in autism diagnoses. One of only two people on the spectrum to testify (the other was Ari Ne'eman, the then president of the Autistic Self Advocacy Network), Michael offered moving testimony that there was "no medical basis" for treating autism like a disease to be cured. "As we all grow, whether we're on the spectrum or not, we need to hear about what we can do," he said, "not what we can't do." Recently, New York University has acknowledged the importance of Michael's message and recognized his talent in communicating it by creating a position for him as its consultant for neurodiversity across its New York, Shanghai, and Abu Dhabi campuses.

Stephen Shore: "They Accepted Me"

Stephen Shore describes his early childhood in this way: His development was typical until he hit eighteen months. That, he says, is when the "autism bomb" hit. His capacity for functional communication vanished, and he stopped making eye contact with his mother and father, who watched, bewildered, as he repeatedly banged his head. He seemed detached and distant and constantly engaged in self-stimulatory behaviors for regulation: rocking, spinning, flapping.

In the early 1960s that combination of challenges was so rarely seen that it took a year for his parents even to figure out where to have him evaluated. When he was finally diagnosed with autism in 1964, the physician who diagnosed him deemed Stephen too "sick" for outpatient treatment. The doctor's only recommendation was to have the boy institutionalized.

Fortunately for Stephen, his parents ignored that advice. Instead, operating only on their own instincts, they began what Stephen says would now be labeled a home-based early-intervention program. At the time it was considered just unusually strong-willed parenting. His mother was determined to keep him engaged, dedicating her days to encouraging his participation in activities with music, movement, and sensory integration. At first his parents attempted to teach Stephen by trying to get him to imitate them. When that didn't work, they began imitating *him*. That drew Stephen's attention and offered the beginnings of his ability to connect in meaningful ways.

"The most important thing about my parents is that they accepted me for who I was," says Stephen, who didn't speak until he was four, "but at the same time recognized there were a lot of challenges to overcome."

As an adult Stephen has dedicated his life to helping people on the autism spectrum and their parents conquer those obstacles and build fulfilling, productive lives for themselves. He holds a doctorate in special education, has authored books, advises governments on policy related to autism, teaches at Adelphi University, and has spoken at the United Nations. He spends much of his time traveling the world consulting and delivering speeches to educate parents and professionals. He teaches piano to autistic children, but not to neurotypical kids since he finds it difficult to understand how they think and learn.

It surprises many people who meet him that an autistic person would spend so much time speaking to large groups of people. But to Stephen a presentation feels like nothing more than a long monologue—just his kind of conversation. When it comes to their enthusiasms, he says, people on the spectrum can talk for days.

That dry wit is part of his appeal. Of the many autistic people I have met, Stephen has one of the best senses of humor about being on the spectrum. One time Stephen and I were on a stroll when he spotted a stick on the ground, picked it up, and held it up to his eyes to examine it closely. "Hey, Barry, great stim toy!" he said, grinning.

His sense of irony comes out when he talks about his marriage.

Stephen met his wife, then an exchange student from China, when they were both studying music and were assigned to check each other's homework. They went on to connect socially, and one day on the beach she held his hand, kissed him, and gave him a deep hug. He explains his reaction in terms of "social stories," the technique developed by my talented colleague Carol Gray that helps autistic people understand and navigate social situations: "I had a social story which says that if a woman kisses, hugs you, and holds you all at the same time, it probably means they want to be your girlfriend." He knew his response could be "yes, no, or further analysis indicated." He decided on yes, and they have been married since 1990.

Stephen's ability to make light of his own mind—and the many challenges he encounters—brings a refreshing sense of perspective, a relief from the belief that autism is predominantly a heavy burden that casts a pall on life for the autistic person and the family.

His sense of humor might be connected to the other distinctive quality that distinguishes him: for an autistic, Stephen stands out as unusually grounded and calm. Most autistic people describe their heightened anxiety, but Stephen's relaxed demeanor is a reminder of the differences that exist among autistic individuals. I have seen him in a variety of situations—before audiences, in smaller groups, one-on-one—and he always is even-tempered, thoughtful, relaxed, and easy to be with. Unlike some autistic people, he loves to explore new and unfamiliar situations.

That is not to say that he doesn't struggle with the same kinds of dysregulation as others on the spectrum. He experiences maddening discomfort on those rare occasions when he has to wear a suit and tie, often wears baseball caps to keep glare out of his eyes, and recalls childhood haircuts as torturous, especially since he was unable to express his discomfort to his parents. He struggles so much with remembering people's faces that when he teaches college courses, he often can't put names with faces, even long into the semester.

On the other hand, Stephen knows exactly what it takes to calm his nerves. One reason for his extensive travel schedule is that he loves the experience of traveling on an airplane. That too is unusual among autistic people, who often find the sensory experiences and the chaos of air travel dysregulating. Children in particular often find the cabins of commercial airliners to be overly confining and find it challenging to be in such close proximity to so many people. But Stephen craves the feeling his body experiences during takeoff. So he keeps traveling.

He also continues to spread the messages that are most important for him to share. Each autistic adult I have met who shares their personal experiences to educate others has particular messages. Temple Grandin emphasizes the potential to turn special interests into careers. Michael John Carley focuses on the need to help those without strong family support and to educate potential employers about autism. One of Stephen's core messages is the importance of disclosure, that is, of informing a child of his or her own diagnosis at the appropriate time and in the most thoughtful way (see Chapter 11).

His sensitivity about that issue may stem from his own parents' care and attention in addressing his challenges. More than almost any autistic person I know, Stephen has a sense of his own story and the importance of "giving back," sharing his unique journey so that it can be of benefit to others.

Central to Stephen's narrative is the story of two parents who, despite being told that there was no hope for their son, followed their own instincts, ignored the "doom and gloom" messages they heard from some professionals, and used creativity and love to raise their child. It seems fitting that the child went on to commit his life to help autistic people and families with similar challenges, and to show parents and professionals that their children and family members, despite their diagnoses, have unimaginable potential.

CHAPTER 10

The Long View

IT's often hard for parents raising an autistic child or anyone caring for an autistic family member to have perspective. Mothers and fathers are so caught up in the day-to-day demands of caregiving that they can easily forget that whatever is happening now represents just a single moment in time. When a person seems stuck in a pattern of troubling or perplexing behavior, it can be difficult to imagine her ever progressing further. Particularly in the earliest years, parents worry that their child might never develop language or might never progress beyond echoing a few phrases. Parents wonder if a daughter will ever stop lining up her stuffed animals in precise order, if a young son might ever display interest in other children or develop friendships, or if a teenager might ever try new foods. What causes so much stress for autistic people also induces stress for parents: uncertainty—in this case, about the future.

It's important to remember that autistic people progress through developmental stages just as we all do. "One does not grow out of autism," explains Dena Gassner, who is on the spectrum and has an autistic son. "One grows into autism." This journey of self-awareness is lifelong for the autistic individual and the family, and no two journeys are alike.

To offer perspective, wisdom, and insight, in this chapter I share the experiences of four families whose sons I knew as preschoolers but have moved into adolescence and on to adulthood. I share the stories of these four not because they are exemplary or a representative sampling but rather because of what I have learned from these young men and from observing, spending time with, and knowing their families. I hope reading how they have progressed, faced challenges, thrived, and found perspective and love will provide valuable lessons for your own journey.

The Randall Family:
"If He's Given a Chance, He Runs with It"

It was Andrew Randall's grandmother who first suggested that his parents have him evaluated, that something might be amiss.

Andy was three years old but had been struggling for some time. When he was twenty months old, his mother, Jan, noticed that the language he had acquired was slipping away. Andy had learned about fifteen words but then stopped using some of them and clearly wasn't adding new ones to his vocabulary. A pediatrician assured Jan that her son was fine. Soon after that, their daughter Allison, two and a half years older, was diagnosed with a seizure disorder, and Jan and her husband, Bob, naturally shifted their focus to managing that crisis.

Meanwhile Jan became increasingly puzzled by the differences she noticed in Andy. He rarely looked at her and wouldn't point at objects or people. Jan's mother, a first-grade teacher, sensed that these were red flags, but when she suggested that to her daughter, Jan at first ignored her.

Then, watching TV in December 1988, Jan caught a segment on *Entertainment Tonight* about a new movie called *Rain Man*. "It was like someone punched me in the stomach," she recalls. "I knew right then and there: that's what was wrong with Andrew."

After a school psychologist evaluated Andy, Jan asked point-blank if her son was autistic. No, the psychologist said, noting—incorrectly—that an autistic child wouldn't demonstrate the strong maternal attachment Andrew clearly displayed. Her diagnosis: severe speech delay.

Jan felt relieved for a time, but Andy kept slipping. By then he didn't speak at all, just pulled Jan or Bob to the refrigerator when he was hungry. His meltdowns could last an hour or more as he jumped up and down with such intensity that the downstairs neighbors could feel their apartment rattle. Fortunately for Jan and Bob, the neighbor was a sympathetic friend. For nine months the boy slept so sporadically that Jan had to post herself on a couch outside his bedroom so she would be available to soothe him.

Andy was nearly five when Jan finally appealed to the school district's special education director for more help. The district referred her to a psychologist—not to help Andrew but to help her develop parenting skills. Hearing Jan's account, though, and meeting Andrew and looking over his evaluations, the psychologist put the pieces of the puzzle together: clearly, she said, he was autistic.

By that point Jan welcomed the news. "It felt like I had been in a very dark room and somebody opened all the blinds," she remembers. "I felt like I was basking in sunshine."

Armed with the diagnosis, she felt newly empowered. She began reading everything available about autism. She sought out other parents. She joined autism advocacy groups. She enrolled Andrew in a full-day special education program.

It took her husband longer to realize how profound his son's disability was. When Jan once mentioned wistfully that their daughter Allison would likely never become an aunt, Bob didn't seem to understand what she meant. "We just were not in the same place," she says.

At the time, the early 1990s, autism was much less frequently diagnosed than today and rarely discussed in the media, so the couple spent a great deal of energy explaining autism to friends and relatives—and fending off criticism. Jan's own father, baffled at his grandson's condition, blamed Jan. She took an active role helping her son to negotiate the world, but other relatives questioned her parenting, saying her coddling was causing the meltdowns.

While the criticism stung, she found support from a handful of other parents of autistic children, who not only understood her plight but encouraged her to raise her expectations of Andrew. The sky's the limit, they told her. Don't put the brakes on yet. Don't underestimate Andrew.

Despite Andrew's challenges, his personality shone through. Around the house he liked to stand on his head on a recliner, laughing uproariously. His parents found it hard not to laugh along. And children were drawn to him. A girl who lived in their apartment building took a particular liking to him, and when Andrew sat alone at the park or playground, she would draw him into the action, pushing him on the swing set or enlisting his participation in games like Duck Duck Goose. He took part amiably, though the rules defied him.

As for Jan and Bob, they tried not to let Andrew's challenges prevent their family from doing anything they otherwise might have done. They made a point of exposing him to a variety of people and experiences from an early age, taking him to church and letting him go on frequent sleepovers at an aunt's house or a neighbor's. Bob took him swimming weekly at the local YMCA, and the couple brought him along to restaurants and social gatherings. Those opportunities helped Andrew learn to adapt to changes and to different people and environments.

Though he used little spontaneous speech, he often communicated with echolalic phrases. A favorite was "We fight all night," a sentence he picked up from a Dr. Seuss book and used when he felt upset or thought someone else was angry. He still relied a great deal on physically manipulating other people in order to communicate, moving them next to objects that he wanted or places that he wanted to go. His struggle to communicate made him so frustrated that he routinely had meltdowns in stores and restaurants. But that didn't stop the Randalls from taking part in the routines of family life.

When Andrew hit adolescence, things became more challenging. Only in retrospect did his parents realize just how much. The private school where he was enrolled used behavioral approaches, and he was miserable there. When he had outbursts, the staff used four-point restraints and even locked him in a padded closet. He developed tics, quick and jerky head and shoulder movements, which the school staff tried to eliminate with behavior therapy, to no avail. A therapist who saw them at home encouraged a tough love approach, urging Jan and Bob to "get in his face" and "let him know who the boss is." Due to all these challenges, he had no afterschool activities.

He was so dysregulated so much of the time that he lashed out at home as well. He punched and kicked holes in the walls of the house. He broke car windshields and windows. He was angry, confused, and overwhelmed.

For a time his parents tried to maintain faith in the private school, which had a good reputation, but eventually Jan's instincts told her his being there was doing Andrew more harm than good. Then a special education consultant helped confirm her feelings, telling her, "Andrew doesn't want to be acting this way. It's terrifying for him, too."

That proved to be a turning point. "All those people who were telling me to be in his face and 'put the thumb on him' when he gets out of control," she says. "They were wrong, wrong, *wrong*. He was hurting. He was treated as less than a person. That's why he was losing it."

They pulled Andrew out of the school when he was twelve. Jan tearfully apologized to her son for what he had been through there, and, remarkably, he seemed to forgive her. "We wanted more for Andrew," she recalls. They found it at South Coast Educational Collaborative, a public special education collaborative in southeastern Massachusetts, where Andrew was greeted by a warm and supportive community, including understanding teachers who welcomed parents' advice. When Jan suggested a reading program she had heard about that was particularly effective for autistic students, the teacher didn't hesitate to try it. On the first day she used the program, Andrew read words for the first time—at age thirteen.

"They understood that Andrew wasn't just a problem—he had skills and potential," says Jan. "They treated him with respect. They valued him as a person. And they respected me as a true member of the team."

That's what made it so difficult when Andrew hit age twenty-two, making him ineligible to continue in the program. Andrew had always been a hard worker; he was happiest when he was busy: taking out the trash, doing laundry, vacuuming. Jan surveyed ten different state-sponsored programs for adults with disabilities. Finding none appealing, she nonetheless signed him up for one since he needed to be in a program.

It proved a disappointment, suffering from poor organization, and was ill-equipped to support Andrew's challenges. His behavior regressed, but Jan and Bob kept hoping for improvement. When it never came, they took him out of the program and arranged to have him back at home, where Jan managed his time and work. A life-skills coach helped him with appropriate workplace behavior and everyday tasks like shopping and using transportation. In his late twenties he worked part time at a supermarket fetching shopping carts.

In his mid-thirties, Andrew is still living with his parents, who say the key to assuring his quality of life is staying open to new opportunities. He receives adult services through what's known as a participant-directed model, which allows Andrew to make many of his own choices with support. For fun, he participates in kayaking, surf therapy, adaptive yoga, tennis, and watercolor painting. After working for several hours a week with a therapist who helped with job skills, he landed a job he enjoys: stocking shelves at a Dollar Tree. With the help of visual supports, he continues to learn. He's most challenged when he's bored and not engaged or physically active. His language continues to grow, with Andrew asking more and more questions and initiating conversations more frequently than previously.

Looking back, Bob admits that it took a while for him to come to terms with having a son on the autism spectrum, to accept that his son wouldn't play Little League, wouldn't drive a car, probably wouldn't have a family. "Once I finally got over all that stuff," he says, "then you just take him for what he is, and I'm proud of the person he has become. If he's given a chance, he runs with it."

A few years ago he started calling his sister Allie "Alliecat," and now appends the suffix *-cat* to the names of many girls and women, a sign he feels comfortable with them. He calls snack mixes "crunch stars," a phrase he heard long ago in Lucky Charms commercials. And when he feels the need to apologize, he sometimes says "Never ouch Mom," a phrase Jan says originated from her response when he would lash out in his early adolescence.

He also has an endearing mischievous streak. Riding in the car of one of the mentors who spends time with him, he sometimes slips bottle caps into the car's vents to playfully test her reaction.

Jan remembers that earlier in life, she was the kind of person who would hear a child crying at the supermarket and wonder what was wrong with the parents. Not anymore. "Andrew's taught me to be patient," she says, "and that good things come in many different ways."

No matter how much autism colors the way Andrew experiences the world, she likes to point out that there's more to him than that. "He is not his autism," she says. "He's an amazing human being."

The Correia Family:
"He Teaches Me How to Live"

When she first sensed that her son Matthew might be autistic, Cathy Correia's initial reaction was fear.

Just after college, Cathy had supervised employees at a sheltered workshop where adults who were autistic or had other developmental challenges sorted jewelry parts. Some of the workers had spent their lives in institutions, a fate she could hardly imagine for her son. "When they started using that word about my own son, I thought, 'What are they going to *do* to him?'" she recalls. "That was my emotional reaction."

That's not to say she hadn't suspected from early on that Matt, the younger of two sons, had his share of challenges. As a toddler Matt was beginning to speak, easily expressing his basic needs, but he didn't react in conversation the way Cathy thought he should. Instead of speaking spontaneously, he would echo whatever he heard. He'd stand in front of the TV, seeming not to notice that his brother was trying to watch. When she raised these matters with a pediatrician, though, the doctor suggested that she not jump to conclusions until Matthew was in preschool and more routinely interacting with other children.

It took just a couple of months of preschool before his teachers noticed his difficulties. At a conference with Cathy and her husband, David, they described how Matt rarely engaged in play with the other children, occupying himself with solitary, repetitive activities and flapping his arms when anxious. Though they weren't surprised by the teachers' descriptions, autism hadn't entered their thoughts. One of their neighbors happened to have a son, a few years older, who had been diagnosed with autism, but that boy didn't speak at all. Matt, in contrast, was a chatterbox, frequently repeating what his parents said.

When a doctor diagnosed him with Pervasive Developmental Disorder (a term then used for Autism Spectrum Disorder), the parents reacted in different but complementary ways. David believed the assessment of his son was accurate but wanted to wait and see how Matt's development progressed. Cathy immediately reached out to other parents and autism groups in search of whatever information and support she could gather.

She found comfort in connecting with other mothers as she

watched her son struggle. At times Matt became so frustrated at not being able to communicate that he resorted to scratching his parents and others. If it was time to leave the house and Matt wasn't ready, he could be defiant, flailing and swinging. At family gatherings he sometimes made his cousins the targets of his swinging arms and scratching nails. Fortunately most of the Correias' relatives responded with love and support.

So did Traci, Matt's teacher for first and second grade, then a new hire at his mainstream public school with a natural ability to draw out her students and find the best ways to engage them. In the initial days of first grade, Matt would cry all day, but Traci supported him by paying attention to what mattered to him. When he once complained about a frightening dream, at his request she let him lead his classmates in acting out the dream, a process that helped him move past the fear the dream induced.

Looking back, David remembers what he calls two different Matts: the locked-in, frustrated boy before he met Traci, and the more expressive, happier boy who emerged. His experience as a father paralleled that development. "It was very hard for me when he was little," David says. "Once he got to the 'other side,' it was a totally different experience."

Another teacher introduced the Correias to the technique of using soft brushes to massage Matt's body as a way to work on tactile and sensory challenges. That sometimes seemed to work with Matt.

In other ways Matt's education proved disappointing and endlessly challenging, especially after second grade. Rather than identifying and addressing his unique style of learning, teachers were content with a one-size-fits-all approach. Like many children on the spectrum, he could decode—read the words on the page by rote—at about grade level, but his comprehension always remained considerably lower.

Cathy became frustrated with teachers who emphasized her son's behavior issues and learning challenges rather than seeking his strengths. She wasn't pleased by the excessive use of behavior-modification strategies, rewarding or sanctioning her son—an approach she found induced stress in Matt more than it helped him. Cathy's continual efforts to educate herself about autism paid off. At one autism conference, she watched a film about how seemingly minor and invisible frustrations could build within a child, eventually causing him to lash out or display problematic behaviors. Teachers in the movie responded in ways that caused the child even more stress and dysregulation. She immediately thought of the tic Matt had recently developed, repeatedly twisting locks of hair in his fingers so frequently that he pulled out clumps. "When I saw that presentation, I realized it wasn't all his fault," she recalls. "It was the situation."

Just a few days later Cathy arranged a meeting with the school psychologist and shared her insight. She suggested a series of changes in Matt's schedule and the school's approach to help alleviate stress and support his ability to regulate himself. To their credit, the psychologist and teachers were open to making the changes. High school proved considerably happier for Matt, who was enrolled in a special education collaborative agency, continuing for three additional years in a program designed to support the transition to adulthood.

Cathy expanded her understanding and knowledge of autism, constantly sifting through what she read and learned for whatever she felt would help Matt to communicate and learn to regulate himself. Meanwhile David took the opposite tack, assiduously avoiding lectures and literature on the topic. "I have never read a *paragraph* about autism, let alone a book," he says. That was not because he didn't want to learn but rather from a determination to focus on his son rather than his diagnosis. "From the get-go, I just wanted to interact with Matt and trust my gut."

The more he did that, the more he discovered a delightful young man: open, innocent, guileless, loving, and eager to connect with others in his own way. He delighted friends and acquaintances with his enthusiasms: time, clocks, the calendar, and sports (especially those that were timed, such as football). The boy who was so uncomfortable and agitated in preschool became a teen and young adult who was calm, easygoing, and, within certain limits, able to function comfortably and independently. When Cathy accompanied him to a memorial service for one of his former school administrators, "He worked the crowd, shaking hands and enthusiastically greeting people and sharing memories with people," she recalls.

He has become self-sufficient in a number of ways. He can walk into a Subway restaurant, choose the ingredients of his sandwich, and pay. He knows the shelves of the local supermarket by heart—a great help on family shopping trips. At home he keeps his belongings organized and participates in planning meals, expressing strong preferences and letting Cathy know when she's purchased an item he doesn't approve of. He's skilled at using a computer and is the keeper of the family schedule.

He still has his challenges, though they are not as powerfully disabling as in the past. Seeing a sign advertising a blood drive, for instance, can make him anxious, and in conversation he still tends to focus on his own interests. He also seems aware of his limitations, whether they are real or self-imposed; for example, he declines offers of driving lessons, despite his remarkable sense of direction and knowledge about cars. "He just knows what's for him and what's not for him," Cathy says. "We're not trying to limit him, but he seems to know what he can and can't do."

Whether he understands the impact of autism is another matter. In his last year of high school the Correias learned that Matt's teacher planned to hold a class discussion about autism. The couple debated how to handle that, then opted to ask that Matt be excused from the session. Cathy had felt a duty to explain to Matt why he had never taken the same school bus as his brother, why he struggles with things that come easily to others, but she had never told him "You're autistic." Matt's teacher argued that understanding his diagnosis would be important to Matt in the future so he could advocate for himself in employment situations and elsewhere. To his parents that potential was outweighed by the thought that learning of his diagnosis might give their son the idea that there was something wrong with him. "The child isn't his diagnosis," David says. "You don't want to interact with your *ideas* about who he is. You want to interact with the person standing in front of you."

When she discusses Matt's challenges with him, Cathy keeps things factual and objective, to help him understand why he sometimes needs extra help. Now in his thirties, Matt now communicates much more freely about his strengths, challenges, and his autism. He has matured in his ability to understand and advocate for himself and routinely asks questions and expresses his feelings in a healthy, positive way. He takes part in The Miracle Project–New England, the theater and expressive arts program I cofounded, readily sharing his ideas and creativity.

He also attends a day program focusing on community activities including delivering meals to local residents, exercise classes, and recreational fields trips. He's admired by program staff and has gained a reputation for compassion and patience, particularly for those who have significant difficulty in communicating.

As for the future, the Correias are in no rush to have Matt live outside of their home, nor does he seem in a hurry to take on the world. They delight in having him at home and Matt enjoys socializing with their many family friends.

When she thinks back on her job working with people with developmental disabilities, Cathy remembers the strong feeling that the individuals with the best quality of life were those who were living at home with their families. For now, she and David are happy to offer Matt that option for the rewards they get in return.

"Living with him, it's a two-way street," explains David, who says he has learned kindness, honesty, and enthusiasm from his son. "Every day he teaches me how to live."

The Domingue Family:
"We Have to Follow Our Gut"

In one of Bob Domingue's most painful memories, his son Nick was four. He could speak but occasionally shut down in silence and at times struggled to communicate. A speech-language pathologist had advised Bob and his wife, Barbara, that it was critical to force Nick to use words whenever possible. One afternoon in the kitchen, Nick approached his father, took his hand, and led him to the refrigerator.

"What do you want, Nick?" Bob asked.

Silent, Nick pulled his father's hand to the refrigerator door.

"What do you *want?*" Bob repeated, following the therapist's advice.

Struggling, Nick said one word: "Door."

Bob understood exactly what his son wanted: a cup of juice. But he pushed further, insisting that Nick use words to tell him. Nick only grunted.

"You want *milk?*" the father asked, holding up a carton.

Grunt. Head shaking.

Bob held up a jar of pickles: "You want a *pickle?*"

Nick, obviously frustrated and downcast, frowned, trudged to the corner of the kitchen, sat down, and quietly began to cry.

Decades later that moment still upsets both Bob and Barbara. "He was *communicating.* Why was I putting him through that?" Bob says. "There was absolutely no need for that."

Barbara says the lesson was clear: that they should trust their own instincts about their son. "If we as parents feel that this is what we should be doing, then this is what we should be doing," she says. "We have to follow our gut."

That intuition has helped the family over a journey of three decades, one that has included its share of challenges, tragedy, and surprises.

The journey began when Nick, the second of the Domingues'

three children, wasn't yet two and seemed to have hearing problems. He didn't respond to his name or even respond to sudden noises such as clapping or the clang of pots and pans. But if his mother called "Popsicle!" from the kitchen, he always came running.

He also made a habit of lining up toys. He flapped his arms and hands. He became upset easily, screaming without apparent reason and once biting his sister Bethany on her shoulder with such force that he drew blood.

Nick was two and a half when a psychologist diagnosed him with autism. The couple knew little about autism, but perhaps because Barbara grew up with a brother who was blind and one of Bob's sisters had developmental delays, they spent little time grieving. Barbara immediately got to work, reading whatever she could find on the topic and even badgering authors and experts by phone for advice. They found supportive professionals and connected with other parents of autistic children through a day program I helped run at Bradley Children's Hospital in Providence, Rhode Island.

As much as the support helped, Nick still had significant challenges. Unable to communicate with words consistently, he was deeply frustrated at times, routinely scratching his parents and once tearing the cornea from his father's right eye. He was also prone to running. On one occasion Barbara left the room where Nick was watching cartoons, then returned to find he was gone—and nowhere to be found in the house. She ran outside in a panic, worried that if he reached a nearby lake he could drown. Fortunately a stranger found him before he got to the water and, suspecting something was amiss, stayed with him until Barbara showed up.

Nick communicated mostly by using echolalia. Sometimes he would surprise his parents with an unexpectedly sophisticated sentence, and Bethany, his older sister, would put things in context, identifying the TV dialogue he was echoing.

From early on, Bob found that keeping a sense of humor and making things fun were keys to Nick's development. Noticing that physical activity was calming to Nick, Bob devised a game called

Stop and Go, in which the children ran wildly around the room until he told them to freeze. Bob also found that when he played tickling games with Nick, his son would be more open to social interactions, so he took those opportunities to connect and teach new skills.

When it came time for school, the family relocated from Fall River to Swansea, Massachusetts, mostly because Barbara felt the town's school district would offer the best services. Both Barbara and Bob had attended Catholic schools and had always assumed their children would too. They enrolled Nick in a Catholic school where he was one of the few children with a disability. To help with his challenges, Nick's teacher created a small, curtained-off area within the classroom where, when Nick felt overstimulated, he could escape, listening to music through headphones.

Though he struggled at times, he also excelled in some academic subjects. He did so well at math that classmates came to him for help. In middle school he was the occasional victim of bullies and once landed in the principal's office for threatening another student in a lavatory, saying "Right in the kisser!" It turned out he was just repeating one of his echolalic phrases, and Bob had to set him straight. "*We* understand, Nick," he told his son, "but when you say that to somebody, they think you're going to hit them."

From an early age he was drawn to video games. As a second-grader he wrote about himself, "If I could I would like to be in video games. I'm happiest when playing Nintendo." When he was about eight, Barbara noticed his habit of holding his hands in front of his eyes, forming a crosshatch. When she asked why he did that, Nick said it helped him to design mazes, running imaginary characters he called "stim creatures" through them in his mind. "If we had eliminated that, we would have been eliminating a creative process," she says. "The behavior might have looked odd, but we asked why he did it, and he was able to tell us."

Nick was in eighth grade when, in an instant, the Domingue family's fate took a tragic turn. They were driving home from a birthday dinner for Nick's younger brother, Nathan, when a truck ran a red light and crashed into their white Corolla, leaving Bethany with a traumatic brain injury just two weeks before her sixteenth birthday. In the hospital and rehabilitation for nearly a year, she survived but was paralyzed, profoundly disabled, nearly unable to communicate.

Though the brothers escaped unscathed, Nick regressed while Bob and Barbara focused on Bethany's recovery. Struggling to come to grips with his sister's fate, Nick wrote a letter to God. "The one thing I want to thank you for most of all is for my sister," he wrote. "She has always been understanding and kind to me. If I could have only one person to be with in the world I would choose my sister, Bethany."

Later he found it difficult to shake the painful memory of the accident. Before the crash Bob had hoped his son might one day be able to earn a driver's license, but when Nick began driving, he experienced such severe panic attacks triggered by memories of the accident that the family put that prospect aside.

Still Nick pursued his own dreams of creating video games, working his way through three different college programs to earn a degree in computer game programming and design. For transportation he mastered the bus system, memorizing schedules and maps. On Nick's first outing, Bob drove the family car just behind the bus, monitoring closely to make sure Nick made the correct transfer.

When Bob and Barbara would check on their son in his bedroom, sometimes they would catch him fastidiously lining up objects or pacing in circles. If they suggested he should be doing his homework, Nick would insist that he was doing just that. "He was processing," Bob explains. "That behavior—the pacing and the lining up—wasn't something we had to get rid of. It was a tool he used to help him think."

By the time he finished his college studies, gaming technology had changed so greatly that much of what he had learned was obsolete. And since Nick wasn't fond of the newer 3D games, he lost interest.

Still living at home, Nick is soft-spoken, compassionate, and low key. In contrast with his younger days, when he was kinetic and distractible, as an adult he is keenly aware of how those around him feel. For several years, he worked part time selling tickets and concessions at a movie theater, where his inflexible thinking and adherence rules sometimes paid off. Once Nick stopped a patron trying to enter an R-rated movie, stubbornly demanding to see identification with a birth date. It turned out the customer was a top manager in disguise. He had high praise for Nick's work.

He also worked part-time as a bookkeeper for Community Autism Resources (CAR), the nonprofit his mother founded and directs, which offers programs and provides assistance for thousands of families across southern New England. There too his thoroughness and adherence to rules has paid off, and he has shown interest in pursuing a certificate in bookkeeping. Nick also helps out as a personal care assistant for his sister—who used to take care of him. Balancing all of that can be difficult, as Nick admits that it can be challenging to remember to do certain things, but visual aids help.

Nick says he hopes to use the money he is earning to achieve a degree of financial stability and has expressed fear over losing his parents. Barbara and Bob find it difficult to think about what will become of their children as they age. Though Nick is an adult, they also still worry that someone's "cruel words" will hurt him.

Barbara remembers one of the first times she reached out to another parent for advice about raising an autistic child. Someone had given her the number of an autism advocacy group, and Barbara told the woman who answered the phone that her three-year-old had recently been diagnosed.

"My son is eight," the woman said. "You will be fine."

It's not so different from the advice Barbara and her parent-professional staff dispense these days at CAR: One day at a time, one step in front of the other. Keep the future in mind, but don't be wedded to any one plan. If anyone knows that, it's the Domingues.

The Canha Family: "You Have to Be in the Trenches Making It Happen"

Maria Teresa still sometimes watches the videotape that shows a family gathering when their son Justin was two. Holding a stick, Justin wanders about aimlessly, seemingly oblivious to his cousins and everyone else. Even when Maria Teresa and her then husband Briant call his name, Justin doesn't look up.

It's difficult to believe that remote, silent toddler grew to be the Justin of today: outgoing, ebullient, funny, an accomplished artist who delights in teaching children to draw and paint.

That transformation has much to do with his parents, who embraced and encouraged Justin's quirky, singular personality—and, when necessary, pushed the people around their son to help Justin make the most of his life.

The younger of two sons, Justin had developed typically until around two, when he lost most of the language he had acquired and seemed to retreat from the world. "All of a sudden," Maria Teresa recalls, "we were back to zero."

A doctor told the Canhas their son didn't have autism; he had Pervasive Developmental Disorder. Looking back, Maria Teresa sees that diagnosis as a disservice: "It took me a year to figure out that it was the same thing."

Not long after that, the parents and son visited my office, then at Boston's Emerson College. I found that while he was not very responsive to people, Justin was curious, alert, and concentrated in his focus. I confirmed that he was on the autism spectrum, but I told his parents that his potential was unlimited, provided they worked to give him appropriate support and keep their expectations high—an approach Briant summarizes now as "high support, high demand."

They found little assistance, though, in Belgium, where the family had relocated for Briant's work. Justin's international school offered little support, and Maria Teresa felt increasingly alone and despondent, wondering if her son would ever speak.

Searching for ways to get through to Justin, Briant employed his artistic talent, creating storyboards and videotaping them to teach basic skills such as toileting and avoiding danger. Justin immediately responded in ways they had not imagined. "I realized then that Justin was smart," Briant recalls. "If we could figure out how to shape the information and get it into his head, he immediately got it."

Still the Canhas knew they required considerable assistance to help Justin make the most of his life. Since they couldn't find it in Europe, they moved back to the United States, settling near family in Rhode Island. There they enrolled Justin in a public school inclusion program, which, after a few years, proved a disappointment. In their opinion the teachers didn't truly make Justin part of the class but rather taught him separately. And the aide assigned to him, whose qualifications for the job were impressive, failed to take a strong personal interest in Justin.

That disappointment brought with it a lesson: that the most effective professionals were those who were invested in Justin. "I don't care what education they have, what background," says Maria Teresa. "If they believe in Justin and they're enthusiastic about working with him, when they teach him according to his interests, it's contagious."

Frustrated in their attempts to find such people in Providence's public schools, the family relocated again, this time to Montclair, New Jersey, where they found a school strongly committed to including children with disabilities and providing an appropriate level of support. In that nurturing environment Justin's personality emerged: his charming sense of humor, his love of and commitment to animals, his strong work ethic and desire to please parents and teachers, his affection for his family. From an early age he loved giving and receiving hugs.

Even before he could speak, Justin drew, and over time it became clear to his parents that he had great potential if they could nurture his remarkable artistic talent. He spent endless hours drawing cartoon characters—his favorites were from Sesame Street, Disney, and Looney Tunes—and his early language was focused on talking about them. That budding ability might have become little more than a hobby if not for Maria Teresa, a tenacious and creative advocate who explored all avenues in search of whatever might benefit her son. "In terms of promoting myself, I'm shy," she says, "but for Justin—no shame."

That meant finding him an art tutor, Denise Melucci, who found ways to push Justin, then ten, beyond his comfort zone, successfully persuading him to expand from reproducing cartoon characters to the more ambitious realm of drawing figures and landscapes (see Chapter 7). Maria Teresa also pursued dedicated and energetic social skills tutors, occupational therapists, and other professionals to maximize her son's potential.

"Parents send their kids to school and think, 'They're taking care of it,'" she says. "It doesn't work that way. You have to have a goal in mind, and you have to be in the trenches making it happen."

Throughout the secondary school years, Justin benefited from the support of an aide in his inclusive public school program. He took part in an innovative post–high school transition-to-adulthood program run through Montclair High School in which students who had been previously enrolled in special education learned to shop for food, use public transportation, and gain employment experience through internships. In social skills workshops, the students learned how to conduct themselves in a job interview and, later, among their coworkers.*

In the process Justin began focusing on a long-term goal: to support himself independently by selling his artwork and teaching art. By his early twenties he was well on his way, represented by New York City's Ricco Maresca Gallery, which sold his paintings and charcoals

---

* Justin and the program were featured in the article "Autistic and Seeking a Place in an Adult World" in the September 17, 2011, edition of the *New York Times*.

and sponsored shows of his work. Justin also began to volunteer as an art teacher in various classrooms, with both typical children and autistic children. But the art market is notoriously unstable, and when Justin emerged at twenty-one from the transition program, he hadn't secured stable employment.

That didn't dampen his determination. Though he continued living at home into his early twenties, he made his way around the New York City area on public transportation, often turning down offers of rides because he was intent on being self-sufficient.

At first his parents focused on finding him jobs that required little social interaction since they knew Justin found that challenging. But when he worked at a series of bakeries, he seemed to seek out opportunities to interact with customers. And he truly shone in the classroom, developing his skills teaching art to elementary school students in Montclair and in a New York City school serving autistic children. He also began earning money designing and decorating birthday cakes and working at children's birthday parties, taking drawing requests from the guests. He has begun to speak in front of large conference audiences, to the delight of those in attendance. If an audience member poses a question he doesn't like, Justin, always direct and honest, blurts out, "Next question!"

In those settings, say his parents, when most people meet Justin they are intrigued by his delightful personality. Ebullient and engaging, he likes singing Disney tunes to himself and is prone to inventive and descriptive language. When he finds someone annoying, he says the person "must be subtracted." When his mother asked about future relationships, Justin told her he didn't plan on marrying "because marriage is too complicated."

His father finds irony in his son's magnetic presence. "We came to realize that his real strength is his communication skill with other human beings," says Briant. "I'm still trying to get over that."

Eager to gain more independence, approaching his late twenties, Justin took the major step of moving into an apartment with his brother, and later into his own unit in a government-subsidized building that houses both the elderly and people with disabilities, where he lives with periodic support. An animal enthusiast from an early age, he enjoys the company of his cat, Tommy.

While he doesn't drive, he uses public transportation independently as well as ride-share services. In addition to his bakery job, he volunteers at a New Jersey wildlife sanctuary, preparing the food for the rescued animals. He also gives tours there sharing his infectious enthusiasm for animals.

As engaged in the world as he is, Justin also enjoys relaxing on his own, playing on his computer, listening to music, and engaging in "self-talk," endlessly repeating scenes from movies and pieces of conversation floating in his head. When he's in her home, it's not unusual for Maria Teresa to suddenly hear a loud, high-pitched voice from upstairs: Justin, playing out yet another scene in his head.

His parents understand that's part of being on the spectrum. Earlier, Briant admits, he expended more effort on helping Justin to fit in social situations, preferring environments where he could be around more neurotypical peers so he could learn from the model of their behavior. Over time that has seemed both less achievable and less important.

That particularly struck him years ago when the parents traveled with Justin to Los Angeles, where he collaborated with Dani Bowman, an autistic artist who runs her own small, independent animation company and eventually contracted with Justin to create storyboards for her. At first the Canhas expected to play an important role in helping Justin and Dani to communicate and relate. But they quickly observed that the two autistic artists had their own language, their own way of collaborating, and had no need for assistance.

To the parents it was both humbling and remarkable to see the son they once watched wander amid his cousins, aloof to the world, now fully engaged and fully himself.

"When you meet Justin, you immediately know he's different," says Briant. "And he's successful not in spite of that, but because of that."

PART THREE

The Future of Autism

CHAPTER 11

Reframing Autistic Identity

I WAS trying to keep a low profile when Mikey blew my cover.

I hadn't yet met Mikey when I visited his fourth-grade classroom one morning to observe him in my role as a consultant, helping his public school's teachers and staff to support children on the spectrum. I'm accustomed to blending in on such visits, so I settled into a child-size chair on the periphery of the morning circle. Knowing that the children would notice a stranger, the teacher smiled and nodded in my direction, casually explaining to the kids that I was there to visit and see all the wonderful things they were learning about.

Clearly intrigued, Mikey kept looking in my direction as I tried to play fly on the wall. Finally, as his classmates made their way to their desks, he rushed up to me. "Hi, Dr. Barry. Are you the autism man?" he asked, eyes wide. Caught off guard, I told that him I come to meet lots of students, and some of them are autistic. At that, he began flapping his arms and stood up on his toes. "Then you must be here to see *me*!" he said in an excited voice. "*I'm* autistic!" He explained that his mom had told him I would be visiting the school to see autistic children. Being autistic, he told me, meant he had a good memory but that sometimes when he got too excited, he had meltdowns. Then he proceeded to inform me in great detail about his favorite football team, the New England Patriots, and their star quarterback.

As Mikey's teacher intervened, directing him back toward his seat, I couldn't help but smile. I was accustomed to being discreet in such situations, but here was a joyful, delightful child who at nine years of age had clearly learned to embrace being on the autism spectrum. He had nothing to hide and everything to share.

Mikey taught me more that morning than about football players. His unrestrained greeting gave me new insight into the remarkable changes in the way autistic people have come to see themselves and the role of autism in their lives. Increasingly, autism isn't viewed as something to hide or whisper about, but rather a significant part of who you are. That evolution in perspective has come about in large part because people on the spectrum are raising their voices, challenging long-held assumptions, and reframing the way autistic people see themselves.

In this chapter we will examine how that revolution, led by people on the spectrum, is addressing and affecting some important and central questions: When and how should an autistic person learn of his or her own diagnosis? What are the best ways to handle disclosing one's diagnosis to others? What does it mean to embrace autism as an identity? How does being autistic overlap with the other aspects of a person's identity? And what can we learn about all of this from a unique group of autistic self-advocates, those who are nonspeakers who use AAC to communicate, and who are now "speaking" up for themselves?

The Two Sides of Disclosure

One of the most common questions parents ask me is: When is the right time to tell my child that he or she is on the autism spectrum?

Should we even use the word autism in the presence of our family member? The issue comes up regarding adults, too. Sometimes there are conflicting opinions about what to do or say when an individual might be on the spectrum, or has been diagnosed but isn't yet aware of it. When to bring it up? And how? That's the first side of disclosure: discussing autism with a person who may not be aware of being autistic. The second side: with this awareness, when should an autistic person disclose their diagnosis to other people in their life who may not be aware of it?

The way we think about these questions has evolved along with our knowledge and understanding of autism. Decades ago, the psychologist Ivar Lovaas, who developed behavioral approaches aimed at "recovering" children from what he viewed as a "horrible" condition, counseled parents and professionals never to discuss autism with their children or students. He felt it would be harmful for a child to be aware of his diagnosis. To this day, many parents are hesitant to share the diagnosis with their child, or even strongly oppose doing so, fearing that placing a label on the child is somehow limiting or feeling (correctly) that the child is far more complex than one word can capture.

I advocate for an approach best described by my friend Dr. Stephen Shore (see Chapter 9), who is on the spectrum and teaches widely on the topic. Instead of working *against* autism, Stephen says, we should work *with* autism. That is, instead of focusing primarily on the challenges that come with autism, we should emphasize the strengths that can characterize autism, not asking what the person can't do, but what they *can*. "If you're going to present to your child that he's autistic, do it in a positive way, not like some of these professionals who say, 'Your child is never going to do this and this and this,'" Anita Lesko (see Chapter 12), another autistic self-advocate, said on a conference panel I moderated. "Present the positives, so the kid can say, 'Hey, I've got this great thing!'" Even if a person has significant challenges, it is always possible to identify relative strengths and positive qualities that can be highlighted.

This approach can help inform our decisions about the first side of disclosure—the process of sharing a diagnosis with an autistic person. Before we ask when to disclose, it's worth asking why. The best reason is that knowing one's diagnosis can foster self-understanding and enhance self-esteem by objectifying a person's challenges. Often, as autistic children gain social awareness, they begin to feel different from their peers and struggle to understand why they find some situations and encounters so challenging. Others come to question their own intelligence and abilities, assuming there must be something wrong with them. "Am I crazy?" one boy repeatedly asked his mother. In still other cases, the person lacks the self-awareness even to notice or be mindful of these differences.

Having a diagnosis—and being aware of it—gives an individual a way of understanding many of these difficulties and frees the person from feeling somehow flawed or responsible for his or her own challenges. It also allows a person or family to connect with others with the same diagnosis who may share similar challenges.

Let me be clear. I have never met an autistic person who felt that being told of the diagnosis—or becoming aware of it over time, even through self-diagnosis—was a negative or damaging experience. To be sure, the responses fall on a continuum. Some recall the moment of suddenly understanding their difficulties, feeling relief that their struggles were not of their own making but rather a result of their internal wiring. Others describe how the disclosure immediately changed their lives for the better, marking a new beginning: "I finally understand myself, and don't blame myself." Adults on the spectrum overwhelmingly share that being diagnosed or self-diagnosing, or having a diagnosis revealed to them brings a sense of comfort, begins the process of erasing negative feelings about oneself. It offers a much-needed explanation for challenges they experience. As noted, it also can help a person understand their strengths and positive qualities.

When is the best time to raise the issue? Parents often avoid disclosing a diagnosis to a child because of their own fears or lack of understanding of the term autism. Certainly, when a child begins to express that he feels different from his peers, or questions why she has such difficulty with things that seem to come easily to others, there is a need to talk about it. When a child or teen makes self-deprecating remarks reflecting his low self-esteem, it's important to discuss the diagnosis. If a child becomes a victim of teasing or bullying, disclosure can help her understand why her behavior or appearance may be seen as being different. When a child or adult meets an autistic peer; this is an opportunity to explain challenges or differences the person and peer might share.

It's helpful to think of disclosure not as a verdict or end goal, but as a process, one that varies for each family and each individual— not an instantaneous revelation but a discussion that transpires over weeks, months, or even years. The "discussion" need not occur only or primarily through spoken conversation. Visual supports such as written words, pictures and icons, pictures drawn spontaneously as part of a discussion, and age-appropriate books about autism can help.

Stephen Shore recommends a four-step process that unfolds over time and that emphasizes an individual's strengths while acknowledging the challenges that may come with autism. (With an adult or a more self-aware child, the individual can contribute to steps 1–3.)

> *Step 1:* Make the child aware of his distinctive personal strengths and positive qualities.
>
> *Step 2:* Develop a list of the child's strengths and challenges.
>
> *Step 3:* Without judging, compare the child's strengths with those of potential role models, friends, and loved ones.
>
> *Step 4:* Introduce the label autism to summarize the child's experience and disability.

Stephen himself undertook this process to disclose a diagnosis for a teenage boy to whom he'd taught music for many years. The parents hadn't raised the topic of autism with their son because they had hoped he would grow out of the challenges they had observed. But when he hit adolescence and his differences became even more apparent, they asked Stephen for his guidance and direct help. At the next music lesson, Stephen began by pointing out the young man's strengths: music, graphic design, computers. Then they discussed his challenges (carefully avoiding the loaded word "weaknesses"): making friends, penmanship, sports. Speaking of "challenges" rather than "weaknesses" isn't a way to sugarcoat autism, but rather to present it in a more objective and less negative way. Also, challenges can be overcome, and using this term helps counter the damage done over many years by so many professionals who delivered the news of a diagnosis along with a list of things the child would likely never be able to achieve or accomplish.

Next, Stephen moved to the second step: lining up the challenges and strengths, and pointing out one or two strengths to accommodate each challenge. Then he made what he calls a "nonjudgmental comparison," mentioning other people in the child's life and their strengths and challenges, while emphasizing that all people are good at some things and not so good at others. Perhaps the boy's sister was better at doing some things, and he was better at others—because, Stephen explained, different people have different brains. He mentioned famous people and historical figures who may have been on the spectrum.

Finally, Stephen pointed out that the boy's particular set of characteristics line up with something called the autism spectrum. In the case of this boy, the initial disclosure process took about twenty minutes. For others, the process can spread out over days, weeks, or months.

One factor that can make the process easier for all is freely using the word "autism" in conversation long before the disclosure rather than intentionally avoiding it or making it a taboo term. Even long before a parent or other loved one chooses to disclose the diagnosis, making occasional mention of autism when pointing out a person's strengths and challenges related to autism presents a more balanced perspective and takes away the stigma that might otherwise be felt.

Understanding one's own diagnosis—at any age—helps the individual or family to seek out accurate information in order to make decisions about what needs to be done and what kind of supports the person might need in order to have a successful life.

The other kind of disclosure that's equally important to consider is when and to whom should an autistic person opt to disclose his or her diagnosis? Or, in other cases, when should the parents or other loved ones of an individual on the spectrum make the diagnosis known?

As Stephen Shore frames the issue, it's important to consider this whenever being autistic might have significant impact on a situation or relationship, highlighting a need for better understanding and if needed, special accommodations and more support. That doesn't necessarily mean you have to disclose your (or your child's) actual diagnosis—that might be too much information to share. Particularly in a work environment, it may be inappropriate, in the same way one wouldn't reveal a health issue or another private matter that wasn't relevant to one's work. But when aspects of being on the spectrum affect your ability to do your job, or a student's ability to work or engage in the classroom, or when a child's participation in an extracurricular activity might be affected, it's often worth disclosing, at least in a limited way.

This question often comes up when an accommodation will enhance an autistic person's ability to do his or her job. Carly Ott (see Chapter 12) found that many of the strengths that came with her neurodivergence helped make her a more effective employee for the bank where she worked. But early on, she also encountered sensory issues that made the workplace challenging for her. The high level of background noise in the open-plan office where she worked made it almost impossible for her to focus, so she found herself staying late every night and completing work after hours. After some time, she requested an accommodation: she explained to her supervisor that she was particularly sensitive to sound, and asked if she could work from home, where she could better maintain her concentration. (This was before the Covid-19 pandemic made such arrangements commonplace.) When making such a request, it's wise to emphasize not the individual's need, but the opportunity to be a better employee or team member.

While it's not usually necessary in such situations to use the word autism or disclose an actual diagnosis, many people find it highly stressful and draining to continually hide or "mask" being autistic. Many speak of "autistic burnout," essentially the exhaustion, extreme dysregulation, and shut-down caused by constantly putting energy into concealing one's true self. In the same way LGBTQ folks speak of "coming out," autistic people weigh the relative merits of disclosing their diagnosis. Of course, every person is different—with unique needs for privacy, a unique level of tolerance of attention, and unique feelings about what to share and what to conceal. Often the decision comes down to an assessment of risk: will disclosing my autism diagnosis make my situation better or worse? The decision to fully or partially disclose one's diagnosis also depends upon the purpose. In Carly's case, it had to do with the need for work accommodations. Another autistic person might choose to disclose in order to educate others about autism, especially if they have inaccurate and deficit-laden perceptions of what autism is and is not.

When the time feels right to share a diagnosis with colleagues, Carly recommends doing so in an almost offhanded way, and trying to emphasize the positive. If a colleague or supervisor compliments what you were able to do because of a relative strength, you could connect that to being on the spectrum: "Oh, that was easy. It really helps that I'm autistic, because that just comes naturally to me." That gives the person hearing it a positive association, and also makes the person more open to helping with accommodations when you might need them in the future. As a secondary benefit, disclosing in this way is a natural way of educating colleagues and others about autism and neurodiversity. We all carry stereotypes of other people and groups, and the best way to overcome them and foster understanding is for people to encounter each other on an interpersonal basis.

Morénike Giwa-Onaiwu (see Chapter 12) is an autistic college professor, writer, and self-advocate. On the first day of a new term, she always covers the topic of ADA accommodations, seizing the opportunity to mention that she herself is on the autism spectrum. Nearly every time, students express surprise, some telling her they've never encountered an autistic teacher—only children or teens. Often, the students follow up by disclosing their own diagnoses, or suspicions that they may be on the spectrum. "They say, 'I didn't know [an autistic person] could be a college professor,'" says Morénike, who replies, "You can be far more than that!"

Disclosing one's autism often starts as a form of self-advocacy— that is, seeking accommodations or supports for oneself. That process often leads to a more general form of advocacy, paving the way for others in the same organization or school who might be on the spectrum, or making colleagues more open to—and informed about— neurodivergent people in the future.

That kind of awareness has also given rise to another evolving issue: the changing nature of autistic identity.

Autism as an Identity

Not long ago I was attending a major autism conference when I witnessed an exchange that captured for me the great culture shift in how our society views autism, and how autistic people view themselves. Across the lobby of the large convention center, I noticed a young woman with a baby stroller. She was engaged in conversation with a middle-aged man with wire-rimmed glasses who was admiring her child.

As I walked toward them, I recognized that the gentleman was John Elder Robinson, author of the memoir *Look Me in the Eye*, and one of the most outspoken and forward-thinking voices in the autism community. I approached and introduced myself to John, being careful not to interrupt his conversation with the woman, who I gathered was on the spectrum and who told John that her daughter was nearly three months old. John smiled and looked at the infant with delight. "I bet," he said, "she will grow up to be a fine autistic tyke."

A fine autistic tyke. That phrase reverberated in my mind. Years ago it might have been considered an insult or even a curse to tell someone their infant might grow up to be autistic. But here was one of the autism community's most prominent figures, expressing the hope to a fellow neurodivergent person that her child would develop to be a member of the extended community they shared.

It struck me how far we have come, and how autism has evolved from something to cure, recover from, or get rid of into an identity to be embraced. To be clear, we still have a long way to go, as much stigma and misinformation remains.

Andrew Solomon, whose celebrated book *Far From the Tree* chronicled the stories of families raising children with a variety of disabilities and differences, has described the challenges he experienced growing up gay and suffering from chronic depression, and how he ultimately found strength in embracing his identity. "Identity involves entering a community to draw strength from that community, and to give strength there, too," he said in a TED Talk. "It involves substituting 'and' for 'but.' Not, 'I am here but I have cancer,' but rather, 'I have cancer and I am here.'" (Of course, having cancer has mostly a negative impact on quality of life and can be life-threatening, whereas being autistic comes with both relative strengths that have the potential to improve quality of life, as well as challenges.)

More and more people on the spectrum have come to embrace autism as their identity, drawing strength from their community, and giving strength as well. That phenomenon is all the more remarkable in light of autism's history, and the long-held assumptions made over the years about autism and autistic people—nearly all of which have been proven wrong. Early researchers in what's known as the Psychogenic School posited incorrectly that autism was the result of emotionally abusive parenting. Leo Kanner, the Austrian psychiatrist, coined the term "refrigerator mother" to describe a parent whose cold, uncaring parenting, he claimed, caused the child to retreat into autism. (He later retracted that assertion.) The psychologist Bruno Bettelheim's book *Empty Fortress* made the case that autistic children were essentially empty shells of humans. Ivar Lovaas, one of the most controversial figures in the history of autism treatment, viewed autistic people as displaying a collection of quirky behaviors. His behavior analytic approach aimed to "modify" behavior that he saw as pathological, without asking the "Why" question. His goal was to make autistic children facades of some hypothetical neurotypical ideal, which he and his colleagues referred to as "indistinguishable" from their peers.

Even the process of disclosing a diagnosis was long fraught with negativity and pessimism. Many parents have stories of doctors or psychologists delivering an autism diagnosis and following up immediately with a list of all the things the child would be unlikely to do: make friends, attend college, hold a job, have a decent quality of life.

Unfortunately, the residual effects of those erroneous, damaging, but long dominant approaches and practices are still with us. Some professionals and approaches still place blame on parents, implicitly or explicitly, for being too lenient or dooming their child's future by not adopting the type of treatment they practice and profit from. Others continue only to pathologize autism. What has changed the landscape and outlook is the self-advocate movement: the effort by autistic people—who, in many cases, have directly suffered from these damaging approaches—to speak for themselves and their autistic community, and embrace autism as integral to their identity.

Years ago, Temple Grandin spoke at the annual conference I helped organize. Someone asked her if her autism could be taken away, would she agree to that? Her response was simple and direct: "If you take away my autism, you take away an essential part of who I am."

That understanding has been reflected in the way the language of autism has evolved. As late as the 1980s, professionals commonly referred to people with intellectual or developmental disabilities using terms such as "retard" and "idiot" (as in "idiot savant"). People on the spectrum were called "autistic," with only a negative connotation. In the 1980s and '90s, a movement arose to use "person-first language," a construction, put forth with all good intentions, aimed at recognizing the whole person and not define an individual by his or her disability. In more recent years, many autistic people have taken issue with that approach, asserting that it denies how essential autism is to their sense of personhood and identity. The more self-advocates have spoken about the autistic experience, the more the majority have expressed the preference for being called "autistic." As one nonspeaking autistic young man, Huan, put it: "My autism is who I am. You wouldn't call me an individual with Vietnamese heritage. You'd call me Vietnamese."

Of course, embracing an identity looks different in different people, and autistic identity falls on a continuum. Some individuals, like those featured in Chapter 12, not only embrace the identity, but come to organize their lives around autism, even creating full careers as autistic advocates. Becca Lory Hector, for example, found that what she had learned in trying to understand herself and get the support she needed was helpful to others, too, so she changed her career path and became an advocate, providing on-line webinars and emotional support services for autistic people. In contrast, Dave Finch, my cohost on "Uniquely Human: The Podcast," says he thinks of himself primarily as a husband, a father, and his primary work is as an engineer; autism is further down his list.

One of the most famous individuals on the spectrum is Greta

Thunberg, the Swedish climate activist. In interviews, Thunberg has said that being on the spectrum has helped her to focus her attention on environmental issues in a way that has allowed her to emerge as an international leader. But while she frequently speaks out on climate change issues, she almost never speaks publicly with a focus on her autism. Clearly the public identity that she puts forth is as a climate activist, not an autistic self-advocate.

Other people who are on the autism spectrum express at various points in their lives that they don't want to be defined by autism, particularly if they associate it with negative experiences. In my speaking engagements, I often share a clip from the HBO documentary *Autism: The Musical*, which highlights the story of five young performers in the early years of the Miracle Project, the Los Angeles program in which autistic youths create and perform musical theater productions. One scene shows Wyatt, then a fifth grader on the spectrum, telling his mother he's upset about his special-education class.

"What's wrong with school?" she asks.

"One-hundred percent of kids are retarded," he says.

When she asks if he'd like to transfer to an inclusive class, he hesitates. "Have you ever heard a bully, Mom?" They discuss bullies for a few moments, then he asks, "Do you think it's because I'm in a special-ed class? Do you think that's why they bully me?"

Like Wyatt at that age, some autistic people come to associate being on the spectrum as a negative, externally imposed identity. It's about what you can't do, where you don't fit in, how the bullies treat you—the result of the stigma that self-advocates are desperate to change.

Even for teenagers and adults, it can be difficult to escape the stigma that comes with autism—the assumptions that the individual is either a *Rain Man*–like savant or someone incapable of being a responsible person. "I'm supposed to be some kind of computer genius or not have any real difficulties in my life," one young man told me. "That couldn't be further from the truth. I'm terrible with computers and I have a lot of difficulties that would categorize my autism as a disability." Unfortunately, the societal stigma associated with autism may become internalized. Scott Steindorff (see Chapter 12), diagnosed as autistic as an adult and now a successful executive director of award-winning films and television shows, says he first felt shame when receiving the diagnosis. Due to the disproportionate value western culture places on spoken language skills, those who do not speak or who have obvious speech and language difficulties are especially misunderstood and victimized by stigma.

What's helpful is rejecting those kinds of external assumptions, constructing your own identity and aligning yourself with others committed to shattering the stigma and misconceptions. Justin Canha identifies as a professional artist who loves animals. Mikey isn't just an autistic fourth grade student, he is also knowledgeable and passionate about sports, and readily shares his expertise. Ron Sandison (see Chapter 12) identifies as a medical professional and an autistic minister, and he speaks in churches, synagogues, and mosques. Danny Whitty (see Chapter 11) is a talented chef and an on-line advocate for nonspeakers. Rather than focusing on the stigma associated with autism, these people construct identities around some of the strengths and interests that come along with being on the spectrum.

Building a positive sense of self is all the more important given that autistic people are at high risk for experiencing secondary mental health issues. Justin and Ryan both have challenges associated with their autism, but they also have a sense of pride in who they are as people, and are seen by others as interesting—even remarkable—individuals.

Many autistic individuals find that when they embrace autism as an identity, they discover communities. It's common for autistic people to find themselves connected with other autistic adults because they share common experiences and challenges. Becca Lory Hector (Chapter 12) was diagnosed at age thirty-six. After she contributed a chapter to an anthology called *Spectrum Women*, she found herself connecting and bonding with a new community of women—of varying ages, in different countries, from a range of backgrounds—who shared challenges, experiences, and outlooks. "It just felt like home," she told me. "Maybe I can have a best friend again—I haven't had one since I was four!"

Part of what creates group identity is humor. My friends Dena Gassner and Stephen Shore, both autistic adults, can make each other laugh about all the social quicksand that neurotypicals create for themselves, rather than being honest, direct, and forthright. A group of autistic friends who met at a camp in Massachusetts even started a comedy troupe called Aspergers Are Us, which became the subject of documentaries on both Netflix and HBO. In their shows they joke about everything but autism, but they say their shared autistic sensibility is what fuels their comedy.

One benefit of the way people on the spectrum are embracing autistic identity is that it can ease the way for those who are newly diagnosed. A young autistic friend, Rebecca, was diagnosed at twenty-two. Before that, she had worked for several years with autistic children. "I saw myself in each one of them," she told me. "We *got* each other in a special way. I always knew that. But, I could not bring myself to believe that the reason for that might be more than [that] I just have a knack for it. Once I got diagnosed, I started to see stigma firsthand, through my own view of myself. It took a while for me to accept this label in myself, because I had internalized the stigma. The stigma around autism is spread in all sorts of ways—even by very well-intentioned people." But then Rebecca added this: "We have absolutely come a long way, and every day we have more and more autistic people sharing their story and paving the way for the future." Rebecca is now teaching neurotypical therapists what it is like to be autistic based on her own experiences so they can change practices that are insensitive to the experience of being autistic, and develop more "autistic friendly" practices.

For Rebecca, and for countless other, the future looks so much more bright and positive.

How Autism Overlaps With
Other Parts of Who We Are

While it's significant and encouraging that so many people on the spectrum are coming to acknowledge autism as central to their identity, being autistic is never one's *sole* identity. Autistic people, like all human beings, have multiple identities. We're all multidimensional, all members of multiple communities. Just as autism has impact on our various identities, those other identities have impact on being autistic.

This concept of overlapping identities was best articulated by Kimberlé Crenshaw, a Black lawyer and civil rights advocate who in 1989 published a landmark paper arguing that one can't understand the reality of being a Black woman simply in terms of being black or being a woman, but rather by the way those dual identities combine and affect each other. Crenshaw illustrated the idea with a metaphor: a person standing at the intersection of two roads, each representing an identity. We can't define the person exclusively by either road, but rather by the combination. The point is that we all carry multiple identities that overlap and intersect.

I should note that the person who explained this concept of "intersectionality" to me most clearly is a remarkable woman who herself carries multiple identities, as an autistic, Black mother of autistic children, a college professor, and the daughter of immigrants. Morénike Giwa Onaiwu's own experience illustrates clearly how overlapping identities can affect each other and determine the course of our lives. She was born in the United States to parents who had immigrated from Nigeria and Cape Verde, the archipelago west of Africa. Growing up, she always felt different from her peers, but she couldn't pinpoint exactly why. She felt "tomboyish," she says, perhaps because she was the only girl surrounded by boys. She was an African-American girl attending predominantly white schools. Even when she was surrounded by Black people, she often felt out-of-place because her family's West African customs were different from those of other Black cultures. Visiting relatives in Nigeria, she felt too Americanized to fit in comfortably.

"I was always trying to figure out, what was that 'thing,' so I could fix the 'thing' and be able to fit in," she said during our discussion on "Uniquely Human: The Podcast."

She was diagnosed with ADHD and depression, but it was only when she was diagnosed as autistic, following the diagnoses of her two youngest children, that Morénike came to understand herself clearly: "I felt this sense of kinship with the neurodiversity community—and autistic people in particular."

Before long, she became an activist, authoring several books about autism and diversity issues, and speaking out about the various ways being on the autism spectrum overlaps with other identities. Speaking from her own experience, Morénike says she displayed early traits that should have clued in teachers and medical professionals that she might be autistic, but they overlooked them, probably because she was Black.

In fact, not just Black women but women in general may well be under-diagnosed because of cultural biases. Autistic males have long outnumbered females—according to the most recent figures by a ratio of four to one. But some studies have shown that might be because the medical and mental-health professionals doing the diagnosing overlook women, don't think to diagnose them until they are much older, or apply diagnostic criteria developed for males and not for females, whose presenting behavioral patterns might differ significantly from males.

Similarly, Black children are less likely to be accurately diagnosed on the spectrum than white children, possibly because white children's behavior issues in school and elsewhere raise red flags. In contrast, teachers or physicians might not pay close attention to the same displays of behavior in a Black child, mistakenly assuming the behavior is a reflection of race and culture, rather than disability.

Then there are the challenges faced by parents who are themselves autistic. Many autistic parents report that teachers or medical professionals often question their competence as parents simply because they are on the spectrum. In some cases, autistic parents live in fear of having social-service agencies or judges declare them incompetent parents and take custody of their children—simply because the parents are autistic. There is no evidence that autism makes a person a less competent parent—in fact, autistic parents are likely to be more sensitive to the needs of neurodivergent children—but assumptions left over from the dark ages of autism persist in many areas, with unfortunate results.

Sorting Through Autism and Gender Diversity

Another significant identity issue that autistic self-advocates are successfully bringing to the fore is the overlap between autism and gender diversity. More and more people on the autism spectrum are openly identifying as transgender, nonbinary, or gender-queer, and the reverse is also true: increasing numbers of undiagnosed gender-divergent people are identifying as autistic.

A major 2020 study found that people who don't identify with the gender they were assigned at birth are three to six times as likely to be autistic as cisgender people, those whose identity matches their birth gender. Just as autistic people fall along a spectrum, gender also occurs on a spectrum. "We're all very, very different," Wenn Lawson, an autistic trans British psychologist who has spoken widely on these issues, said in a talk. "You've got girly girls, you've got tom-boy girls, and all of those in between. And it's the same for the male gender."

Wenn knows the subject well. Female at birth, Wenn was diagnosed with an intellectual disability at age two, didn't speak until five, then was labeled schizophrenic at seventeen. It wasn't until age forty-two that Wenn was diagnosed as autistic. While that came with the comfort of a new level of self-understanding, Wenn continued to experience discomfort for reasons Wenn couldn't pinpoint.

Wenn felt uncomfortable about having breasts, about experiencing menstrual periods, about being in women's dressing rooms, but for years Wenn put those sensations in the same category as Wenn's aversion to certain noises and textures. "I thought that was a sensory thing," Wenn has said. "But in fact, that . . . was a gender thing."

As Wenn came to learn, what Wenn was experiencing was gender dysphoria: though Wenn knew innately he was male, he was physiologically a female. It wasn't until Wenn was sixty-two that a psychiatrist confirmed that Wenn's true gender identity was the opposite of the one he was assigned at birth. That began a process over several years of making the physical transition to make his body conform physically to his gender identity. As he now explains, "I am a more whole and complete person. I'm home—which I had never experienced before."

Wenn continues to speak out and tell his story, in large because of the high rates of depression and other mental-health issues experienced by non-binary and gender-questioning individuals on the spectrum—often because of the difficulty and stress that can come with camouflaging one's true identities. Asked at one appearance what parents can do to support their children who might be struggling to understand their own gender identity, Wenn was clear in his answer: "Just listen to us. Walk beside us. Support us all the way. And if things change, change with us."

Nonspeakers Speaking Up

In February of 2018, I paid a visit to the University of Virginia in Charlottesville that opened my eyes and shifted my understanding about a remarkable subculture of the autism community. Over two days, I spent time with a group called the Tribe, nine young adults, all autistic, all identifying as nonspeaking, and all of whom had learned to communicate as teenagers by pointing to letters on letter boards or keyboards to spell their messages, with the support of aides called

Communication Regulation Partners (CRPs). They all were thought of as significantly intellectually disabled as children, even well into their teen years.

What I saw and what I have learned since gave me new insight into one of the most misunderstood and marginalized populations in the world of autism. It's estimated that between thirty and forty percent of autistic people are nonspeakers—meaning they cannot use speech as their primary means of communicating. (An important word about language: others refer those who don't speak as "nonverbal." But "verbal" refers to those who use a language-based system, whether through speaking or other ways of communicating, such as sign language or writing. One can be verbal, but also nonvocal.) Some aren't able to vocalize, some vocalize but don't produce intelligible speech. Others have minimal or "unreliable" speech, which may not be under their volitional control, in the same way people with Tourette's syndrome or those who have had strokes often can't control their speech.

To be clear, not speaking is not an inherent characteristic of autism; it is a co-occurring condition that is neurologically based—often referred to as a motor-speech disorder.

In our society, we equate speaking with intelligence, assuming that the way someone communicates through speech reflects how intelligent they are, and that someone who can't communicate by speaking is probably less intelligent. For decades, people—including professionals and educators—wrongly made such assumptions about many autistic and neurodivergent people who were not able to communicate through speech. We know that many people who suffer strokes or who have cerebral palsy retain the capacity to take in and process information, though they may not be able to produce intelligible speech. In the same way, for many autistic people, the inability to produce meaningful speech does not reflect the workings of their minds.

Why can't these people speak? Producing intelligible speech requires the most demanding motor coordination human beings

achieve. It requires us to synchronize our breathing with the movement of the articulators—the tongue, lips, teeth, palate, and jaw—to
produce particular sounds and sequences of sounds heard as words.
In some autistic people, neurological impairment prevents the brain
from sending signals to the body parts for speech articulation resulting in speech production. In short, what's impaired is the ability to
move from thought to speech.

What is rapidly changing is that more and more people on the
autism spectrum are accessing approaches—both high-tech and
low-tech—that enable them to circumvent this neurological challenge and communicate in ways other than speaking. Newly empowered, these people are using their newfound voices to speak up
and shatter stereotypes, in the process joining the conversation and
creating their own subcultures and identities.

That's what I experienced on my visit with the Tribe. Over two
days, I sat among nine autistic young adults who are part of a program coordinated by Elizabeth Vosseller, a speech and language pathologist who developed an approach in which an individual points
to letters on a letter board or keyboard, with support from a CRP,
who reads the letters, and then the fully formed words and sentences,
aloud. In some cases individuals who have some ability to produce
speech on their own speak some words while spelling.

Some forms of Augmentative and Alternative Communication
(AAC), as it is known, have attracted controversy over the years, in
large part because methods of communication that require support
from a partner led some to question whether what is being communicated is purely the authentic, volitional expression of the autistic
person. The concern was, who was the author of the messages, the
support person or the nonspeaking person being supported? I had
my own questions, but kept an open mind, and urged others to do
so as well in a book chapter I wrote in 1994.

My visit with the Tribe helped answer my questions and made
me realize the remarkable potential of this kind of communication,
a form of AAC I had not yet observed. Even though I had known

and consulted for many autistic individuals over the years who communicated through low- and high-tech non-speech communication approaches, I had never witnessed the degree of sophisticated conversational communication I engaged in with members of the Tribe, individuals who had been so misunderstood for so many years.

I saw with my own eyes and heard with my own ears as these young people "talked" to me and among themselves. Significantly, their partners provided no direct physical assistance, only holding the letterboard or keyboard, calling out the letters and words and, with their presence, helping the people on the spectrum to communicate with intention and stay well-regulated and focused. That's essential, Elizabeth explains, because even people who are able to speak find that when they're upset, ill, or otherwise dysregulated, they can have trouble with speaking and other motor-control issues. Why shouldn't nonspeakers also need support?

I was particularly struck by Ian Nordling, with whom Elizabeth had worked since he was a young child, and whom I later interviewed for our podcast. Now in his twenties, Ian describes how, unable to communicate as a child, he had endured countless hours of therapy that he found "pointless." "Have you ever had one of those nightmares where you are stuck in a horrible situation and you try to speak but nothing comes out?" he asked. "That was me, but I was awake."

Not that a miracle happened and he learned to communicate overnight. The same sorts of motor-control issues that interfere with speech can also affect skills such as pointing to a letter on a board. So, while Ian knew how to spell, it took him many months and years of practice to achieve fluency using the letter board. "This has come with years of motor practice and communication," Ian said of using the letter board.

Most of us who can speak think of speech as something automatic, requiring little thought or practice. The truth, of course, is that none of us come into the world speaking, and we learn to speak only through many years of practice, training our minds and various body parts to do the work of producing speech. Elizabeth compares it to a child learning baseball, first batting with a tee and learning to throw and catch only with hours of practice. What's essential, she says, is to presume competence—that is, to assume that what's blocking the ability to communicate is a neurological issue, and if we can find a way, the person will have much to share.

That was certainly the case with another nonspeaker I have met, Danny Whitty. After Danny was diagnosed with autism at age three, his family moved from Japan to San Diego, where his parents hoped to find better options for an autistic child. Soon after he learned to speak, he lost that ability, and doctors said he had apraxia, a type of motor speech disorder: essentially his neural and motor systems are not well aligned, so he struggled with the fine-motor skills required for speech. For many years he could not communicate most of what he knew. "School was awful and humiliating and traumatizing," he said in an interview for our podcast. "Not being able to communicate and living in a society that saw little worth in me was soul-crushing."

He has warmer memories of a loving home, with parents and two sisters who supported him. He came to love helping his mother in the kitchen, though his physical limitations made it difficult to do anything but basic tasks. But he absorbed the details of cooking and in his teens pored over fancy culinary magazines like *Bon Appétit* and *Food & Wine*.

Then in his twenties, he made contact with Elizabeth who connected him with an instructor in San Diego. It wasn't until the Covid-19 pandemic lockdown, when his sister Tara moved back in with the family, that she began assisting him with communication and, at thirty-four, he became a fluent speller, sharing his thoughts, dreams, wisecracks—and recipes.

Being able to make himself understood transformed his life. "Even small things like choosing my outfit each day, to huge, monumental topics like grief and future dreams and advocacy for nonspeaking autistic people," he said. "It is all open to me for the first time in my life."

He's hardly alone. Stories like Ian's and Danny's, and their advocacy, are changing the way nonspeaking people are perceived, and opening up more and more opportunities and options for them to communicate using various forms of AAC. While working with letter boards is increasingly popular, nonspeakers are using a variety of modalities: typing on a keyboard or tablet computer, writing, pointing to pictures. Others on the spectrum are able to vocalize but prefer to type or write out their thoughts first, then read them aloud. That gives them the opportunity to formulate what they wish to say when well-regulated without the stress and anxiety that can come with trying to vocalize while interacting with others.

Nonspeakers are now organizing to advocate for themselves in remarkable ways. The International Association for Spelling as Communication is a group of spellers and allies working to advance communication access for nonspeaking individuals through training, education, and research. And another group, Communication-FIRST, cofounded by Tauna Szymanski, a disability rights attorney, works more broadly to protect and advance the rights, autonomy, opportunity, and dignity of people with both developmental and acquired speech-related disabilities, especially nonspeakers, including those on the autism spectrum.

While these organizations and others work to advocate for communication as a basic human right, people like Ian, Danny, and Jordyn Zimmerman (see Chapter 12) are advancing the cause by sharing their life stories. Their advocacy work is in expressing their truths and making themselves heard. "The very most loving thing you can do," says Ian, "is to hear my words and believe them."

CHAPTER 12

Giving Back,
Leading the Way

O NE of the most significant shifts in the autism community in recent years is the recognition that it's essential that people on the spectrum be centrally involved in any discussion of autism—that autistic people ought to speak up for themselves rather than being spoken about or spoken for. Indeed, it's autistic people who, through their words and deeds, are forging our understanding of the autistic experience.

Over the past two decades, I have been privileged to meet and collaborate with a number of remarkable individuals on the spectrum who are not only speaking up but also taking prominent public roles as activists and advocates, pushing for societal and legal change, promoting autism awareness among healthcare providers and others, and moving to action by working to empower autistic people in myriad ways. And, of course, each of these self-advocates does this work in his or her own unique way. They most often use their unique interests and strengths in their mission, demonstrating the power of being uniquely human.

To me, these people are the unsung champions who are leading the autism community—and the rest of us—into the future. I have been fortunate to get to know and work with each of these people and have been awestruck by their personal stories of significant struggle and, in most cases, great resilience and persistence. Many of them express gratitude to mentors and collaborators they've encountered along the way. Here are six of their stories.

Carly Ott

"Without autism, I'd be out of a job"

- Bank executive
- Autism Society of America Volunteer of the Year
- Expert on how to out yourself as autistic
- Mentors autistic people on how to thrive at work

When you meet Carly Ott, it's not difficult to be impressed. She's articulate and confident, a vice president and senior operations manager at one of the country's largest banks; she has become an active volunteer and advocate, serving on the board of the Autism Society of America and of several other nonprofits. She's also a mom.

Given all of that, you might be surprised to hear that in her mid-twenties, she could barely function, living on government benefits and leaving her tiny apartment only occasionally to see her therapist or pick up groceries.

Carly—whom I first met several years ago when she was president of the Autism Society of Ventura County, California—is testimony to how difficult life can be for autistic people before they're aware that they're on the spectrum, and also how being autistic can provide the keys to finding fulfillment and success—if the individual finds the right setting and supports.

Looking back, Carly had many traits common to autistic people.

As a child, she flapped her hands, she craved deep pressure, and liked to wrap herself tightly in blankets. She struggled with social understanding. Once, seated behind a bald man at a cinema, she told her sister loudly enough for anyone to hear, "I'd be enjoying this movie a lot more if this *giant watermelon* weren't sitting in front of me!"

Having no inhibitions could also be helpful. When her high-school biology teacher tapped her to give an Earth Day speech in front of the governor, it didn't occur to her to be nervous.

On the other hand, she struggled so much to make friends that she had to change schools repeatedly, and by seventh grade felt suicidal. "It's more acceptable to be a socially unacceptable boy than a socially unacceptable girl," she says, "and mean girls are real."

Her social challenges continued until she graduated from college, landing in New York City, where the direct and blunt way many locals communicated made her more comfortable.

Before long, though, she was suffering from what she identifies in retrospect as "autistic burnout"—exhaustion from the effort of trying to fit in. Relocating to Los Angeles, she was diagnosed with major depressive disorder, and mostly stayed in her small, cluttered apartment feeling barely able to care for herself.

Then came a breakthrough. One day at a grocery checkout counter, she picked up a magazine. The cover story was on autism. "When I read it, a light bulb went off," she says. She marked up the article with a yellow highlighter and took it to her therapist. "Oh my gosh," the woman said. "This is you!"

Just after her twenty-eighth birthday, she got an official diagnosis, which qualified her for support services through the state's system. Realizing she was on the spectrum also gave her new perspective on her many years of struggles. *Now it all makes sense*, she remembers thinking.

Feeling newly empowered, she landed a job in property management, and then, at the height of the 2008 mortgage crisis, at a major bank, where she worked in property preservation.

She soon moved to a department where a manager quickly recognized that Carly understood business and technology in a way practically nobody else did—precisely because of the unique way her mind worked.

Fortunately, she also benefited from managers and colleagues who appreciated her unusual strengths and also were compassionate about her challenges.

As she rose in the ranks, she balanced her desire to be open about being on the spectrum with her choice at other times not to disclose her diagnosis and instead keep that personal information to herself. She spent countless hours studying TV shows and movies to understand the subtleties of neurotypical behavior in social interactions that seemed to come naturally to others.

"I created a Rolodex in my head of the appropriate ways to respond in every possible situation I could ever encounter, she says. "Whether it's what to do if somebody spills the milk or what to do if there's an alien invasion—it's all in my Rolodex."

On the other hand, she found value in being "out" with other colleagues in order for her to do her job well and avoid awkward conflicts. She found it so difficult to get work done in the office, where coworkers were in cubicles and she was distracted by the ambient noise—that she would work into the evening, when it was quieter. When that was too burdensome, Carly got an accommodation to work from home.

"Being able to control my environment means that I'm not exhausted from masking all day, so I can focus on work," she says.

Still, she says, many women find it easier to mask their autism in the workplace for fear of being ostracized. "The vast majority of us learn to mask as a survival function," she says.

That same societal bias prevents many women from seeking out an autism diagnosis until they're much older, and also makes medical and mental-health professionals biased against diagnosing women on the spectrum. Carly has been vocal about trying to change that.

For those who do want to share with coworkers that they're autistic, Carly suggests putting a positive spin on it. "If someone compliments you on something, that's related to a strength that comes from your neurodiversity," she says, "Just say, 'Oh yeah, I'm autistic, so that comes naturally to me!'"

For Carly, that's not hyperbole. She firmly believes that people on the spectrum have much to offer in the workplace—one reason she became active in the Autism Society of America, which named her Volunteer of the Year in 2018. She also serves on several museum boards, using those positions to advocate for the inclusion of people with disabilities.

Thanks to her determination and grit, what once caused her such heartache and confusion became, in short, her superpower. "If somebody offered me a cure and a million dollars to take it, I wouldn't," she says. "I credit my autism for being able to think outside the box and come up with solutions to problems that others are stumped by. Without autism, I'd be out of a job."

Becca Lory Hector

"Autism colored my world with vibrant possibility"

- Blogger and speaker
- Advises and counsels autistic people on quality-of-life issues
- Shares self-help tools with people on the spectrum

Becca Lory Hector has always had a special interest in weather, so she remembers that it was a sunny, spring afternoon with low humidity for Long Island when she got her autism diagnosis.

She was thirty-six years old.

As she sat in the passenger seat of her mother's car, digesting the news, her mother asked, "Are you okay?"

She pondered the question. She thought about how much of her life she had spent sad, angry, confused. Or resentful. The anxiety, the panic attacks, the depression.

"No, I'm not. And I haven't been," she said, "But maybe now I will be."

It took about a year before she was ready to move forward. Since then, Becca has been an unstoppable force. And she says what happened that sunny day has made all the difference.

Becca became a friend as we worked together on a project in Colorado, and I became impressed with her intelligence, her strong sense of self, and her commitment to challenging long-held misunderstandings about autism. Her resolve to do away with inaccurate assumptions about autism is embodied in a powerful piece of her writing with an arresting headline: "Autism Saved My Life."

She explained that before her diagnosis, she had suffered from depression, failures, and disappointments. But understanding her diagnosis changed that. This is what she wrote, in part: "Autism colored my world with vibrant possibility which before had been a swirling vortex of chaos and confusion. The world was making sense to me through the lens of autism and I was finally ready to live life on my terms. Layers of society's constraints and demands piled high over the years were slowly peeling away and underneath was me. . . . I was getting to know myself in a way I had not been able to before and I liked this version of me. I liked this version of life. I liked this version of MY life."

Despite the relief of that revelation, she also came to understand that all too often, people diagnosed on the spectrum as adults find themselves with information but no tools to act. Newly diagnosed children can benefit from school programs, therapies, and activities with peers, but adults often find themselves on their own. "You're given this huge life-changing piece of information," she told me. "And then you have nothing to do with it."

For one thing, she says, autistic people often don't know how to ask for help. Requesting assistance is itself a learned skill, and people on the spectrum need to learn from examples both how to ask for help and how to advocate for themselves.

In fact, she found, what most parents and professionals emphasize most is encouraging people on the spectrum to become more independent. "That's the biggest lie in the entire world," she says. "I don't know anybody independent in my life."

Instead, she prioritizes the idea of *interdependence*—learning whom to ask and how to ask for what kinds of help, and when it's best to ask.

"I would go to my grandfather for financial advice, because he was an accountant," she says by way of example, "but I'd never ask him about what clothes I should wear. That would be foolish."

To learn about help, she did a close examination of the literature, assembling some of the most popular self-help books on the market and carefully studying them for wisdom. She discovered patterns and repeated themes: boundaries, taking time for yourself, understanding your own value. She took the accumulated wisdom and repackaged that advice specifically for people on the spectrum.

"As autistics, we need patterns and rules—so you're essentially rewriting the rules for your life," she says.

One prime example was Jon Kabat-Zinn's description of mindfulness. Autistic people tend to worry about the future or ruminate about the past, she says. "If instead you pay attention to the present moment, it lifts the worry," Becca says, "because right now is actually the only thing you have any control over."

In the process of sharing her accumulated wisdom, she has also found a community—a cadre of fourteen autistic women spread across the globe, all of whom contributed pieces to an extraordinary anthology called *Spectrum Women: Walking to the Beat of Autism.*

It's natural after an adult diagnosis to feel alone, as if you're the only person dealing with the set of challenges and understandings that come with being autistic. But connecting with other women on the spectrum made her realize that she could have close friends for the first time in her life, Becca says. "You find out that not only are you not broken, you're actually a pretty good autistic, and there are other people like you, as weird as you are. You can be weird with them and they'll be weird back."

And maybe that's the greatest self-help tool of all: the ability to connect with others, to be interdependent, to have people in your life who accept and love you exactly as you are. Becca Lory might not have been okay yet on that sunny day on Long Island. But she certainly is now.

Chloe Rothschild

"I love helping people"

- Coauthored book about interoception, the eighth sense
- Advocates for acceptance and promotion of a variety of AAC methods for autistic people to communicate, even though they may be able to speak

I first connected with Chloe Rothschild not long after the first edition of *Uniquely Human* was published. She emailed to tell me two things: (1) My book was the one hundredth book about autism she had added to her personal library, and (2) she was grateful for my openness to the many ways autistic people use to communicate.

After that, I shared time with Chloe, then in her early twenties, at a number of national conferences. Each time I found our interactions meaningful and delightful. She was articulate, self-aware, and passionate about advocating for herself and helping others on the spectrum. While she is fully able to communicate by speaking when well regulated, and is engaging and entertaining as a speaker, she often prefers to use alternative means of communication, such as typing her thoughts on an iPad and then having the device generate the speech or reading aloud from the iPad herself. Other times she uses pen and paper and reads back what she's written. Over time, she has become an outspoken advocate for those who use alternative and augmentative communication (AAC) methods, and she pushes back against those not allowing speaking autistic people to use AAC if it is their choice to do so.

What's even more remarkable is that she uses these various methods to communicate important and original messages. Chloe has a rare ability to describe both the positive and challenging aspects of being autistic—in all their color and nuance.

While the Chloe you encounter is likely to be joyful, enthusiastic, and self-confident, being on the spectrum hasn't always been easy for her. Chloe struggled early in life. She was born prematurely and her mother, Susan Dolan, remembers her as a colicky baby. Chloe had a serious visual impairment—she was legally blind—in addition to displaying behavioral differences that caused concern for her mother. When she was three, a neurologist diagnosed her with developmental apraxia—a neurologically based motor speech disorder that impedes the ability to produce intelligible speech. Several years later, another doctor said she had ADHD and "signs of Asperger's syndrome."

Sue vividly recalls the doctor's fatalistic declaration: "They told me to take her home and love her—like there was no hope."

As Chloe, who has an intimate knowledge of her own personal history, tells it, the next step was more matter-of-fact than painful. "We went back to my pediatrician, and he said, 'Who are we kidding? She's autistic,'" recalls Chloe. That was diagnosis enough.

At first the diagnosis was of little use, says Chloe's mother, because her Ohio school district would make accommodations for only a single disability per child, so her parents opted to accommodate for her visual impairment. "Otherwise," says her mother, "she wouldn't be able to get the large-print books she needed."

Chloe spoke early, but she showed little interest in other children. On playdates, she gravitated toward her mother and the other parents. She also had sensory challenges. She had a fear of wind, so an adult had to carry her when it was windy. She was clumsy, injuring herself frequently in falls—including a memorable one right in her pediatrician's office.

"I don't know if it was because of visual problems or because I didn't know where my body was in space," Chloe says.

High school proved difficult. Teachers frequently assumed she was seeking attention or being purposely manipulative. "There was much more to it," she says. "Behavior serves a purpose in communication."

A turning point came in her early twenties, when she suffered a traumatic experience while at summer camp. She found herself unable to communicate what had happened—even to the people who were closest to her. Later she was diagnosed with PTSD. What most traumatized her was that she wasn't able to speak up or explain herself. "A year later, she said, 'I want to speak because I don't want anyone else to go through what I went through,'" recalls her mother.

She wanted to write a book to explain her experience of the world, to bring understanding of the autistic experience. Struggling to communicate, she began by giving talks to medical students, using preprogrammed messages on an iPad. She was far more fluent and articulate using that method than speaking spontaneously, so she continued communicating using a variety of modes.

Besides developing more effective ways of communicating and supporting others in their communication, she also focused on self-regulation, using anything that worked: a weighted blanket, a sensory room in her family's basement, a small version of Temple Grandin's squeeze machine. "I have so many sensory fidgets that it's not even sad anymore when I break one," she says.

Eager to share her experience and perspective, Chloe also coauthored a book, *My Interoception Workbook*, written with Kelly Mahler, an occupational therapist, and Jarvis Alma, another person on the spectrum. She explains interoception as the eighth sensory sense, the one that helps you feel your body and inner organs and tells you when you're hungry, thirsty, tired, in pain, or other sensations. With visual supports and other strategies, she is now better able to understand the "messages" that her body is communicating to her.

"I love helping people," Chloe says.

Susan, Chloe's mother, has a clear message for other parents of autistic kids: "to understand that your child can do everything or anything that they really want to—they just may need a little more help and we just need to trust our instincts."

And Chloe has a message of her own. "Presume competence," she says. "Don't assume that people can't do something. Get to know them and give them a chance. They're probably extremely capable."

Anita Lesko

"It is not about falling down; it is about getting up"

- Nurse anesthetist and aviation photographer
- Diagnosed at fifty
- Working to educate health care providers to better serve autistic people

Anita Lesko likes to say she discovered she was autistic by accident. She was fifty years old when a coworker's son was diagnosed with Asperger's syndrome. It was the first time she'd heard of it. Curious, Anita asked to see a piece of paper the friend had brought from the appointment. It was a questionnaire asking about certain traits.

"It said if you have ten out of twelve of these, you have Asperger's syndrome. I had all twelve," she says. "All of a sudden, all the pieces of the puzzle fell into place."

Three weeks later, she visited a neuropsychologist who diagnosed her. "It was the greatest gift I had ever received," she says, "to finally know the answers to the mystery of my life."

On the way home, she stopped at a bookstore and purchased a handful of books on the subject. That night, she didn't sleep. She stayed up reading Tony Attwood's *The Complete Guide to Asperger's Syndrome.*

Her predominant emotion was relief. All her life, Anita had felt alone and different from everyone around her—like she didn't fit in. When she was in fifth grade, she listened while her school's principal told her mother that Anita would never amount to anything. Her mother was defiant and always supportive. She was also a best friend for Anita, who over many years never learned to make or keep friends.

"When I was six or seven, I was a little lost soul," she says. "There was a lot of falling down, but it is not about falling down, it is about getting up. Always remember that—there's always the next day to work towards your goals."

In fact, she has pursued her goals with determination. At age twenty-two, when she showed interest in anesthesia, a doctor suggested she become a nurse anesthetist. She pursued that path, graduating from Columbia University with a master's in nurse anesthesia, a field in which she's worked for more than three decades. She specializes in anesthesia for neurosurgery, trauma, organ transplants, burns, and orthopedic joint replacements.

She's also had a longtime interest in aviation photography, dating back to the first time she saw the movie *Top Gun* in 1995. That led to work as a military aviation photographer—and, on one occasion, a flight on an F-15 fighter jet.

Anita has also made a name for herself in the autism world, authoring books, including a memoir, *When Life Hands You Lemons, Make Lemonade.* We met in 2013 when we both presented at the United Nations on World Autism Awareness Day and have collaborated at several conferences since.

Her passionate desire to address healthcare issues resulted in her publication of *The Complete Guide to Autism & Healthcare,* and her goal is to become an international autism advocate, working to radically improve how healthcare professionals and systems serve people on the spectrum. Too often, she has observed, doctors and others don't give the same credence to what autistic patients say about their health as they would to neurotypical patients, so her primary focus is educating health care providers to communicate more effectively with people on the spectrum.

Perhaps her proudest accomplishment, though, is her 2015 marriage to Abraham, who is also autistic. Stephen Shore served as officiant at the first "all-autistic wedding," which took place during the national conference of the Autism Society of America and was open to the public—part of an effort to raise awareness that people on the spectrum have the same need for love and relationships as everyone else. "Having [Abraham] in my life, being able to talk to him after a long day, the two of us together give the feeling of peace, comfort, and security," she says.

Conner Cummings

"If my today try does not work,
I know I have my tomorrow try waiting for me"

- Successfully lobbied for a law benefiting adult children with disabilities whose parents divorce
- Famous for testifying before Congress wearing Mickey Mouse ears

The first thing you should know about Conner Cummings is that he is the force, with his mother, Sharon Lee Cummings, behind Conner's Law, a Virginia statue passed in 2015 that closes a legal loophole to allow single parents of adults with disabilities to receive child support.

The second thing is that he has testified in the U.S. Congress wearing Mickey Mouse ears. He has more than fifty sets of the Mickey-ear hats, accumulated during his semiannual trips with his mother to Walt Disney World. He chooses to don the mouse ears whenever he's in big crowds practically wherever he goes, because they make him feel more comfortable and confident. "It's no different from someone wearing a ball cap with their favorite team on it," he says.

His advocacy and his Mickey ear enthusiasm are both important.

Conner, with whom I've maintained regular contact since we collaborated on an Autism Society of America panel several years ago, has unique ways of expressing himself and staying well-regulated. These combine to make him an estimable activist with an infectious personality. In recognition of his volunteer efforts, the Autism Society of America presented Conner with its Outstanding Advocate of the Year Award.

Earning that kind of honor wasn't what anyone would have predicted when Conner was diagnosed as autistic as a toddler. At age four, he still wasn't speaking, and doctors told his mother that he would never would—or be able to follow more than a single simple command. He started in inclusive classrooms, but struggled. "I was like an outsider," he told me. "I had the desire to make lots of new friends . . . but then I felt like I didn't have any because my social and communication skills were lacking."

To make matters worse, his teachers showed little faith in his abilities and didn't offer accommodations to support him. After one of them intimated that Conner's mother was doing his schoolwork for him, Sharon pulled him out of school, eventually hiring a former classroom teacher to instruct him at her home, where the relative quiet helped him to focus. All along, Conner showed remarkable persistence and drive. As he explains it: "I try things, and if my today try does not work I know I have my tomorrow try waiting for me."

Homeschooling also helped him come to understand his own unique learning style. "It was easier for me to learn by seeing (visual) to help me understand better than hearing," he wrote of his education. "My mom told me that it's okay to learn or do things differently. It does not make me less—in fact, just the opposite, she said companies pay big money for people to look at things 'out of the box.' I am a gift."

At age seven, he began speaking in complete sentences, though to this day he prefers to express himself in writing, which gives him more control and time to process what he hears and formulate what he wants to communicate. That communication style has not limited

Conner, who has studied French and Spanish. His teacher also helps him with life skills: shopping. comparing prices.

Mostly, though, he credits his mother with helping him to maximize his potential. "My mom is very supportive of me. She never gives up on me and she loves me no matter what—and we do fun things together," he says.

That includes frequent visits to Walt Disney World, which he says makes him happy and gives him a magical feeling.

She was in the midst of her divorce from Conner's father in 2013 when she asked for child support. Because of a legal loophole, she lost. Her lawyer said her only choice was to get the law changed. He was half joking, but the idea inspired her to get to work doing just that. She enlisted the help of a state senator, but it was only when Conner himself began speaking out that the proposed law got traction.

Mother and son spoke at Virginia's capitol in Richmond multiple times—Conner always wearing his Mickey ears—making themselves well known among the state's legislators. The law passed with bipartisan support in both houses of the legislature, and when then Gov. Terry McAuliffe finally signed it into law, Conner celebrated by presenting the governor with an autographed pair of Mickey Mouse ears.

In addition to his advocacy, Conner is a talented photographer who has worked as a still photographer on three movie sets. He plays piano, has won Special Olympics medals for ice skating, and has appeared in 911 preparedness videos, designed to help law-enforcement officials understand and interact with people on the spectrum.

As for advice for people on the spectrum Conner is adamant: "Be proud of who you are and not letting anyone tell you different, neither be afraid to take a stand, and also to love and accept themselves never give up and try to learn different things."

That doesn't mean things necessarily get easier.

"Every day there is a challenge for me, but now I face and I welcome them and I look forward to overcome all of my challenges because I am a very positive person," says Conner. "There is absolutely nothing that I can't do."

Ron Sandison

"It takes hard work; it takes love and compassion and vision"

- Hospital psychiatric-care specialist and ordained minister
- Author of books celebrating the diversity of autistic experience

Some people look at life and see only the curses. Then there's Ron Sandison, who focuses on the blessings. Ron's rare combination of optimism, determination, faith, and a drive to help other people on the autism spectrum are infectious and inspiring.

Ron works as a hospital psychiatric-care specialist, but his real passion is empowering people on the autism spectrum. An ordained minister, he speaks regularly about the intersection of autism and faith at churches, synagogues, and mosques. He's also a husband, a father, and the author of three books, all aimed at informing and empowering autistic people and helping others to understand them.

Those accomplishments are even more remarkable in light of Ron's early years. As he tells it, his early development was unremarkable, but sometime after eighteen months, he lost even the most basic words he had learned and stopped making eye contact with his mother.

He struggled in his efforts to interact with other children and had frequent meltdowns. A doctor diagnosed him with an emotional disorder, but Ron's mother didn't accept that assessment. She took him to a neurologist, who diagnosed him as autistic.

Professionals told his parents that Ron was unlikely to read beyond seventh-grade level, wouldn't attend college, and probably wouldn't be able to have meaningful relationships.

Determined to prove the experts wrong, his mother, Janet, "quit her job as an art teacher and became a full-time Ron teacher," says Ron. She used art and other activities to engage him and help him learn.

One year for Christmas, she gave him a stuffed prairie dog he named Prairie Pup. That sparked a special interest, as Ron became fascinated with the minute details of prairie dog life. He'd constantly carry an animal book in his right hand and Prairie Pup in his left.

Following Ron's lead, Janet seized upon that enthusiasm, incorporating Prairie Pup into reading and writing lessons and to engage him socially. Ron would dictate fictional stories about his stuffed animals. He illustrated them and she wrote them down, in turn teaching him reading comprehension and spelling.

School, on the other hand, was difficult. "My speech was so delayed that my brother would introduce me to people and say, 'I think Ron's from Norway,'" he told me. "No one knew what I was saying." His sensory challenges and difficulty reading social cues made it difficult to develop friendships.

He still recalls some of his more awkward social moments, such as the time he learned that the Detroit Lions' football coach, Wayne Fontes, had been fired. "He came to the car wash where I worked, and I handed him a job application and said, 'Wayne, you don't have to be unemployed anymore—we're hiring right here!'"

What helped him connect with peers and find friends were new enthusiasms: he trained so hard that he became a star athlete, running track and cross-country, and also became a devout Christian, memorizing thousands of Bible verses.

That propelled him to an athletic scholarship to a small Christian college, then an academic scholarship at Oral Roberts University, where he earned a master's in divinity.

He credits his parents for recognizing his talent even when others couldn't and for advocating for him. He calls his mother a "mama bear." "She always made sure her cub got what he needed."

And he still keeps Prairie Pup close by. (When we met via Zoom for our Uniquely Human podcast, he proudly held him up to the camera.) Over time, he replaced the original with a series of other stuffed animals. On his honeymoon, he picked up a stuffed honey badger, and for company during the Covid-19 pandemic, a Tasmanian devil.

Over the years, though, his enthusiasms have evolved, he says, "I went from animals to art, to track and cross-country, to preaching, to speaking to people about autism."

He preaches in about twenty-five churches annually, also speaking at conferences and seminars, in keeping with one of the 15,000 New Testament verses he has committed to memory: "Each one should use whatever gift he has received to serve others, faithfully administering God's grace in its various forms."

He sees his gift as educating people about autism and helping people with disabilities to find their own purpose and get the support they need to thrive. In addition to his talks, he has done that in his books, including *Views from The Spectrum*, based on his interviews with twenty extraordinary people on the autism spectrum—from Armani Williams, the NASCAR driver, to Tarik El-Abour, the professional baseball player, to Rachel Barcellona, the activist and beauty-pageant contestant.

"Ninety percent of success in life is connections and people with autism are like worn-out Velcro, we don't connect well," he says. "But if we can learn how to connect well and use our gifts or resources, then we're going to be able to accomplish amazing, awesome things."

It's not always easy to be so optimistic, but Ron's life serves as a reminder that so-called experts' early assessments can often be wrong, and that the support parents, mentors, and others can make all the difference.

Ron speaks a great deal about religion, but when asked what advice he gives to parents and individuals on the spectrum, he says achieving success in life takes more than faith. "It takes hard work; it takes love and compassion and vision; and it takes never giving up," he says.

Surely his life is testimony to that.

Jordyn Zimmerman

"When I started being able to share my thoughts
and aspirations my life changed dramatically"

- Misunderstood and underestimated for years, learned to communicate by typing
- Working to "shift the narrative" for her fellow nonspeaking people on the spectrum

When Jordyn Zimmerman looks back on her early school years, she recounts a relentless and painful mix of isolation, forced ABA therapies, and boredom. One elementary school year, she was put in a class in which students did little but played video games all day. In high school, she was assigned tedious, repetitive tasks: putting cards with teachers' names in alphabetical order, washing bus windows, putting clothes on hangers.

"I was so miserable," she said on our podcast, as she communicated by typing words on an iPad using a text-to-speech app.

Because Jordyn didn't speak, most of her teachers expected little of her, and those who did make efforts found her particularly unmanageable. "She was probably one of the most challenging children I've ever worked with," Wendy Bergant, an autism-program director with three decades of experience, said of Jordyn in an interview in *This Is Not About Me*, a documentary film about Jordyn.

Jordyn recalls a fourth-grade aide discussing her issues in front of her, as if Jordyn weren't there. Even as a girl, Jordyn had aspirations of becoming a teacher, but seeing how her own instructors underestimated her, she says, "I questioned whether my dreams would ever come true."

Middle school was worse, with the sensory overloads triggering meltdown after meltdown. Seeking to contain Jordyn, her high school used a closet as her classroom, isolating her from other students as she received individual instruction from a single aide or teacher.

Frustrated and misunderstood, Jordyn would respond most often in two ways: self-injurious behavior such as banging her head against a wall, or running. When Jordyn ran, teachers and aides would chase her and then restrain her—a pattern that repeated itself for years.

That continued until one teacher, Christy LaPaglia, intervened, taking a particular interest in Jordyn and posting signs around the building to remind Jordyn that if she ran, head for Christy's office. There, Christy would dim the lights and Jordyn would sometimes take refuge under a desk, staying put until she could calm and regulate herself. "I would write her a note: 'How can I help?'"

Others tried to offer communication tools, but Jordyn recalls the options as limited and simple. One book she used in tenth grade, for example, contained words, phrases, and pictures she could point to. But the phrases were generally simple demands and statements: "I want," "I smell," "I see." And the only food option was a cookie. Asked in the film what happened when it was impossible to communicate her feelings or needs, Jordyn said simply, "I would get very frustrated."

That led to the running, the lashing out, the self-injury, the meltdowns.

A breakthrough finally occurred when she was eighteen. It wasn't in a flash, but over time, Jordyn began learning to communicate by touching displays on an iPad. Her progress was halting, starting with images and symbols, and then moving to letters and words. But increasingly, she gained the ability to express her thoughts and feelings, and after a year, she was a nonspeaker communicating effectively on her I-Pad with a text-to-speech app.

"When I started being able to share my thoughts and aspirations," she said, "my life changed dramatically."

In turn, people's perceptions of her also changed. For years, teachers and others had assumed from her silence that Jordyn was unintelligent, unreachable, and incapable. What emerged as she gained fluency in communicating was a bright, funny, and sensitive young woman who was eager to engage with the world despite enduring years of the trauma of being isolated and misunderstood.

With rapidly developing communication abilities, confidence, and support, she graduated high school and went on to college at Ohio University, where she founded an inclusive college cheer team, the Sparkles, and earned a degree in education policy. Determined to pursue a career in education, she went on to Boston College, where she is working toward a master's degree in curriculum and instruction.

"People can no longer say they think they know what I want without asking me and giving me time to provide an answer," Jordyn says.

She has also become deeply involved in advocacy, educating and supporting others, keynoting conferences, and speaking out for the rights of nonspeaking individuals to have access to various modes of alternative and augmentative communication.

While she often types freely and seems to communicate her thoughts and intentions with ease and fluency, it's not always easy. "I still have many gaps I have to work through," she admits. "For example. I know many more words in my head than I can spell."

And then there are the external barriers. In 2019, when she had a summer internship in Washington, D.C., with an advocacy group, the National Disability Rights Network, Jordyn visited the U.S. Supreme Court during a hearing. But a security screener refused to let her bring her iPad inside, after some negotiation offering a pen and paper—which were of little help. "It goes to show how the highest court in the land is not expected to be held to a standard of providing communication access," she says.

That experience underscored the importance of the work she has made her personal mission: increasing opportunities, options, and access to meet the communication needs of nonspeaking people. Her goal: to "shift the narrative about our own lives and what is possible."

While she aims for that lofty goal, Jordyn has more practical advice for educators and families who come in contact with nonspeaking people. She points out that too often, people often have short attention spans. Holding a conversation with someone who types like Jordyn can entail silent pauses of several minutes while the person formulates and types what they wish to say. Sometimes, she says, the listener simply walks away before the answer comes. Her suggestion is both simple and profound. "Probably the most important advice," Jordyn says, "is to be patient."

Scott Steindorff

"I love how I perceive life, I love how
I'm creative, and I love my sensitivity"

- Overcame alcohol and drug addiction to find success in Hollywood
- Diagnosed late in life, he aims to raise awareness of neurodiversity to help others on the spectrum lead successful lives

Growing up in a small town in Minnesota, Scott Steindorff never felt like he fit in. He had difficulty speaking, his motor skills were awkward, he avoided looking people in the eye.

"I remember my father telling my mom I was just slow," he says.

Unable to account for his unease and seeming disconnectedness, a teacher told his parents that ten-year-old Scott might be taking drugs.

His obvious challenges made him the victim of incessant bullying—until he finally retaliated, punching one of the bullies so hard that the others backed off.

From an early age, Scott also escaped through writing, taking refuge in the process of creating imaginary worlds with words. He found another outlet in athletics, becoming a competitive snow skier and committing so fully to the sport that he landed a spot on the U.S. Ski Team.

It was when days as a skier ended that he grew depressed, turning his energies to making money in real estate, and then like many neurodivergent people facing personal struggles, he took comfort in alcohol and eventually drugs. "Cocaine made me feel powerful and whole—like I had never felt before," says Scott, who ended up more than once in an emergency room. "I knew if I kept doing this I was going to die."

Finally landing in rehab, he experienced what he calls a shift in consciousness, and sought out less harmful outlets. He devoured books, taking in three or four a week. He got married. He started a business. None of that did away with his sense of inadequacy.

"I still felt like that ten-year-old boy, getting bullied and teased with low esteem and low self-worth," he says.

Still, knowing he might not survive another encounter with alcohol or drugs, he was determined to stay sober. He was also committed to professional accomplishment, forging a career as a television and film producer specializing in adapting literary bestsellers for the screen. He built a portfolio that includes such hits as the films *The Lincoln Lawyer* and *Chef* and the Emmy award–winning TV miniseries *Empire Falls*, coproduced with Paul Newman.

Even with that success, he continued to struggle. Doctors diagnosed him as a highly sensitive person (HSP) and with ADHD.

But it wasn't until one of his daughters, diagnosed with ADHD, was working with a therapist that she suggested to Scott, then in his sixties, that he was on the autism spectrum.

His first reaction was shame, but the more he investigated, the more the diagnosis made sense. "I started working with a therapist and started to understand what was going on with me." The more he learned, the more he came to understand challenges he had experienced: difficulty in relationships and in understanding his own emotions, avoiding looking people in the eye in business meetings, an aversion to attention.

"I started a process of uncovering and discovering who I was, and my perception of my past changed drastically."

His daughter told him she had been embarrassed to invite friends home because Scott spoke so loudly, missed social cues, and would sometimes leave a conversation mid-sentence.

Over time, he came to embrace being on the spectrum. "I am unique, I'm not damaged," he says.

He also came to appreciate that he could attribute much of his success—at sports, at business, at writing—to his wiring and his ability to focus like a laser on a topic or project. "Somebody asked me, 'Would you have changed it?' " he said of his autism diagnosis. "No, because I love how I perceive life, I love how I'm creative, and I love my sensitivity."

What he does regret is that no one helped him come to that realization earlier in life. With appropriate knowledge and support, he says, "so many of my life's problems could have been averted."

Which is why Scott has dedicated himself to bringing attention to autism and to making mental-health professionals and educators more attuned to neurodivergence. He's on a mission to increase recognition of autism and related conditions in the general population, as he believes neurodivergent individuals too often either live their lives undiagnosed and misunderstood or choose to remain "in the closet." Through a neurodiversity program at Arizona State University, he is also working to raise sensitivity and awareness of autism among students. Having produced entertainment for NBC, Netflix, and HBO Max, among others, he's determined to use his influence in Hollywood to help remove the stigma and shame commonly associated with being on the spectrum.

His aim is to help people on the spectrum experience the success—both personal and professional—that he has finally been able to achieve himself. "This is the most important thing in my life," he says. "I'm autistic and I'm proud."

CHAPTER 13

Energize the Spirit

SOMETIMES a question is a revelation. Some years ago I was at the parent retreat I help to facilitate when a mother seated beside me tapped on my arm to get my attention. It was the first retreat for Cynthia, a parent whom we think of as "new to it all." Her son, then just two and a half, had recently been diagnosed, so most of what she was hearing was new and unfamiliar information. Over two days she had taken in the discussions among parents, many with years, even decades of experience with autistic loved ones. She had listened as some parents recounted their children's enthusiasms and idiosyncrasies, and others discussed battles with school administrators and the challenges of navigating disorganized support systems. She had met one mom who expressed gratitude for discovering a suitable residential school for her nineteen-year-old and another who spoke openly about the challenges of balancing work with motherhood.

Then, just before the retreat's emotional closing circle, Cynthia turned to me. "Dr. Prizant," she whispered, "I have a question for you." She told me about a website she had come across that claimed its online program helped autistic children in such extraordinary ways that some had "recovered" from autism. She wanted my opinion. She described the testimonials she had read from parents whose children had made remarkable strides in reducing the symptoms of autism within weeks or months merely by following the recommended activities. The cost? Nearly a thousand dollars. "What do you think, Dr. Prizant?"

Her question reminded me of the many times parents have approached me with a related query. "If money weren't an object," they ask, "if I weren't bound geographically by my career or family, where would you suggest that we relocate to get the best services for our child?" These parents harbor the belief that somewhere out there is a mecca of autism services. There's a school or a doctor or a therapist that just might be able to rid their child, and thus the family, of all of the challenges associated with autism.

Where, they ask, should we go? What city, what school?

The answer: It's not that simple. There is no one professional or clinic, no magical place, no treatment approach offering all the answers and the plan to render a child "normal" so that families can put autism behind them and move on with their lives.

Nobody would blame Cynthia, the mother of a young child, for pursuing all options in her quest to give her son the best possible life. Nor would anyone fault families for seeking out the best services available. They want what all parents want: for their children to be happy, to lead fulfilling lives, to make the most of their potential, and to progress through their teen and adults years as respected, engaged, and valued members of their communities. In short, parents want what's best for their children. But when the challenges associated with autism and co-occurring conditions enter the equation and become the primary focus, it's easy to lose track of what's important.

The Question of Recovery

Some approaches to autism make "recovery" their explicit goal—the notion that a person can overcome autism the way one might conquer cancer or rebound from a heart attack or stroke. Whether that is possible, or even desirable, remains an open question. A 2019 study published in the Journal of Child Neurology followed 569 children found that, over time, a very small percentage of children experienced such improvements in symptoms that they no longer met the *DSM* autism-diagnostic criteria, but most still had "difficulties that required therapeutic and educational support." The study found no way to predict which children would show such gains, or why.

This view of autism defines recovery as reducing the number of "autistic symptoms" below a certain threshold to such a degree that a person no longer meets the DSM criteria for diagnosis. Yet many of the most successful people on the autism spectrum I know well (Temple Grandin, Stephen Shore, Michael John Carley, Becca Lory Hector, Dave Finch, Dena Gassner, and now hundreds of others), who by all measures enjoy full lives, do not refer to themselves as having recovered. They have fulfilling careers, are active community members, and some have families with children. Others who were once considered to have recovered from autism as children later identify and self-diagnose as being autistic adults. And many other autistic adults, even some who say they are free of most obvious symptoms or have learned to expend great energy to "mask" their autism and therefore are largely able to pass for "neurotypical," resent the emphasis on recovery, many viewing autism as an inseparable, integral part of their identity.

A person can enjoy a good quality of life whether or not his behavior meets the criteria for autism. As one teenager told his parents when they first broached the topic of his diagnosis, "I *love* my autism."

Whether or not "recovery" is possible, pursuing it as a singular goal and viewing it as the principal marker of a successful outcome can be emotionally and financially exhausting for parents and stressful for autistic children and adults, particularly when the treatment focus is on reducing "autistic behaviors" or learning how to mask or hide them. And when professionals present "recovery" as likely— despite research indicating it is rare, as well as considerable controversy as to how "recovery" is even defined and whether its pursuit is desirable—they violate ethics of professional practice, especially when they make such claims to promote their services.

Maintaining hope in the prospect of minimizing the challenges associated with autism and achieving good quality of life need not be inextricably linked to "recovery." (Some simply call it "making great progress," "overcoming challenges" or "enhancing quality of life.")

When families make recovery their preeminent goal, they can miss the beauty of the child's developmental breakthroughs and unique characteristics, just as a driver focused only on the destination doesn't notice the beauty of the scenery along the way.

In contrast, I have watched many parents derive great enjoyment from the small gains and daily progress their school-age and adult children make—precisely because they are focused on the journey across the life span. The incremental gains add up to large transformations that improve the quality of life for autistic people and their families.

Sheila described that distinction better than anyone I've met. Her son Pablo was a sweet ten-year-old who had high anxiety and sensory sensitivities. He could speak, but his dysregulation made it difficult to keep him consistently engaged. For years Sheila felt desperate to change him and rid him of his autism, trying a multitude of alternative diets and various other treatments. It was only when she came to our parents retreat, met parents just like her, and heard of their struggles and triumphs that she paused and saw her efforts in a new light.

With tears in her eyes, she shared with the group her epiphany: "I keep trying and trying to fix Pablo, and what I've learned is that he's whole and he's happy." Voice quivering, she added, "We do need to pursue whatever we can to make our children's lives more comfortable and happy, but they really are whole—and *they* can fix *us*."

Different Families, Different Dreams

Focusing on the journey looks different in every family, just as it does for parents raising any child. As part of my private practice, I once visited two different families for consultations in their homes within a few days. Each set of parents had a child under three recently diagnosed with autism. My role in each case was to confirm the diagnosis, and then to begin a conversation about what the future might hold and how the family might proceed.

After the initial discussion of the diagnosis, the first father asked me a question: "Do you think he'll ever go to college?" That was his top concern: Would his son succeed academically?

With the second family, our initial discussion was almost identical, but then the boy's mother asked me her own question: "We want to know, will our daughter be happy?" That question led to more: "Will she have friends and be around people who love her? Will she be a respected member of her community?"

Every family is different. Same diagnosis, same stage in the journey, very different priorities.

My friend Barbara Domingue (see Chapter 10) once gave me a framed print I hung in my office. It's a surrealistic picture of a man on a tightrope walking toward a distant, sun-like light. Only one end of the rope is secured—the end behind him. The segment of the rope extending in front of where he stands he's holding in his hands, so his next step is into thin air. In Barbara's interpretation, the man represents a family just after receiving an autism diagnosis for their child: the parents realize they are beginning a long journey, but it's one they will have to invent with every step. Choosing each and every step can be fraught with anxiety and the fear that one misstep may result in doom for the child and family. Unfortunately, some professionals whose role is to be helpful, actually instigate and perpetuate that fear.

Such feelings may extend beyond the time of diagnosis in childhood. In fact every part of the journey can feel that way. Even when things are stable, even when parents feel like they're walking on solid ground, at any moment things can change—a beloved therapist moves away, a school program is a bad fit, a child approaches puberty and adolescence with a transition to a new school—and the parents become tightrope walkers again.

To extend the metaphor, there is a complicating factor: as you improvise your way, trying to keep your balance, all kinds of people offer advice and direction, too often resulting in distraction and even guilt.

"Make a right turn here!"

"Take a left turn there!"

"Now, do a double flip and land on your feet!"

Parents and caregivers can feel chronic stress as they constantly second-guess whether they are making the best choices for their children or family members. At many junctures there is no clear answer, no certain choice. A professional might insist that the child needs forty hours of therapy per week. A parent asserts that a particular treatment that did wonders for her child would surely do the same for yours too. One swears by inclusion; another home-schooling; another insists on a private autism school; a fourth declares that a gluten-free diet is a must. Parents can feel that one misstep, one wrong choice (or failure to make a choice) will cause irreparable harm.

All of that can make it difficult to look toward the future, for parents to consider *What is it that we're walking toward, anyway? What is my light? What are our hopes and dreams for our child? How should we make the right choices to fulfill them? Is this what my child wants and needs?*

Every parent answers differently. Every family has a unique set of priorities, goals, and dreams. And of course, many autistic teens and adults, and even young children have their own goals and desires for the future.

Small Steps, Shifting Perspective

It's natural to have anxiety about the future. The mother of a five-year-old boy told me recently that she sometimes wakes up in the middle of the night, filled with worry about what her son will be like when he's fifteen. Other parents say they don't allow themselves to get caught up in worry about the future. When Justin Canha was a teen, someone asked his mother about his future life as an adult. "I just can't go there," she said. "One step at a time."

Parents often express concern that if a child hasn't reached a certain developmental milestone by age three or five or seven, it's too late. Somewhere they have heard that if a child doesn't speak a certain number of words by age five, hope is lost. Or that the focus should be only on speech because using AAC (Alternative and Augmentative communication) isn't *real* communication. Or that a young child's IQ or academic achievement can predict the child's future. (All not true.)

When the challenges seem greatest, hope can be in short supply. I have met many parents whose children have not developed speech at a young age. They've heard either that if a child doesn't speak by age five, she will likely never speak, or that introducing AAC will prevent speech development and speech training is the only hope. Both are not true; development continues throughout life, and not only can AAC be a very effective means to communicate, in some cases it may actually support speech development. Still these parents feel desperate to see the child develop speech as quickly as possible. When that doesn't happen, they feel discouraged. They feel burnt out. Their hope dissipates. Overly focused on a particular goal, they see everything through that prism, and it becomes difficult for them to perceive the strengths, the accomplishments, or even to see the child. Unfortunately, in some instances the child's happiness and emotional well-being is the casualty as the pursuit of recovery results in chronic stress for both the child and family.

What helps in those situations is reframing. Even when a child is not speaking, there are often signs of engagement: he might be intentionally looking at his mother or father; she has started pointing or waving. These are initial indications of social interest, a foundation for and stepping stone to more advanced communication abilities supported by multimodal means to communicate (gestures, sounds, words, AAC systems). Often parents are so singularly focused on getting the child to speak that they don't notice such promising indicators. When a child takes her mother by the hand to bring her to the refrigerator, she is not merely "using a person as a tool," as some dismiss such actions; it is intentional communication, a starting point from which to build. As much as we dream about major leaps, often it's these small steps that indicate progress and offer hope.

It's also helpful for parents or caregivers to get to know families that have been down the same road. At our parent retreat, the mother of a three-year-old might meet the father of a teen or young adult who had the same challenges at a young age. The young adult might not speak but uses an iPad or spelling board to communicate. Her parents maintain a positive attitude, they surround her with love and affection and helpful supports, and it's clear she leads a happy, self-determined, and fulfilled life.

Amir is a young man with minimal speech who runs a business baking cookies that are sold in local shops and at the community theatre managed by his parents. His parents admit that when he was a teenager, they could not have imagined him doing such a thing. He has a good quality of life. He has a purpose. He is involved with his community. He takes pride in his work. He feels good about himself. And his parents say they cannot imagine life without having their adult son living at home.

It's a reminder that human development is a lifelong process—and that priorities shift. What seems critically important at one stage might feel less so in a few years.

Happiness and Sense of Self, or Academic Success?

Parents want to know what a child's school program should focus on to guarantee the greatest success when he becomes an adult. What abilities and qualities are important for a person to have to help assure the best quality of life? Here are my top priorities: building self-expression and self-esteem, instilling happiness, creating positive experiences, and emphasizing healthy relationships. It's also important to increase self-awareness, and the ability to emotionally self-regulate and when needed, accept support from others.

When you have positive emotional experiences, it motivates you to learn and explore, builds self-confidence and the desire to connect with other people, set personal goals, and seek out more varied experiences. In other words, it enhances your quality of life. Being happy also makes you a more desirable person to be with. It makes people seek you out. This becomes obvious when you watch children interact in groups. When a child is anxious and edgy or sullen and dour, others avoid her. But if the same children encounter a child who is perceived as approachable: cheerful, smiling, playful, and well-regulated, they are drawn to him. Happiness is a natural connector.

Yet many parents, educators, and therapists prioritize academic achievement over instilling happiness, even if it greatly increases stress and dysregulation. In fact I have heard a prominent proponent of behavioral approaches take issue with the idea of emphasizing happiness, arguing that for autistic children, it is far more important to develop skills than to be happy. In other words, measuring happiness is not relevant, we should be measuring skills.

Not only is this way of thinking misguided, but it misses the point. Children—and all human beings—learn more readily when they are happy. They retain and recall information more effectively when they feel positive emotion. When we try to learn under persistently stressful situations, we are more on guard, retain less, and it's more difficult for us to access what we learned. But when we're feeling positive emotion and trust the world we live in, we're more primed for learning experiences and our learning is deeper and far more meaningful. When we enjoy and trust the people around us, we feel more motivated to learn and to take risks.

Again and again I have encountered educators who push students too hard, stressing academics instead of considering the big picture. Often educators are under pressure from administrators following policies that measure success only in terms of academic performance. In extreme cases the result is school refusal—the child resists going to school. Other children simply shut down. At the very least the pressure creates stresses and negative emotional memories that can be difficult to overcome. Instead of narrowly focusing on academics or letting the standard curriculum be the guide, it's essential to consider the development of the whole person and to make the necessary accommodations and choices that foster happiness and availability for learning and engaging. *That* results in the best quality of life.

The Importance of Self-Determination

I was once invited to present a workshop in Christchurch, a picturesque city that is among the largest in New Zealand. I learned it was customary for representatives of the local indigenous people of Polynesian descent, the Maori, to open such events with a brief prayer service. When I arrived at the crowded conference hall, an organizer introduced me to the Maori elder, a tall, broad gentleman holding a carved wooden staff. I felt humbled and honored when the elder invited me to take part in the brief ceremony. It opened with the participants greeting one another, each pressing his nose and forehead against the other's, proceeding down a line. The exchange, called a *Hongi*, symbolizes the ritual of sharing your spirit when you greet another person.

Then, seconds before I was to begin my presentation, the elder approached me, leaned over, and with his lips practically touching my ear, whispered a short sentence: "I trust that you will convey the message that in order to advance the mind, we must first energize the spirit."

As I took in the words, I felt a vibration shoot through my body. For in that sentence he had summed up much of what I believe about the lives of autistic people: that the best way to help autistic and neurodivergent individuals progress toward fulfilling, meaningful lives is to find ways to engage them with deep respect, to help them build a sense of self, and to foster connection and joyful experiences.

We must energize the spirit. Each year I meet dozens of autistic people. When I think about these encounters, it's often in terms of spirit: *He's got a great spirit. She's a spirited child. They're such free spirits.* These are the kinds of people who draw people to them, who can fill a room with joy and wonder. Others seem lethargic, passive, cautious, disengaged, or even fearful or traumatized. About those people we might say, *His spirit has been broken*, or *We need to lift her spirits.*

The difference may be caused, or at least greatly influenced by innate factors, such as severe sensory or biomedical issues, but more often the more spirited individuals are those who have been given choices and opportunities in life, with the right supports. Their enthusiasms have been honored and nurtured. They have been given a say in their own situation. That doesn't mean they can live their lives without support; for some that's possible, and for others it's not an immediate goal. In fact, it may be wrong to elevate "independence" as the most desirable goal. Increasingly, we are learning from autistic people, such as Becca Lory Hector, that quality of life may be more highly correlated with *interdependence*, having secure and trusting relationships and knowing how to rely on other people and communities for support. What is of critical importance is *self-determination*—a personal sense of identity, recognition of what one loves and wants, and some degree of say over one's own life—not being controlled by someone else, not being expected to endlessly comply and respond to prompts.

Some parents begin thinking about self-determination only when their autistic children are entering the late teen years and adulthood and weighing the options that are available or can be created. But the conversation should start earlier—as early as preschool. In raising, teaching, and supporting young people on the spectrum, we ought to ask constantly "What can we do that will ultimately help this child or adult to lead the most self-determined, fulfilled life possible?" That's why it is essential to offer choices whenever possible instead of forcing a particular expectation on an individual. The goal shouldn't be to fix the person or make her appear "normal" (whatever that is), but rather to help her develop the ability to make her own decisions, to exert control over her own life.

When Jesse, who had once been deeply dysregulated, got the opportunity to deliver mail and organize recycling with friends, contributing to his school and enhancing his pride as a middle schooler, he was taking steps toward self-determination.

When Scott, who had been so annoyed by his previous therapist, forbade me from using the term "Good job," he was expressing his self-determination.

When Ned, who was afraid to ride the ferry, was given the chance to opt out but instead decided he would be brave, he was learning about being self-determined.

When Justin was commanded to make eye contact and have good manners by his autistic friend, and he responded, "Manners suck," he was exercising his self-determination.

When Ros wouldn't come to dinner until she'd had her chance to jump on a trampoline, she was demonstrating what it means to be an adult with full self-understanding and control of her own life.

When parents and teachers and members of extended communities offer choices, create opportunities, and empower autistic and neurodivergent people, we not only help to advance their minds; we also energize their spirits.

EPILOGUE

EVERY year when our autism parent retreat concludes, the moms and dads who have joined together express a mix of elation and longing. On the one hand, they have delighted in these few days of connection, understanding, and being understood. On the other, as they head back to their homes and their day-to-day lives, they wonder how they can ever recreate what they have found in this place and with these people with whom they have shared, laughed, cried, and smiled.

"The retreat showed me how important it is to gather together and share experiences or just be present in a place where all the members understand your glories, frustrations, and griefs," said Juan Carlos, father to two children on the spectrum.

Some parents speak of how meeting other families dealing with similar stresses and challenges made them feel less isolated, literally saving their marriages. Other parents emphasize how important it was to meet and learn from the autistic adults we invite as guests. In short, what they have experienced at the weekend we offer with our partners, the parent-professionals of Community Autism Resources, is the power of belonging to a community of support—a community that sees you, hears you, understands you, and values you just as you are.

It strikes me that coming to the end of *Uniquely Human* isn't so different from departing the retreat. The world is full of negative messages and misunderstandings about autism, and too often the people who are supposed to be helping and uplifting autistic people and their families instead portray autism as tragic, painful, and difficult. In these pages, we've tried to show another side—what it means to be uniquely human and live in a uniquely human family. Getting to know Ros Blackburn and Justin Canha, hearing the voices of Morénike Gina-Onaiwu and Jordyn Zimmerman, learning from Stephen Shore, Carly Ott, and Chloe Rothschild, you may wonder, how can I bring these extraordinary people and their outlook and message into my life? How can my family and my loved one be recognized and appreciated and valued for being uniquely human as these people are?

The best answer I have is by finding communities of support. Places physical, social, spiritual, and even virtual where you can connect and learn and talk and where you can be appreciated and valued and supported just as you are. I'm not talking about therapeutic enterprises that are focused on making autistic people look more "normal" or trying to fit round pegs into square holes. I'm talking about communities where you and your family are seen and understood, where you share humor and experiences and insights.

Where to find such communities? Some of the best I have experienced are performance and expressive arts programs such as the Miracle Project programs in Los Angeles and New England, Elaine Hall's creation, where autistic and neurodivergent kids and teens and their neurotypical peers collaborate in creating musical theater productions and other inspiring activities. Where parents take pride in the creativity of their family members. Even as the Covid-19 pandemic raged, the Miracle Projects continued to forge bonds via Zoom, giving the participants a way to connect, see each other and be seen. "Sure the coronavirus is scary," one of the actors, Nick, wrote, "but it is amazing that we are all in this together."

Programs that I am proud to be a part of, like the Miracle Project, and Spectrum Theatre Ensemble, an adult professional company, create opportunities for participants to connect over shared interests and having their voices heard, giving each a shared sense of membership. "It's a place where I can follow my love of acting without being criticized or bullied for my disabilities," said Julia, an actor in Spectrum Theater Ensemble. "It's for the people who understand me and don't mind if I mess up my lines."

Performing arts groups are just one kind of community. The right school can be a community of support. So can a group that gathers just to talk. Becca Lory Hector told me she found community among the other women who wrote pieces for the essay anthology called *Spectrum Women*. She has never met most of them in person, but through their stories, through emails and texts and Zooms, these autistic women have transcended time and geography to connect in real and deep ways.

Whether on your block, in your neighborhood, in your city, in your community of worship, or in some virtual form—or in occasional gatherings like our parent retreat—communities are out there, and they are the best ways to create and foster quality of life for people who are uniquely human and for their families.

Of course, one of the great ironies about autism is that for so long, autistic people were portrayed as living in their own world, having no social instinct or awareness, no compassion, no desire to connect with other human beings. Nothing could be further from the truth. The more we listen to people on the spectrum the more we know that they desire social connection as much as anyone else, are as much in need of the validation, love, and appreciation that all human beings crave. In fact, because the social constructs of society can make such connections so difficult, they often crave connection even more.

The good news is that supportive communities are out there— communities where you and your loved one can be appreciated, respected, accepted, and embraced not in spite of being uniquely human, but because you are uniquely human.

I'll give the last word to my friend Dena Gassner, an autistic mother of an autistic son and an internationally known expert on autism, a social worker, college professor, and mentor to countless autistic people. When Dena was on "Uniquely Human: The Podcast," I asked her about what messages she shares with the autistic people she mentors and those who have not yet connected with the autistic community. Her poignant words spoke to the power of supportive community, and to the beautiful ways that, more and more, autistic people and their families are there for each other.

"We're waiting for you," Dena said. "Your community is waiting for you. We are your culture. We are your family. We are your tribe. And we're waiting for you."

My wish for you is that you, as an individual or a family, find the community that embraces you as the uniquely human people you are.

FREQUENTLY ASKED QUESTIONS

N OT long ago I traveled to the emirate of Dubai to present a workshop on autism. Parents and professionals had flown in from all over the Middle East and as far away as Nigeria. In appearance the audience hardly resembled the kinds of groups I'm accustomed to addressing in the United States, Europe, or Australia. Many of the women were dressed in burkas, and some wore the traditional head coverings known as niqabs. But their questions were practically identical to those I have heard from parents, educators, and therapists in places as varied as mainland China, New Zealand, and Israel: Why does my child spin and rock? Should I let my son have so much time with the iPad? Will my daughter ever speak? How can I get my spouse to accept that our child is autistic and he won't just "outgrow" it? What can I do about a girl in my class who won't engage with other children? How can I get my student to stop biting his hand? How can my adult son's deep interests lead to job opportunities? Parents the world over want the best for their children and family members, educators want answers, all kinds of professionals and support staff want the best information available. To help, here are some responses to some of the many questions I most frequently receive.

How can you tell if a person has high-functioning autism or low-functioning autism? What about Asperger's syndrome?

At just two and a half Eric can assemble puzzles too complex for most four-year-olds. But he can't speak yet, and he communicates mostly through gestures. Is Eric high-functioning or low-functioning?

Eight-year-old Amanda is able to function academically at grade level in her fourth-grade class. But if she doesn't have the assistance of an aide, she can become so anxious that she bolts from the classroom, or even out the door of the school. Is Amanda high-functioning or low-functioning?

Dominic, who is fifteen, doesn't speak, communicating instead with a speech-generating device. He spends half of his school day in a special education classroom. His classmates and teachers love and appreciate him, and he enjoys greeting his many friends on the playground. Is Dominic high-functioning or low-functioning?

Layla is an artist in her thirties whose pet portraits are in great demand on her online shop. Yet she experiences cycles of severe depression and rarely leaves her parents' basement due to paralyzing challenges with social anxiety and sensory sensitivities. Is Layla high or low functioning?

Though these terms have become commonplace, I do not use them. I have long been a student of child and human development, and I am keenly aware of how simplistic these characterizations are. People are infinitely complex, and development is multidimensional and cannot be reduced to such a simple dichotomy.

Besides that, the terms are so imprecise as to lack meaning. "High-functioning" and "low-functioning," along with "severely autistic," "profoundly autistic," and "mildly autistic," have become pseudo-diagnostic categories without commonly accepted definitions or any corresponding diagnostic criteria. The most recent edition of the *Diagnostic and Statistical Manual of Mental Disorders*, the *DSM-5*, provoked controversy when it abandoned all subcategories of Autism Spectrum Disorder, so that Asperger's syndrome was no longer a distinct diagnosis. Long before that there was debate about whether Asperger's and high-functioning autism were the same or different since no clearly defined diagnostic boundaries existed.

I have often observed how terribly inaccurate and misleading the terms *low-functioning* and *high-functioning* autism are when applied to children and adults I have known well, and using them seems disrespectful and too often, only represents brief snapshots in time. When mothers and fathers hear the term *low-functioning* applied to their children, they are hearing a limited, piecemeal view of their child's abilities and potential, ignoring the whole child. Even when a child is described as "high-functioning," parents often point out that he continues to experience major challenges that educators and others too often minimize or ignore. Furthermore, those who appear more capable or even neurotypical when well regulated are often judged more harshly, as are their parents, than individuals who have more obvious disabling conditions.

When professionals apply these sorts of labels early in a child's development, it can have the effect of unfairly predetermining an individual's potential: if "low," don't expect much; if "high," she'll do fine and doesn't need support. The label often becomes a self-fulfilling prophecy. Yet children who appear more challenged (and therefore need more support) early in their lives often make wonderful developmental progress over time. Some kids are later bloomers, and all development is lifelong. Instead of focusing on vague and imprecise labels, it's better to focus on the person's relative strengths and challenges and to identify the most beneficial supports.

I've heard that the window of opportunity for helping an autistic child closes after age five. After that is it too late to expect any meaningful progress?

In short, no. Many parents hear from another parent or from a therapist or they've read on a website that it's important to do as much early intervention as possible because at some point the opportunity for improvement vanishes. Some parents hear that if a child isn't exposed to a particular form of therapy for a certain number of hours by age five, the opportunity for progress has been missed. This makes parents feel guilty that they are letting down their children if they fail to provide the recommended level of intensive therapies.

The truth: There is no evidence that a window of opportunity closes at age five. Research does indicate that one of the predictors of better outcomes for autistic children is earlier intervention with family support, but it simply doesn't follow that if you don't start early, there is little hope for meaningful ongoing progress. Many parents notice significant growth and progress between eight and thirteen years and far into adulthood. It's also true that there are critical periods in human development for some abilities; for example, if you're not exposed to a language early in life, it becomes much more difficult to master it later. In many other areas, however, development is truly a lifelong process of increasing competence and gaining skills—for all of us, including autistic people. In fact, many autistic people who are initially misdiagnosed or never diagnosed in childhood report that some of their greatest gains in quality of life occurred following a professional diagnosis or self-diagnosis as adults, often as late as 50 or 60 years of age!

I strongly encourage starting early with a well-coordinated, comprehensive plan that is a good fit for a family's lifestyle and culture. Yet many parents tell me that advice they received caused them such worry about missing the "critical window" that they poured money and energy into therapies that were not appropriate choices for their children. Many parents follow a prescribed plan, no matter how stressful or disruptive, out of anxiety and fear. That's not necessary, and it can cause stress on parents and children alike. At one of our parent retreats, a mother described how she surfed the Internet until 3 a.m. every night in search of the next breakthrough for her four-year-old son, not realizing her habit was having a debilitating impact on her family and marriage. A well-coordinated plan is just as relevant for adults on the spectrum. The plan should align with the individual's goals and lifestyle, and can incorporate living circumstances, vocational and leisure-time opportunities, and social connections.

As a guideline, research on preschool- and school-age children indicates that twenty-five hours per week of active engagement, focused on social communication, emotional regulation, and learning is optimum. These hours can be *a planned part of everyday activities and routines*, as simple as brushing teeth or making popcorn, or playing with siblings, not just therapies provided by professionals. Piling on additional hours of one-to-one therapy does not necessarily add value.

Some autistic people seem hyperactive, but others appear lethargic. What explains that?

Autism is called a *spectrum disorder* because the abilities and challenges of autistic people fall along a continuum, and no two people manifest autism in the same way. One individual seems so revved up all the time he can't settle down, while his autistic classmate often seems sluggish and spacey.

This phenomenon is known as *arousal bias*. All humans navigate through various states of physiological arousal on a daily basis. The pediatrician T. Berry Brazelton described these "bio-behavioral" states in infants that are relevant for all humans.

The states range from the low end (deep sleep or drowsy) up to the high end (agitated, anxious, even giddy or elated).

We all have a bias in one direction or the other. The challenge for many autistic people is that they are either too "low bias" or too "high bias"; that is, they tend to be either under-aroused (too low) or overaroused (too high) too much of the time. When the task or setting calls for a quiet, focused state, the child is agitated and easily distracted. When the situation requires being active, the child is drowsy or unfocused. To complicate matters, people sometimes shift rapidly from being too high arousal to too low arousal, sometimes within a few hours.

Autistic people often have difficulty navigating between different arousal states to meet the requirements of an activity or the environment. A kindergartner's high-arousal state works well on the playground, but then she gets so revved up that she can't come down to a quiet alert state when it's time to sit for circle time. The goal is to find the right supports to help a person maximize her time in a state that is appropriate for the specific activity.

In working or living with an autistic person, it's important to be mindful of that person's arousal bias, which manifests itself in multiple sensory channels: tactile, auditory, visual, olfactory. A low-arousal, young hypo-reactive child might experience sound such as the human voice as so indistinct that it's difficult to get her attention when calling her name. A high-arousal, hyperreactive person might be so sensitive to sound and touch that even noises at normal intensity can be overwhelming and the pain from a small scratch can be excruciating.

How can a parent or teacher help kids who are too high or low energy or too under- or overreactive? Often what a child needs is a complement to his natural bias. If the child is lethargic, be energetic; if the child is anxious and hyperkinetic, be a calming presence. As always, the best approach isn't to try changing the person but to change our approach to be the most supportive and effective. This requires a sensitive reading of the person's signals so we can make the appropriate adjustments in the environment and our own behavior. (When natural supports are not effective for individuals with extreme high activity and anxiety, medication prescribed and monitored by a physician may play a supportive role as part of a comprehensive plan.)

What is the single most important thing I can do to help a person on the autism spectrum?

In my experience, the best thing parents, educators, and other partners can do for an autistic child or adult is to get them out in the world—with the appropriate supports. Of course that's true of all people, not just those on the autism spectrum: the people who progress the most, who develop to their fullest potential, are those who are exposed to a wide variety of experiences.

Parents of young autistic adults and older teens who are successful in handling everyday challenges invariably agree about what made the most significant positive difference in their child's life: that they always made an effort to get the child out, to avoid sheltering the child—to make the child part of the mainstream of life. Autistic adults agree. They feel that having varied experiences with appropriate supports has allowed them to feel confident in seeking out, coping with, and enjoying new situations. By doing so they are exposed to challenges and offered opportunities to learn coping skills to stay well-regulated. No parent wants to experience their child having a meltdown amid the crowds and noise at an amusement park or be on an airplane with a child who needs to move constantly to stay well regulated. But when you shelter a child from all the bumps of life, you're preventing him from opportunities for social and emotional growth. No autistic person wants to be cast into dysregulating "sink-or-swim" situations that are challenging and unfamiliar without having many experiences that prepare them to be actively and successfully engaged in such activities and environments. David Sharif, a young adult on the spectrum, identifies his enthusiasm as being a world traveler. He attributes his strong problem-solving abilities, flexibility, and comfort in taking risks to his traveling experiences. Ros Blackburn, my autistic friend from England, has progressed from avoiding air travel due to her anxiety, to traveling with a companion, and eventually with careful planning, to traveling solo.

An autistic person might feel anxious and frightened about going into a noisy restaurant or experiencing a particular amusement park ride. But if she tries, and receives appropriate support, it can be a learning experience and even quite enjoyable. Next time, the parent or caregiver can say, "Remember last time? You were anxious about it, but it turned out you were fine." If the person never gets the opportunity to try, how can she progress? And if that person tries a new experience and finds it challenging, it's okay to leave or shorten the time of the visit. There's always an opportunity to add appropriate supports and try again next time. And whenever possible, a person should be given choices based on her sense of how she is feeling.

Can a child who is loving and cuddly still be on the autism spectrum?

Autistic people display a wide range of responses to physical contact and affection. Many children experience sensory challenges that make physical contact so overwhelming that they avoid it, appearing to shun all social contact, especially when dysregulated. Others have a strong desire to be physically close, seeking out hugs and cuddling, especially from their parents. In fact many of these children must learn not to hug strangers or, say, the UPS man. Others enjoy holding hands, leaning against others, and other forms of closeness and affection. Some of my adult autistic friends love to give and receive tight hugs.

For some, the key issue is control. While a child might enjoy a hug when he is the one initiating, if the hug is unexpected and is imposed by someone else—even someone with whom the child feels emotionally connected—it can provoke anxiety (however loving and kind the hugger's intentions). It is important to be mindful of the person's particular sensory sensitivities, state of regulation, feelings, and preferences. Most important, the choice to reject a hug should not be mistaken for a lack of desire for emotional closeness or social connection.

Many parents and family members report that it's incredibly stressful to endure the judgmental glares of strangers when their autistic loved one displays unexpected behavior in public. What to do?

Nearly every parent and sibling of an autistic child or adult faces this reality at one time or another; even professionals and caregivers experience it in a different way. A child has a meltdown at the playground, comments openly about a neighbor's haircut, brusquely collides with a stranger without apologizing, or bolts around the auditorium during a school assembly. An adult runs to the aisle that has her favorite cereal at the supermarket. The parents wonder: Should I explain? What should I say? Do I have an obligation to share my loved one's diagnosis? Or might that actually be wrong? In the moment, a parent or sibling might feel a surge of emotions: embarrassment, confusion, defiance, anger, sadness. Some parents move quite naturally into explaining and educating, while others are far more private and reticent. They ignore the stares as they don't see the value of sharing such information, or even how they might do so in the heat of the moment.

One experienced and creative mother told me she had developed a four-tiered system for such situations, offering explanations that varied depending on the individual's relationship with her child and the family, and the likelihood that they will encounter the person regularly (it's equally relevant for older individuals):

Level 4: strangers who react negatively. Sometimes the reaction is obvious—a comment or glare—but sometimes it's more restrained or even hidden. It's safe to assume that the reaction is more a reflection on the other person than on anything about the parent or child, so there's no need to respond.

Level 3: a familiar person, perhaps a neighbor. With such a person, whom you are likely to encounter again, it's sometimes best to offer a simple, neutral explanation: "My child is on the autism spectrum. That's why he does that."

Level 2: friends and acquaintances who aren't in your inner circle. If the person is open to it, it's often worthwhile to explain at a convenient time what underlies the child's behavior and how the person might react most supportively.

Level 1: grandparents, other close relatives, and teachers who will certainly be close to the child. It's worth deciding how much energy is appropriate to allot to making such people comfortable with the child and able to be most supportive. This may require a discussion over time.

Some schools or agencies provide their teachers and staff with business cards to carry with them on field trips, community visits, and other occasions when the students or clients are likely to be in public. When a person's behavior draws attention, a teacher hands onlookers a card with the school's contact information and, on the flip side, a paragraph explaining that the recipient of the card has just encountered an autistic person and that the accompanying staff is trained in providing appropriate support and intervention.

Another creative approach many families use in place of explaining is wearing T-shirts and other clothing with logos and names of autism organizations. Other T-shirts are designed to explain or educate with messages such "Please be patient with me, I have Autism," or "Autism is my Superpower." If strangers are observant enough to notice those, they'll either ask fewer questions, identify themselves as having a friend or family member on the spectrum, or ask questions to learn something about autism. However, the autistic person must feel comfortable, and when of an appropriate age, give consent for family members to disclose publicly that the person is on the spectrum. With increasing public awareness, it has become more common to talk openly about autism than just a few years ago.

Is it a mistake to let an autistic child "stim"?

The terms *stim* and *stimming* (short for *self-stimulatory behavior*) used to be used by neurotypical professionals mostly with a negative connotation. They did not ask "why," instead viewing stims as undesirable "autistic behaviors" that needed to be discouraged or "extinguished." I have never believed that. We all have specific strategies to stay well-regulated emotionally and physiologically. Many autistic children and adults engage in certain behaviors, some more intense, unconventional, or publicly displayed than what is usually observed in non-autistic people, that give them comfort or help them be more alert: staring at objects, shaking their hands, spinning, fluttering their fingers, flapping their arms, jumping, repeating phrases, or lining up toys. There's nothing inherently wrong with any of these.

When a person needs to engage in such behavior excessively

or if the behavior is potentially harmful or particularly stigmatizing, that may be problematic. If a child sits alone, flicking his fingers in front of his eyes for long periods, having difficulty engaging socially, he needs assistance developing other ways to stay regulated, or we need to modify or change the activity. Changes to the environment, such as lessening noise and visual clutter, can also help. But when the behavior patterns are more limited—occurring during a break or at the end of a long day—there is less need for concern (unless the behavior is harmful to the person or others, or destructive). Some teachers and parents now allow for designated "stim" or break times to allow a person "to chill" during a busy day, which may actually support more successful participation and active engagement in activities at other times.

Often the parent's concern is that such behavior attracts glares or makes others avoid the child. In that case it's sometimes best to explain why a person is doing that while helping the individual learn other ways to self-regulate that don't draw negative attention. For children and teens with more social understanding, it's sometimes worth explaining that, while there's nothing wrong with their behavior, *other* people may not understand it or that it might be distracting to others. Perhaps the person might want to replace finger flicking with doodling or squeezing a ball to stay calm or to request a movement break when she feels unable to focus. It's also worth using a "time and place" strategy, helping the child to understand that it's fine to indulge in such behavior at the time and place that's least disruptive.

Is it better for an autistic child to learn in a regular, fully inclusive classroom, a substantially separate or self-contained special education classroom, or a private school?

No two autistic students are alike, and no two educational programs are alike, so there's no such thing as a one-size-fits-all program. Children learn as much from watching and engaging with their classmates in the flow of everyday activities as they do from the formal classroom learning experiences. The more sophisticated their peers' social and language modeling, the better—as long as it is not too far beyond a child's abilities. That doesn't mean it's always better to be surrounded by neurotypical classmates than by students who also receive special education services. What is most important is that a student feels a sense of belonging and respect.

In many cases the choice isn't only between self-contained special education classrooms with many supports and accommodations and a fully inclusive classroom program with fewer supports. Some schools offer a continuum of inclusive experiences, from all-day special education classes, to spending only part of the day in a smaller group and part in more socially integrated environments, to inclusion much of the day with the full- or part-time support of an aide. Some communities have public agencies or private schools that are self-contained, serving only children or adults with developmental disabilities. What is most important is the match between the types of supports a student needs and can benefit from. Supports may include friends who also can be social models, teaching strategies and accommodations, qualities of learning environments, and what is provided and available in the educational setting.

Should a very bright student with an Asperger's profile always be in an inclusive classroom with neurotypical peers?

Not necessarily. Often such students find themselves completely misunderstood, or even overwhelmed, in inclusive environments that do not have the appropriate supports in place. A system with inflexible rules and teachers or support staff without appropriate training may misconstrue a student's behavior as stubborn, oppositional, or withholding, resulting in a very stressful educational experience for all.

In some successful programs, a class of six to ten students serves as a home base, providing extra academic or emotional support and fostering a sense of community. There, individuals who share a diagnosis can be open to sharing their feelings and experience, growing together and learning from the challenges and victories each child experiences. In stark contrast, some autistic students who have succeeded in inclusive school settings say they have no desire to be around others with developmental challenges and needs.

What's most important is looking at the student's larger environment and considering the various kinds of social opportunities she encounters throughout the day and week and the potential for developing friendships and meaningful relationships, rather than viewing the classroom as the whole picture. Does the student have a sense of belonging to the community of students, or feel isolated and misunderstood? A child with many siblings, out-of-school activities, or connections to children in their neighborhood can benefit from the social experiences of day-to-day domestic life. A child who is involved in a theater, music, or expressive-arts program, a church or synagogue or mosque program, or a sports program with neurotypical peers may have less need for an inclusive school environment, particularly if it presents its own challenges. And many autistic individuals, especially older school age teen and adults, greatly benefit socially and emotionally from connections with other autistic and neurodivergent people, through both formal and informal group connections.

Is there such a thing as too much therapy?

More time in therapy does not automatically mean better quality therapy—or better progress.

Parents often hear from professionals that in order to benefit from a particular kind of approach, a child will need at least thirty or forty hours of weekly, individualized therapy. The underlying message is that the more hours spent in therapy the better, and that a child who doesn't meet a certain time threshold will miss out on its potential benefits. But the number of hours alone does not determine a program's intensity or effectiveness. What's most important is the quality of the approach, including the relationships among the child, family, and service providers, how well it is coordinated across settings and people, and the relevance of the goals and objectives to a child's or adult's life.

Intensive, individualized therapy and support may be an initial, important part of a larger plan for very young and individuals with greater challenges. The danger is losing sight of the big picture, the many different parts of a child's life. A kindergartner who receives intensive outside therapies might be too exhausted to participate in classroom activities. The parents might be shuttling the child daily after school to speech therapy or occupational therapy, or bringing a behavior therapist into the home, but after a while it's all just too much for the child and the family.

Sometimes an agency or therapist will push for more hours of therapy, but the child is resistant. The professional might acknowledge the resistance, referring to it as non-compliance, and suggest that it's important to fight through it. Once again it's essential for parents to trust their instincts and think about the emotional reaction of the child and the larger needs of the family. When a child experiences overload and displays stress, exhaustion, and resistance to participating, it's important for a parent to ask, "Why are we doing this? And why are we doing so much of it?" If the parent is feeling exhausted and pulled in a million directions, that may trickle down, having a undesirable impact on their autistic child as well as any brothers or sisters.

Often the problem isn't the quantity of time devoted to a particular therapy but rather that the therapy is disconnected from the child's life and significantly interferes with the family routines. The key is looking at the big picture and choosing approaches that are in line with the overall goals, objectives, and strategies that are appropriate for the child or adult, and the family. The time allotted to any one therapy is far less important than taking a team approach, having everyone on the same page, and keeping the big picture of the needs of both the autistic person and family in mind. Whenever possible, the autistic child or adult should also have input into decision making.

How can I deal with a teacher or therapist who seems ill equipped—or unwilling—to teach an autistic child?

Some regular education teachers are open to the idea of including an autistic child in their class but feel they lack the necessary support of administrators, aides, or others. Another, more challenging problem is when teachers are highly resistant to teaching autistic children, perhaps feeling that they do not have the training or that it is simply not part of their job.

In either case, the crucial factor often is not the teacher but the school's leadership, and whether or not there is a true team approach. A principal who is committed to leading a school that is inclusive and that supports and values every student will make every effort to support the classroom teacher and the student, and to foster teaming that includes family members and the autistic student. When such a principal comes across a teacher resistant to including an autistic student, she will make it clear that the teacher is part of a team and needs to support the student. However, the school must help such teachers by providing training and support.

It's also essential for parents to understand that they play an indispensable part in the child's success in school. If a well-meaning teacher doesn't feel properly supported, the parents or caregivers should try their best to make sure they have done all they can do to help. They can share their perspective and provide specific strategies that they have learned that helps their child to stay well-regulated and learn. If necessary, they can advocate for more support if it is clear more is needed, not only for the student, but for the staff.

Instead of pressuring teachers, parents should acknowledge, when it's relevant, that a child's reactions can be challenging at times and that if the child has a difficult day, the teacher isn't to blame. In short, parents should send the message that they are partners—active, interested, and involved partners—willing to collaborate with school professionals. They should also make it clear that they expect teachers to be collaborative as well.

Sometimes the match between student and teacher just doesn't work. Then, rather than blaming the teacher or the school, parents should take an active role in solving the problem and seeking the best possible placement for the child whether in another class or educational setting, or in a home-schooling arrangement with educational support.

Many children and adults who have difficulty speaking learn to communicate instead with iPads, other devices, or low-tech options such as picture-symbol systems, letter boards, or sign language. Doesn't that prevent them from learning to speak?

It might seem logical that teaching a child or adult alternative ways to communicate with AAC systems would inhibit their potential or motivation for using speech. The option to use sign language, picture communication systems, letter boards, photographs, and speech-generating devices would presumably take away a child's incentive to learn to speak or an older person's motivation to use speech.

My experience, though, indicates that using these methods to aid social communication actually *supports* speech development—a finding supported by many studies. The reason is simple: the motivation to learn to speak comes from success in communicating. The more a person is successful in relating to and connecting with others, even if it isn't through speech, the more desire the individual has to communicate in the way that most people do: through speech. There are adults whose first intelligible speech developed as adults after learning to be successful through spelling using letterboards or other AAC approaches (see Chapter 11).

It is important to recognize that some people prefer to use alternative or augmentative means of communicating even though they can speak. Multi-modal communication, using different ways of communicating, enables a person to use the most effective way to communicate in different situations and with different people. For example, Chloe Rothschild, a young adult, is capable of communicating by speaking but at times prefers to use a text-to-speech iPad app. (See Chapter 12.) She feels strongly that it's a person's right to communicate in a way they prefer, which might vary at different times.

Research indicates that successful social communication helps a person to stay better regulated emotionally. In turn the person can express social control by requesting or protesting through more socially desirable communication, rather than through undesirable means when becoming upset or dysregulated. When a person becomes a competent and confident communicator, regardless of how he is communicating, he is more available for learning and engaging, which also includes learning how to pay attention to people speaking, and therefore learning how to speak.

What role should siblings play in the life of an autistic child or adult?

Brothers and sisters can play a very important role in understanding and supporting an autistic sibling, but research shows how this is accomplished can vary greatly. Asking a brother or sister to do too much—and essentially act like another parent—may not be developmentally appropriate and often leads the non-autistic sibling to feel resentment. At the other extreme, parents generally shouldn't tell siblings that they need not be involved or concerned at all. In general, siblings who adapt best are those who are given some age-appropriate responsibility and a degree of choice in how to be helpful.

It is important to recognize that siblings go through their own developmental phases in how they relate to an autistic brother or sister. I knew a young girl who enjoyed helping, and even teaching, her older autistic brother. As she approached the early teen years, however, she avoided spending time with him, especially in public. Two years after that she became more involved again, and even more caring. Just as with typical children, sibling relationships are complicated and evolving. It is always helpful to have open communication and let brothers and sisters know that parents respect their feelings and will listen.

Does autism cause divorce?

A perennial myth is that when there is an autistic child in a family, 80 percent of marriages end in divorce. More recent research indicates that in the U.S., the divorce rate in families with an autistic child is only slightly higher than the general population's rate of about 50 percent.

What we do know is that unresolved stressors in a relationship cause divorce. Raising a child on the spectrum can be one of those stressors. If there are already cracks in the foundation of a marriage, then having an autistic child adds additional pressure, and that could be one factor, among others, that contribute to divorce. But it's rarely the lone or primary factor. In some cases, of course, separation or divorce is not a bad thing if it results in a more stable and peaceful home environment, which ultimately is of great benefit for most children. In the short term, however, separation or divorce can certainly be especially confusing—even overwhelming—to an autistic child who thrives on stability and predictability.

Some parents feel that having an autistic child strengthens their marriage and the entire family. Faced with the need to solve problems, make tough decisions, and find the best help and opportunities for a child, couples can learn to negotiate, communicate, and work as teammates more effectively. Parents frequently say making such difficult decisions makes them feel more confident in their ability to face other challenges. And when things are going well, families join in celebrating successes.

Still, it is not uncommon for parents to have contrasting perceptions about their autistic child, particularly early in the journey. Frequently one parent perceives that something isn't right with the child's development, and the other parent is dismissive, telling his partner not to be alarmist. One parent might be concerned about the child's future, while the other takes a wait-and-see approach.

These differences don't end in the early years. One parent might feel embarrassed by a child's behavior in public, while the other is immune to such feelings. One might be drawn to a particular therapy or educational approach, while the other favors a different one. Teachers and other professionals frequently find themselves drawn into a couple's marital differences when partners ask for marital advice in the guise of asking about a child. Parents need not agree all the time but should seek to find ways to face the challenges that come with autism and use them to strengthen the marriage rather than letting them cause greater rifts. The parents I have known who have successfully done so have put their families on positive journeys of growth and fulfillment, improving the lives of every family member.

Autistic people can sometimes be so direct that it comes across as rude. How to deal with this?

Different people and cultures have different standards of bluntness and honesty. I grew up in Brooklyn, and while New Yorkers are rarely put off by my manner, my wife, who grew up in a small town in Connecticut, sometimes finds my direct way of speaking impolite. Dena Gassner and Carly Ott, two of my autistic friends, have both told me that aside from the sensory issues, they found New York City a much easier place to live than elsewhere because the locals communicate so directly and are accepting of their own directness.

Like Brooklynites, autistic people can often speak with an honesty and directness that others—particularly those who don't know them or don't know them well—may find jarring. They may simply not understand that being too direct or giving unsolicited opinions may be off-putting to neurotypical people. If it's our loved one who's doing this, we don't want them to feel badly about themselves, but we also don't want people to incorrectly see them as rude.

One question is to consider is whether the directness or honesty is helpful in a given situation. If it's not, you can say to the other person, "you may find that [the person] sometimes has a direct way of communicating."

In dealing with the autistic individual, rather than overtly correcting the person, which implies that what they've done is simply bad behavior, it can be helpful to model the expected way of communicating. In some cases, direct coaching can be effective, as long as we make clear that what the person was doing was not bad or wrong, just different.

Linguistics literature uses the term code-switching: speaking a certain away to people with a certain status and switching their style when speaking with others. Most of us learn to speak one way to a job interviewer and another when we hang out with our friends. I know many autistic people who have learned to code-switch, seeing neurotypical conversational norms as different from theirs. They may use their more innate direct manner with other autistic people and close friends and be more indirect and "polite" in neurotypical culture. Of course, we hope that our loved ones will feel accepted and understood in both cultures, but not at the expense of feeling badly about themselves or believing that there's something wrong with them.

What is masking? And how is it related to code-switching?

When people on the autism spectrum make efforts to hide or camouflage their autistic traits for fear of being ostracized or discriminated against, it's sometimes called masking. Individuals may not be aware of their own masking, which may be driven by social conditioning. But it can take a toll.

People mask through the way they communicate or by repressing their innate reactions—such as stimming or fleeing overwhelming social environments—because they fear those reactions might be misunderstood and be stigmatizing. Sometimes autistic people whose natural instinct is to be truthful and forthright feel pressure to engage in small talk, act deceptively (i.e. tell "white lies"), or laugh along with others who engage in deception. These are also forms of masking. Children often expend significant effort trying to "hold it together" and display "good behavior" in school when they really need breaks and time to be alone or stim. Adults sometimes try to fit in the workplace by copying or emulating the behavior of neurotypicals, or simply being "one of the gang" even though it is stressful and draining to do so.

In short, masking is an effort to hide one's authentic identity to avoid being seen as different. Repressing your natural reactions in this way can cause great stress and anxiety, sometimes leading to emotional and physical exhaustion some people on the spectrum call "autistic burnout."

If masking is a way of hiding, code-switching is a way of communicating effectively. Code-switching is about adjusting one's communicative style verbally and through behavior—to meet the expected convention of a given situation or context (formal vs. informal, polite vs. casual, etc.). It's generally understood to be a voluntary choice to support effective communication and social cohesion, and is *not* driven by the desire to avoid being ostracized, discriminated against, or bullied, or primarily by the perceived need to fit in. Code-switching is a choice made to increase efficiency in communicating, but not typically to avoid negative consequences. For example, employment training for autistic individuals often involves practicing for interviews by answering questions succinctly and not going into too much detail, and learning to ask appropriate questions about a job when it would not be that person's natural inclination to do so.

A GUIDE TO RESOURCES

THERE has been an explosion of autism publications and online resources that have emerged in recent years, with many becoming much far more specific in the topics they address. This selective list includes some of the most helpful books, websites, and organizations for and about autistic people their families and professionals. Many are contributions by autistic people and the organizations with which they are affiliated. While the resources are grouped by audience and category, many have relevance to multiple categories. I apologize to those authors or organizations whose work may not have made it onto this listing, and encourage readers to pursue other resources that address their issues of concern or interest.

Resources for Professionals

Published Work

Alderson, Jonathan. *Challenging the Myths of Autism: Unlock New Possibilities and Hope.* Toronto: HarperCollins Canada, 2011.

Attwood, A. *Complete Guide to Asperger's Syndrome.* London: Jessica Kingsley, 2012.

Baker, Jed. *No More Meltdowns: Positive Strategies for Managing and Preventing Out-of-control Behavior.* Arlington, TX: Future Horizons, 2008.

Blanc, Marge. *Natural Language Acquisition on the Autism Spectrum: The Journey from Echolalia to Self-Generated Language.* Madison, WI: Communication Development Center, 2013.

Donvan, J. & Zucker, C. *In a Different Key: The Story of Autism*. New York: Broadway Books, 2016.

Goldstein, Sam, and Jack Naglieri. *Intervention for Autism Spectrum Disorders*. New York: Springer Science Publishers, 2013.

Gray, Carol. *The New Social Story Book*. Arlington, TX: Future Horizons, 2010.

Greenspan, Stanley I., and Serena Wieder. *Engaging Autism: Using the Floortime Approach to Help Children Relate, Communicate, and Think*. Cambridge, MA: Da Capo Lifelong, 2006.

Hall, Elaine and Diane Isaacs. *Seven Keys to Unlock Autism*. New York: Jossey-Bass, 2012.

Hodgdon, Linda A. *Visual Strategies for Improving Communication*. Troy, MI: QuirkRoberts, 1996.

Kluth, Paula. *You're Going to Love This Kid*. 3rd Edition. Baltimore: Brookes, 2022.

Luterman, David. *Counseling Persons with Communication Disorders and Their Families 5th Edition*. Austin, TX: Pro-Ed, Inc., 2008.

Marquette, Jacquelyn Altman, and Ann Turnbull. *Becoming Remarkably Able: Walking the Path to Talents, Interests, and Personal Growth for Individuals with Autism Spectrum Disorders*. Shawnee Mission, KS: Autism Asperger, 2007.

Mirenda, Pat, and Teresa Iacono. *Autism Spectrum Disorders and AAC*. Baltimore: Paul H. Brookes, 2009.

Myles, Brenda Smith, Melissa Trautman, and Ronda L. Schelvan. *The Hidden Curriculum: Practical Solutions for Understanding Unstated Rules in Social Situations*. Shawnee Mission, KS: Autism Asperger, 2004.

Prizant, Barry M., Amy Wetherby, Emily Rubin, Amy Laurent, and Patrick Rydell. *The SCERTS Model: A Comprehensive Educational Approach for Children with Autism Spectrum Disorders*. Baltimore: Paul H. Brookes, 2006.

Rogers, Sally, and Geraldine Dawson. *Early Start Denver Model for Young Children with Autism: Promoting Language, Learning, and Engagement*. New York: Guilford, 2010.

Wetherby, A. M., and Prizant, B. M. *Autism Spectrum Disorders: A Developmental, Transactional Perspective*. Baltimore: Brookes Publishing, 2000.

Winner, Michelle Garcia. *Thinking about You, Thinking about Me*. San Jose, CA: Think Social, 2007.

———. *Why Teach Social Thinking? Questioning Our Assumptions about What It Means to Learn Social Skills*. San Jose, CA: Social Thinking, 2013.

Wolfberg, P. J. *Peer Play and the Autism Spectrum: The Art of Guiding Children's Socialization and Imagination* (IPG Field Manual). Shawnee Mission, KS: Autism Asperger Publishing Company, 2003.

———. *Play and Imagination in Children with Autism* (2nd Edition). New York: Teachers College Press, Columbia University, 2009.

Websites

Autism Institute on Peer Socialization and Play: www.autisminstitute.com

First Words Projects, Florida State University: firstwords.fsu.edu

Amy Laurent: www.Amy-Laurent.com

PrAACtical AAC (Augmented and Alternative Communication): http://praacticalaac.org/

Barry Prizant: www.barryprizant.com

Emily Rubin: www.commxroads.com

Tony Attwood: https://tonyattwood.com.au/

Morènike Giwa-Onaiwu: https://morenikego.com/

SCERTS Model: www.scerts.com

Social Thinking: www.socialthinking.com

Interdisciplinary Council on Developmental and Learning Disorders: www.ICDL.com

Resources for Parents and Family Members

Published Work

Christensen, S. *From Longing to Belonging: A Practical Guide to Including People with Disabilities and Mental Health Conditions in Your Faith Community.* Minneapolis: Inclusion Innovations, 2018.

Dalgliesh, Carolyn. *The Sensory Child Gets Organized: Proven Systems for Rigid, Anxious, and Distracted Kids.* New York: Simon & Schuster, 2013.

Kerstein, Lauren H. *My Sensory Book: Working Together to Explore Sensory Issues and the Big Feelings They Can Cause: A Workbook for Parents, Professionals, and Children.* Shawnee Mission, KS: Autism Asperger, 2008.

Kranowitz, Carol Stock. *The Out-of-sync Child: Recognizing and Coping with Sensory Processing Disorder.* New York: Skylight Books/A Perigee Book, 2005.

Reber, Deborah. *Differently Wired: A Parent's Guide to Raising an Atypical Child with Confidence and Hope.* New York: Workman, 2020.

Robinson, Ricki G. *Autism Solutions: How to Create a Healthy and Meaningful Life for Your Child.* Don Mills, Canada: Harlequin, 2011.

Sussman, Fern. *TalkAbility: People Skills for Verbal Children on the Autism Spectrum. A Guide for Parents.* Toronto: Hanen Program, 2006.

Sussman, Fern, and Robin Baird Lewis. *More than Words: A Parent's Guide to Building Interaction and Language Skills for Children with Autism Spectrum Disorder or Social Communication Difficulties.* Toronto: Hanen Program, 2012.

White, Yasmine, and Sonia Belasco. *Autism and the Power of Music: A New Approach to Help Your Child Connect and Communicate.* Arlington, TX: Future Horizons, 2021

Wiseman, Nancy D., and Robert L. Rich. *The First Year: Autism Spectrum Disorders: An Essential Guide for the Newly Diagnosed Child: A Parent-expert Walks You through Everything You Need to Learn and Do.* Cambridge, MA: Da Capo, 2009.

Websites

AuSome Book Club: https://notanautismmom.com/tag/that-au-some-book-club/

Autism Navigator: https://autismnavigator.com/

Bright and Quirky: https://brightandquirky.com/

First Signs: www.firstsigns.org

Shelley Christensen: Inclusion Innovations https://inclusioninnovations .com/

Paula Kluth: www.paulakluth.com; https://inclusionrules.com/

Robert Naseef: http://alternativechoices.com/

The Hanen Center: www.hanen.org

TILT parenting: https://tiltparenting.com/

WrightsLaw (Special education law and advocacy) www.wrightslaw.com

Resources by Autistic People

Published Work

Carley, Michael John. *Asperger's from the Inside Out: A Supportive and Practical Guide for Anyone with Asperger's Syndrome.* New York: Perigee, 2008.

Carley, Michael John. *Unemployed and on the Spectrum.* London: Jessica Kingsley, 2016.

Endow, Judy. *Autistically Thriving: Reading Comprehension, Conversational Engagement, and Living a Self-Determined Life Based on Autistic Neurology.* Lancaster, PA: Judy Endow, 2019.

Garcia, Eric. *We're Not Broken: Changing the Autism Conversation.* New York: Harcourt, 2021.

Grandin, Temple, and Richard Panek. *The Autistic Brain: Thinking across the Spectrum.* Arlington, TX: Future Horizons, 2013.

Higashida, Naoki, David Mitchell, and Keiko Yoshida. *The Reason I Jump: One Boy's Voice from the Silence of Autism.* New York: Random House, 2013.

Lesko, Anita. *The Complete Guide to Autism & Healthcare: Advice for Medical Professionals and People on the Spectrum.* Arlington, TX: Future Horizons, 2017.

Mukhopadhyay, Tito. *How Can I Talk If My Lips Don't Move? Inside My Autistic Mind.* New York: Arcade, 2008.

Pena, E. (Ed.) *Communication Alternatives in Autism: Perspectives on Typing and Spelling Approaches for the Nonspeaking.* Jefferson, NC: Toplight, 2019.

Price, D. *Unmasking Autism: Discovering the New Faces of Neurodiversity.* New York: Harmony Books, 2022.

Shore, Stephen M., and Linda G. Rastelli. *Understanding Autism for Dummies.* Hoboken, NJ: Wiley, 2006.

Shore, Stephen M., and Ruth Elaine Joyner Hane. *Ask and Tell: Self-advocacy and Disclosure for People on the Autism Spectrum.* Shawnee Mission, KS: Asperger Autism, 2004.

Tammet, Daniel. *Born on a Blue Day: Inside the Extraordinary Mind of an Autistic Savant: A Memoir.* New York: Free Press, 2007.

Willey, Liane Holliday. *Pretending to Be Normal: Living with Asperger's Syndrome.* London: Jessica Kingsley, 1999.

Websites

Becca Lory Hector: https://beccalory.com/

Michael John Carley: www.michaeljohncarley.com

Temple Grandin: www.TempleGrandin.com

Stephen Shore: www.autismasperger.net

Judy Endow: www.judyendow.com

Anita Lesko: www.anitalesko.com

Neuroclastic: https://neuroclastic.com

International Association for Spelling as Communication: https://i-asc.org/

CommunicationFirst: https://communicationfirst.org/

Books Written by Parents and Parent-Professionals

Fields-Meyer, Tom. *Following Ezra: What One Father Learned about Gumby, Otters, Autism, and Love from His Extraordinary Son.* New York: New American Library, 2011.

Grinker, Roy. *Unstrange Minds: Remapping the World of Autism.* New York: Basic Books, 2007.

Hall, Elaine, with Elizabeth Kaye. *Now I See the Moon: A Mother, a Son, a Miracle.* New York: HarperStudio, 2010.

Naseef, Robert A. *Autism in the Family: Caring and Coping Together.* Baltimore: Brookes, 2014.

Park, Clara Claiborne. *Exiting Nirvana: A Daughter's Life with Autism.* Boston: Little, Brown, 2001.

Suskind, Ron. *Life, Animated: A Story of Sidekicks, Heroes, and Autism.* New York: Kingswell, 2014.

National Organizations Providing Information and Support

Autism National Committee: www.autcom.org

Autism Research Institute: www.autism.com

Autism Self-Advocacy Network: www.autisticadvocacy.org

Autism Society of America: www.autism-society.org

Global and Regional Asperger's Syndrome Partnership: www.GRASP.org

Spectrum Theatre Ensemble: https://www.stensemble.org/

The Miracle Project: www.themiracleproject.org

ACKNOWLEDGMENTS

T HIS updated and revised edition of *Uniquely Human* could not have been written without the assistance and support of many people. I wish to express my deepest gratitude to the following people.

My collaborator, Tom Fields-Meyer, who came through once again with his friendship, support, sense of humor, and great literary talents in helping to capture all I have learned over the past five decades. A special thanks to Tom's family, Rabbi Shawn Fields-Meyer, Ezra, Ami, and Noam.

My wife, Dr. Elaine Meyer, whose interest and loving support initially inspired the writing of the first edition, and now, the new edition of *Uniquely Human*. Her innovative and compassionate work training health care professionals and at our parent retreat weekend has been an unending source of learning and of inspiration. Her TEDx talk on "Being Present, Not Perfect" is highly recommended: www.youtube.com/watch?v=phUUjk_btiY.

My son, Noah, for his love and his continued deep interest in *Uniquely Human* and in my work. When writing the first edition commenced, he was starting his undergraduate education, and as of this writing, he is just starting medical school. We are so proud of the caring young man he has become. I continue to pray he can find the same degree of fulfillment in his life's work that I have been blessed to find in mine.

My father, Sam, of blessed memory, who always trusted in me to make the right choices and whose pride always buoyed my spirits. And my mother Taube, of blessed memory, who only lived long enough to know me as a young child, but whose love and influence has surely helped me become who I am.

My sister Debbie, for her love and support, and ongoing interest in my work.

My perky companion Nicki, who with her Toto-like spirit, always greets me with positive energy even before the sun rises.

My dear friend Wally Zembo, who continues to help me keep my life in rhythm as he has done over the past thirty-five years.

Our fantastic literary agent, Betsy Amster, for believing in this project from the outset, for her valuable contributions and expertise, and for cheering us on every step of the way.

Our wonderful editor at Simon & Schuster, Lashanda Anakwah, for embracing this updated and revised edition of *Uniquely Human* and shepherding it through the editorial process with skill and great enthusiasm.

Our readers, Michael John Carley, Dr. Elaine Meyer, Eliza Beringhause, Rabbi Shawn Fields-Meyer, and Mary Hanlon, whose insightful input on our initial effort informs this new edition.

My SCERTS Model collaborators, Amy Laurent and Emily Rubin. So many of the values expressed in *Uniquely Human* reflect the ideals and practices we have infused in the SCERTS Model. I am so proud of what we have accomplished.

My career mentors, Drs. Judy Duchan, David Yoder, John Muma, and David Luterman, who believed in me and provided the support, values, and skills to pursue a most meaningful career. Special thanks to David L., who persistently encouraged me to write "*your* [expletive] book."

My former colleague and dear friend Dr. Adriana Loes Schuler, of blessed memory, truly one of the most gifted and unique humans I have ever known. Our initial common interest in echolalia and her brilliant work into cognitive styles of autistic people blossomed into a deep and enduring friendship that I will always cherish.

Barbara and Bob Domingue, our valued friends and retreat partners extraordinaire, and all parents who have attended our weekend retreat over the past twenty-five years and make it the remarkable experience it has become. I am so grateful to have the privilege of witnessing, learning, and being inspired by their incredible stories, their love for their children, their sense of humor, and their generosity in helping other parents.

The professionals, paraprofessionals, parents, and school and agency administrators across the United States and abroad who have chosen to devote their lives to helping children and families. I so appreciate their trust and the opportunity to work with and learn from them. Special thanks to my colleagues who serve children and families "in the front lines" every day, and especially my partners at Brown University and in The Miracle Project–New England: Anna Zembo, Julie Strandberg, Rachel Balaban, Shelley Katsh, and Amy Laurent.

My dear friends Elaine Hall, founder and artistic director of The Miracle Project, and her husband, Jeff Frymer. When Elaine and I first considered a creative theatrical work inspired by *Uniquely Human*, I knew it would become a reality, and the musical film "Journey to Namuh" was born. The great talents of Elaine, and the leadership of The Miracle Project, and most of all the autistic and neurotypical artists brought the themes and values of *Uniquely Human* to life.

My friend and colleague, Dave Finch, my "partner in crime" in producing and co-hosting "Uniquely Human: The Podcast." Dave's great sense of humor, his audio engineering talents, and his curiosity about his own autism and the lived experiences of our guests have made our podcast project so special. And to Taylor McMahon, who helps to make our podcast possible by keeping us in line and on schedule with great humor and patience.

The Canha, Correia, Domingue, and Randall families, who were so generous in allowing me to update their personal journeys so that other families could learn from their wisdom.

All the autistic individuals and their families who have been such a vital part of my life and my learning, and who have generously shared their stories. Not possible to mention them all, but special thanks to Michael John Carley, Stephen Shore, Ros Blackburn, Dena Gassner, Morènike Giwa-Onaiwu, Becca Lory Hector, Chloe Rothschild, Carly Ott, Anita Lesko, Conner Cummings, Danny Whitty, Jordyn Zimmerman, Scott Steindorff, Ron Sandison, Ian Nordling, and Justin Canha. So many have become colleagues, friends, and mentors and have provided me with the great privilege of a deep and meaningful lifelong career. To them my gratitude is truly boundless.

—B.P.

I am grateful to Dr. Barry Prizant for giving me the opportunity to collaborate in bringing his life's work to these pages. As the father of an autistic young man, I have learned that the most helpful people in my son's life are those with compassion, wisdom, and love—the same qualities I value as a writer. Barry has all of those in depth and abundance, and it has been a privilege to learn from him and create with him. Thanks also to his wife, Dr. Elaine Meyer, and son, Noah, for their warm hospitality and friendship over the years of our collaboration.

I am fortunate to have a stellar literary agent in Betsy Amster, who has become a trusted advisor and friend and whose counsel is always pitch perfect. I'm grateful to our editor for this updated edition, Lashanda Anakwah at Simon & Schuster, who brought fresh eyes, insights, and an open mind.

I am indebted to my friend Elaine Hall, who has done much for neurodivergent people and their families, including ours. It was Elaine who suggested that Barry and I meet, setting in motion this book, which has spread even more benefit and understanding.

During the course of our work on this updated edition, I lost my father, Jim Meyer, an extraordinary man who did much to improve the lives of countless people. One of the many lessons he taught me was to approach all kinds of people with an open mind and a compassionate heart. He took a particular interest in autism, not just as a

grandfather but as someone who thought everyone deserved a digni-
fied and meaningful life. I'm grateful to my mother, Lora Meyer, who
carries on that legacy of interest, caring, and support, rarely missing
the chance to share a news story or radio segment about some new
wrinkle in the world of autism. I'm also indebted to my in-laws,
Sandey and Del Fields, constant sources of support and love.

I thank my sons, Ami, Ezra, and Noam, for their love and support, their music, their editorial input, and for making me laugh.
Most of all I am grateful to—and for—my wise and wonderful wife,
Shawn Fields-Meyer, who encouraged my involvement with this
project from the outset, who listens to all of my ideas with patience
and insight, and who supports me with a smile in everything I do.

—T.F.-M.

INDEX

ABOUT THE AUTHORS

Barry M. Prizant, PhD, CCC-SLP, is among the world's leading authorities on autism and neurodevelopmental conditions, and is recognized as an innovator of respectful, person- and family-centered approaches for autistic and neurodivergent individuals and their families. With more than five decades of experience as a clinical scholar, researcher, and international consultant, he is a visiting scholar at Brown University, a certified speech-language pathologist, and director of Childhood Communication Services (a private practice). He serves on the panel of Professional Advisors of the Autism Society of America, and on the advisory boards of The Miracle Project and the Spectrum Theatre Ensemble. Barry is coauthor of *The SCERTS Model: A Comprehensive Educational Approach,* now being implemented in more than a dozen countries. He has published four books, more than 140 articles and chapters and has received many awards, including the Honors of the American-Speech-Language-Hearing Association (their highest recognition), the Princeton University Eden Foundation career award for improving quality of life for persons on the autism spectrum, and the Divine Neurotypical Award of GRASP, the world's largest autistic self-advocacy organization. He has been a two-time featured presenter at the United Nations on World Autism Awareness Day. The first edition of *Uniquely Human: A Different Way of Seeing Autism* (with Tom Fields-Meyer) has been published in 22 language versions, and he cohosts and co-produces "Uniquely Human: The Podcast" with autistic author and audio engineer Dave Finch.

Tom Fields-Meyer is author of the memoir *Following Ezra: What One Father Learned About Gumby, Otters, Autism, and Love from His Extraordinary Son*, a finalist for the National Jewish Book Award. He has coauthored many books, and his journalism and essays have appeared in numerous national publications. He lives in Los Angeles, where he teaches in the UCLA Extension Writers' Program.